Samoan Islands

10   20   30   40

N

S

O C E A N

OFU

TUTUILA

TAU

PAGO-
PAGO

APIA HARBOR

OUR SAMOAN
ADVENTURE

OUR SAMOAN ADVENTURE

By Fanny and Robert Louis Stevenson

WITH A THREE-YEAR DIARY BY MRS. STEVENSON
NOW PUBLISHED FOR THE FIRST TIME,
TOGETHER WITH RARE PHOTOGRAPHS FROM FAMILY ALBUMS.
EDITED, WITH AN INTRODUCTION AND NOTES,

By Charles Neider

HARPER & BROTHERS | PUBLISHERS NEW YORK

Library of Congress catalog card number: 55–8035

To the memory of Austin Strong

Table of Contents

Contents

1892

1893

1894

"Yes, if I could die just now, or say in half a year, I should have had a splendid time of it on the whole"—a ball at Vailima—Louis struggles with *St. Ives*—plans for the Edinburgh Edition—dictating *Weir of Hermiston*—death of Louis on December 3rd.

Pages 233-241

The illustrations, grouped in a separate section, follow page 104.

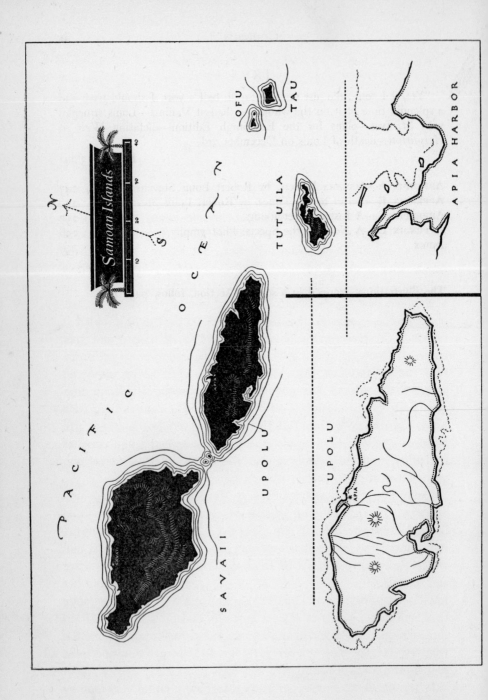

Introduction

The Samoan adventure of Robert Louis and Fanny Stevenson has long captured the imagination of a wide public. Stevenson's side of the story is well known from his letters, but Fanny's has yet to be heard, after a silence of more than sixty years. Although entirely different in tone—as different as her American background from his Scotch, and her quiet efficient manner from his romantic swash-buckling one—her account is fascinating in its own right, in what it reveals of Stevenson's remarkable wife as well as of himself and their island existence. Inasmuch as Stevenson was used to literary collabora-tion (he collaborated with W. E. Henley, with Lloyd Osbourne and with his wife), it is no offense to his memory to have him collaborate now. I have thought it fun to sidelight Fanny's diary with Louis's version of events. Not that the diary requires it; but it will be seen, I believe, that each of the reports illuminates and enriches the other, and that the result of the combination is something greater than the two parts.

Fanny Stevenson was born Frances Matilda Van de Grift, March 10, 1840, in Indianapolis. When she was seventeen she married Samuel Osbourne in that city, Sam being twenty. The Osbournes soon moved to California, where they lived a semi-pioneer life, and where Fanny amply displayed those qualities of hardihood, courage and love of nature which her diary reveals and which Louis and her friends have often noted. Before long it became apparent to Fanny that Sam was undependable as a husband, and in 1875 she and her three children, Belle, Lloyd and Hervey, sailed for Europe, where the youngest, Hervey, died at a very early age. In France, Fanny and Belle took up the study of painting.

It was in Grez, France, in 1876 that Fanny and Louis met by

chance and fell in love. Louis, born in Edinburgh November 13, 1850, was ten and a half years her junior. He came of a family of engineers and lighthouse builders, and had studied law. A charming, ebullient, very slight and frail young man, with a definite romantic flair and remarkable large eyes, he was at this time quite unknown to a general public but beloved by those who knew him and who believed that a genius moved him.

Two years later Fanny returned to the United States, won a divorce from Sam and settled in Monterey, where Louis joined her in the fall of 1879. They were married in May, 1880. In August they sailed with Lloyd (Belle having married) to England, a trip which was followed by several others over a period of years in a search for Louis's health, he being tubercular—to Davos in Switzerland, to Scotland, to Hyères in France—until the Stevensons determined to seek sunnier lands. They reached New York September, 1887—Louis was by now famous —and Louis spent some time at Saranac in the Adirondack Mountains, until their plan for sailing in the South Seas matured.

The Stevensons, with Louis's mother and Fanny's son, sailed from San Francisco for the South Seas June 28, 1888, on the chartered yacht *Casco*. They spent some time in Hawaii, where they saw Fanny's daughter, her son-in-law, and her grandson, Austin, then sailed on the schooner *Equator* for the Gilbert Islands the latter part of June, 1889. Samoa was first sighted by them in the early part of December of the same year, and they stopped in Apia in a rented cottage, purchased ground for what was to become their estate, Vailima, and left orders to have a patch of jungle cleared and a temporary dwelling built. Then, in February, 1890, they took the *Lübeck* to Sydney, Louis and Fanny planning to return soon to England.

Sydney's climate did not agree with Louis, and he fell seriously ill. Inasmuch as he had felt well at sea, and especially well among the south Pacific islands, it was considered by himself and Fanny imperative to get him to sea again. He, Fanny and Lloyd booked passage on the *Janet Nichol* and cruised for more than three months among the islands, Louis recovering and becoming enchanted, and they visited Apia a second time on May 1, 1890. Back in Sydney, Louis fell ill again, and it was then determined that his best chance for good health was to make his permanent home in Samoa.

Fanny was in the habit of keeping diaries—partly for her own use and pleasure, partly so they could be used when needed to refresh Louis's memory of events and places for the benefit of his various literary projects—essays, novels, letters public and private. Such a diary concerned her cruise with Louis on the *Janet Nichol*. It was published in 1914, but the published version was a good deal rewritten and dressed up for the public occasion. The present diary, kept from the beginning of their stay at Vailima in September, 1890 until the end of July, 1893, is a truer if less varnished record of her thoughts and actions. In fact, because of the political stress under which parts of it were written, Fanny had some qualms, as she states in the diary, of its being "overhauled."

After Louis's sudden death in December, 1894, Fanny and Belle lived for a short while at Vailima. When they left Samoa the diary was overlooked. Eventually it reached the hands of an English-woman, Miss Gladys Peacock, who sent it to Lloyd Osbourne some years later with the comment, "Of course I have not read it." It was read and quoted by Nellie Sanchez when the latter wrote her biography of her sister Fanny, and eventually came into the possession of Belle, who had become Isobel Field of Santa Barbara, California. It was Mrs. Field who deeded it to the state of California.

The manuscript was received by the state on May 20, 1949, and placed in the permanent custody of Stevenson House in Monterey, an old adobe now a state museum, where Stevenson is supposed to have boarded some time during the fall of 1879. It is written in an unpaged ledger, 8″ x 12½″, with marbled cover and burgundy calf spine, in a hand that is usually hurried and at all times rather difficult to decipher. The original ink is now brown. Unfortunately portions of the manuscript have been crosshatched out by a modern pen using blue ink, whose ownership is only surmised. Attempts have been made to bring the original to light and in most cases they have succeeded. I have marked the places where these over-inkings occur.

All entries by Stevenson with the exception of those which state otherwise are from his *Vailima Letters*, written to his friend Sidney Colvin[1] when the latter was Keeper of the Prints and Drawings at

[1] English literary and art critic (1845-1927), later knighted.

the British Museum, London. The others are from his *Letters*, edited by Colvin. The *Vailima Letters* were not originally conceived by Stevenson to constitute a diary, although they were never letters in the ordinary sense, being rather journal packets written at from time to time in between outgoing mail steamers. By them Stevenson hoped to convey to his friend a full picture of his island life. It was in June, 1892, that he first became aware of their posthumous value, or at least first mentioned this awareness to Colvin. "It came over me the other day suddenly that this diary of mine to you would make good pickings after I am dead, and a man could make some kind of book out of it without much trouble. So, for God's sake, don't lose them, and they will prove a piece of provision for my 'poor old family,' as Simile calls it."

Vailima, the Stevenson home on the island of Upolu in Samoa, means the place of five streams or waters. Fact has it that there were only four, but Stevenson apparently liked the sound of the name and hoped to justify its adoption by discovering a fifth stream in due time. Despite Stevenson's comparative youth (he died at forty-four), Vailima came to be something of a mecca and a symbol, recalling Tolstoy's Yasnaya Polyana. Henry Adams found it appallingly primitive. Other visitors were charmed by it, particularly sailors from visiting British men-of-war, who, like the natives, were always welcome, and some of whom when ill were nursed there. About ten years after her husband's death, Fanny Stevenson wrote:

"The house at Vailima has been contradictorily described as a place where the master sat enthroned amid hordes of obsequious vassals, and as a sordid, poor place in the jungle, where food was scant, and poverty sat at the elbow of the jaded novelist spurring him on to continual, feverish exertions. Neither was true. The house at Vailima was a plain, large wooden building, with wide verandahs and many doors and windows. Our house-workers, who did not consider themselves servants, but members of the family, were efficient, as a rule, especially Talolo, the cook. We had our own furniture, linen, plate, and china brought from home, and lived very much as we would in England, with a few American innovations. To a man just off a cruise among the islands, no doubt an evening spent at the house in Vailima, with its waxed floors and antique rugs, its rooms blazing with lamps, the glitter of glass and silver, and the flower-bedecked, noiseless house-boys, would seem like a glimpse into paradise. On the other hand, a tourist fresh from the colonies or San Francisco would accept all this as a matter of course, but would note with disapproval the bare feet of our butler, and be much annoyed when the shoes, put out over night to be blacked, showed by their sodden condition in the morning that they had been washed, inside as well as out, under the garden hose. . . .

"A fortnightly service of steamships brought us ice, fresh oysters, and other supplies from the colonies or San Francisco. There was a good baker and butcher in Apia, and fish to be bought on the beach. Eels and fresh-water prawns abounded in our streams, wild pigeons could be shot from our back door, and the chickens and eggs of our own raising were excellent. Without any extraordinary expenditure we were able to live very comfortably.

"Socially, Samoa was certainly not dull. Diplomats and officials, many of them accompanied by their families, rented houses in the vicinity of Apia and entertained as they would at home. I have known Apia to be convulsed by a question of precedence between two officials from the same country, who each claimed the place of honour at public functions; burning despatches on the subject were written, and their respective governments appealed to. Well has Apia been called 'the kindergarten of diplomacy.'

"Besides native feasts, we had afternoon teas, evening receptions, dinner parties, private and public balls, paper-chases on horseback, polo, tennis parties, and picnics. My husband joined in all these festivities, once coming in second in a paper-chase over very rough country. Being an invalid child, he had never been taught to dance. To hold aloof from the balls in Apia, that were attended by almost the entire white population, was like an assumption of superiority; to go and sit out the evening was tedious. So, at the age of forty, he learned to dance, though I do not think he ever attempted more in public than a plain quadrille.

"These social diversions did not interfere very materially with my husband's literary work. It was his usual habit to begin in the fresh, cool hours of the early morning, when the house was quiet. One of the native boys was always on the alert for the study bell, and at the first tinkle would hasten to prepare Tusitala's breakfast, which was served to him in his bed. After that it would be at least two full hours before the household was astir. . . .

"The study was a small room off the library, in reality an enclosed bit of the upper verandah. Two windows opened seaward at the front, and one at the end gave a view of Mount Vaea where my husband now lies. Shelves laden with books ran round the room on all sides. The only furniture was a large deal-table, a couple of chairs, a locked stand of six Colt's repeating rifles, a narrow bed, where my husband might recline at his work, and a patent table that could be swung over the bed and raised or lowered at will."[2]

It was in May of 1952, during a walking tour of Monterey, that I first became acquainted with Fanny's diary. After having driven from the Sierras across the great valleys to the old Pacific capital, I paid my respects to Stevenson's memory with a visit to Stevenson House; and it was there, in a glass case, that I saw the folio manuscript. Soon afterwards I had an opportunity to read it, and was convinced that the diary was worth making available to a wide public.

It is only fair to demand of an editor how heavy a hand he has laid upon his materials. Even the casual reader will notice, in Fanny's text, discrepancies between the pages reproduced photographically and those in print, and the less casual reader will ask for an accounting of what has been done. Fanny's manuscript gives much evidence of having been written hurriedly and in snatches and, possibly, with an eye to saving paper. There are almost no margins in it, and few paragraph breaks. The material is like an undigested mass, with errors of grammar, fact, and with numerous inconsistencies. As it stands, it makes difficult reading.

One of the first tasks was the preparation of a reliable typescript. After a preliminary script had been made by Stevenson House, I

---

[2] From her preface to *St. Ives*, Biographical Edition of Stevenson's *Works*, Charles Scribner's Sons, publishers.

and my wife collated it with the manuscript, and the new typescript became my working copy. Time was spent in deciphering Fanny's sometimes erratic scrawl. Her spelling was often eccentric, particularly in regard to Samoan words and names, and there was a frequent necessity to identify persons and places. Often her spellings of the names of Samoan friends and servants differed broadly from Louis's. In the interests of simplicity I have tried when feasible to make her spellings in this regard consistent with those of Louis's collected works. The final task consisted of punctuating, paragraphing, and making obvious corrections.

I have tried to avoid violating any of the canons of good scholarship, and at the same time, if such a juxtaposition is possible (which I leave for the reader to judge) I have striven to make the end result a pleasure to read. By no statement or reticence have I meant to leave the impression that the diary as it now stands is a collaboration between myself and Fanny. I have merely tried to give its debut the care I am certain she would have given it had she published it in her lifetime. The virtues and the flaws are all Fanny's, and there is no question but that the same preponderance of virtues would be clear to see if the manuscript were published just as it came from her hurried hand. I trust I have taken no unnecessary liberties. I have spared no effort to determine the precise phrase, meaning, or intonation she had in mind, but at the same time I saw no reason to inflict upon the general reader the various difficulties of perusing such a manuscript; therefore I edited in the manner I thought most fitting. I have suppressed not a word, and I have taken care when some inconsistency appeared in her text.

I shall not be surprised if some readers question the value of all this effort. I myself have done so. Who, after all, was Fanny Stevenson that her diary should warrant such care? The full answer, I believe, can only be apparent through a reading of the diary, for it turns out that Fanny was not merely the diminutive, dark, energetic wife of a great English stylist and fine human being, but an unusual human being in her own right, frank as few are frank, courageous in the extreme, and—quite unexpectedly—a writer of sharp observations and of high descriptive power, a writer in the best American traditions, although she may not have been aware of the fact. There are the honesty and self-appraisal and love of nature of *Walden* in her book, as well as some of the humor of *Roughing It*.

Eighteen pages of the manuscript are partially affected by the suppressions. Of the 198 pages of the diary a total of about 2½ are over-inked, and of these substantially all have been deciphered, with about ten lines, none presumably important, remaining still unread. Although there is nothing improper in the passages suppressed, even from a Victorian point of view, it is clear why they caused concern: they are too revealing of discordant notes in Fanny's Vailima life. Apparently the unknown censor thought it desirable to impress upon the reader a sense of harmony in the diary; and certainly Fanny's thoughts about her mother-in-law could be discordant notes in the supposed domestic idyll. What a mistaken notion this ghostly censor labored under if he (or she) believed such revelations to be a blot on either Fanny's or Louis's memory. When Fanny complains of Louis's childish behavior in acting condescendingly toward Lloyd while caught up in emotion regarding "her blessed majesty the Queen," the moment brightens and deepens her, as it humanizes Louis. When she speaks pathetically of her wounded vanity because Louis has told her that she has the soul of a peasant and not of an artist, one sympathizes, and understands that it is part of the domestic music, in which discordance has a time-honored place.

The suppression of such passages bespeaks a mind intent on idealizing relations which, with the possible exception of the sexual sphere, must have been earthy, judging by the evidence. From the modern point of view they are desirable records in that they broaden, deepen, and dramatize an unusual marriage. But even if they did not mirror certain vital moments of Fanny's life it would have been regrettable to have lost them, for they are among the finest lines, stylistically speaking, of the diary, and Fanny at her finest is a good writer and a moving human being. They are subjective and illuminating and beautiful, and the effort taken to bring them to light has fortunately been amply justified.

The particulars of this case of literary detection may have some interest for the general reader. At first, on the advice of an expert, I tried a magnifying glass on one of the least difficult passages, a task in which I was aided by my wife—this despite my early hope that infrared or ultraviolet photography might bring the suppressed passages to light. After many sittings we were successful, but headaches were so frequent and progress so slow that I knew it was fruitless to attack the other passages with the same technique, many of them being so heavily over-inked that little of the original ink was visible. The same expert assured me that infrared and ultraviolet photography were useless for my purpose. The lesson to be learned here was, as usual, beware of the "expert" who theorizes, and go to the craftsman who thinks with his hands. Such a craftsman, a photographer, tried color filters without success, then infrared film with some success (but the grain was too heavy in this), and finally ultraviolet light, which brought to the surface with some clarity many of Fanny's scrawlings.

Even after the passages had been photographed by ultraviolet light special difficulties presented themselves, and the process was often tedious, painful—and unsuccessful. Science was a fabulous but sometimes unwilling handmaiden. By an odd coincidence the passage which presented to the naked eye an absolutely hopeless appearance responded best to the photographic treatment, and it was possible to make it out even in the print made by infrared film. This was the first passage attempted, because it was the worst, and the success attained raised many false hopes. All the other passages, which seemed so ready to fall victims to the camera's revealing eye, gave trouble, and it was only patience, repeated effort, and an intimate knowledge of Fanny's hand that made any progress possible.

One struggled letter by letter, using enlargements when necessary, tracing out the results, and often one would have a word or a phrase ready for use without being aware of it. An hour away from the work, and suddenly the words would leap up plain as bread and forever after seem easy to recognize. Eyestrain and headache were part of one's reward. Curiously, it was found that working with the passages upside down often diminished the chance of headache and increased the chance of success—probably because meaning and content could be distractions when what was most necessary was a liberal concentration on evanescent strokes of the pen set down some sixty years before. More than once I wondered if the effort I was making was not a sign of idiocy, but the suspense was a thing in and for itself, exciting and enervating, and I saw that passivity before it was the happier if lesser part of wisdom. And then there was the sense of letting Fanny finally have her say, as fully as possible.

It has been a puzzle to me why Fanny's children, who published their memories of Vailima, did not, for the sake of their mother's memory if not in the interest of the whole story, publish her diary. No doubt they had their reasons; however, they might have served her memory well had they published it. In my opinion the diary makes clear many of Fanny's virtues and thus illuminates her marriage to Louis, which otherwise might seem as strange as it did to many of his friends, among them Henry James. It presents a striking portrait of the Scotsman's American wife, and I am convinced will establish her as a strong and admirable personality, to be reckoned with by the large public interested in the domestic surroundings of literary genius.

The Samoan political situation, in which Stevenson deeply involved himself, requires a brief explanation. At the time that Stevenson settled in the islands the government, while technically Samoan, was actually in control of the three great powers which had interests there, and which had come to a determination at a convention in Berlin some few years previous. These powers were Germany, England, and the United States. Under the convention Malietoa Laupepa, previously deposed by the Germans, was reinstated as king, and Mataafa, a popular kinsman with considerable claims to the throne, who was especially obnoxious to the Germans, was overlooked and left in the position of pretender. The distance between the kinsmen grew as native feelings were stirred under the influence of the occupying powers, and war was continually threatened by both camps.

In Stevenson's judgment a native war would be calamitous and would only profit the white officials manipulating the scene. He believed that Laupepa and Mataafa would willingly live in peace if permitted to do so, and it was his notion that Mataafa ought to be

given a very high post in the government, to which he believed Laupepa would not object. Stevenson had no illusions concerning the
abilities of some of the occupying officials, in particular of the Chief
Justice, a Swedish gentleman, and of the president of the Municipal
Council, an Austrian nobleman, and he proceeded to make himself
a thorn, sending letters to the *Times* of London, in which he detailed
his views, his object being to have the two officials removed.

The officials were eventually recalled, but it is difficult to say just
how much influence Stevenson himself was actually able to bring
to bear. His efforts to aid the natives and to avert the impending war
were climaxed by the publication in July, 1892, of his *A Footnote
to History*, a small volume on the Samoan trouble. The war, however, was not averted, and Mataafa's forces were defeated and
Mataafa sent into exile.

I wish to express my indebtedness and gratitude to the persons
and institutions which aided in the preparation of this volume. Pri-
marily I am indebted to the state of California, which authorized
me to edit and to publish the diary which Fanny Stevenson kept in
Samoa and the manuscript of which is now the property of the state.
Specifically I am grateful to Newton B. Drury, chief of the Division
of Beaches and Parks, under whose jurisdiction state monuments
such as Stevenson House, Monterey, are administered; to J. T.
Chaffee, district superintendent of the Division; to Mrs. Amelie
Kneass, curator of Stevenson House; and to Miss Myfanwy Lloyd,
assistant curator of Stevenson House. I am particularly indebted to
Mrs. Kneass, whose disinterested efforts smoothed my labors in many
ways.

The Henry E. Huntington Library and Art Gallery, of San Marino,
California, was of great help to me in the matter of deciphering over-
inked passages in the manuscript. I am indebted to Herbert C.
Schulz, curator of manuscripts of the Library; to Miss Phyllis Rigney,
assistant to the curator of manuscripts; to Miss Gertrude Ruhnka,
assistant to the librarian; and most of all to Erwin F. Morkisch, di-
rector of the department of photographic reproductions, who labored

long, conscientiously, and intelligently, and who is largely responsible for bringing the over-inked sections to light.

It was during my residence at the Huntington Hartford Foundation, Pacific Palisades, California, in 1952 that I first became acquainted with Mrs. Stevenson's diary. I am grateful to the Hartford Foundation for all the aid and facilities which it has placed at my disposal, during my first residence, from March, 1952 to January, 1953, and also during my second, from September to December, 1954.

To Joan Merrick, my wife, I am indebted greatly—for suggestions regarding the introduction, for aid in the collation of typescript with manuscript, for aid in deciphering over-inked sections, and above all for making my life at Monterey and Carmel so pleasant that the weeks of work seemed to fly by. They were idyllic afternoons that we spent under the plum tree in the garden of Stevenson House, reading Fanny's diary aloud as we collated it with the first typescript.

Stevenson House, of Monterey, California, and the Yale University Library generously placed at my disposal a number of photographs for use in this volume. A number of rare photographs are included through the great generosity of Mrs. Austin Strong, the residuary legatee of Mrs. Isobel Field. Mrs. Strong gave me free access to family albums and was very helpful to me in many other ways. The full-page photographs of Fanny, and the ones of Louis shaving, of Louis on horseback, and of Louis with Tin Jack on the stairs, are among the many provided by Mrs. Strong. Stevenson specialists will find, I believe, that a large proportion of these photographs are published here for the first time.

I wish also to thank William James; Alan and Lou Osbourne; Edwin J. Beinecke; Miss Elizabeth Lawrence of Harper & Brothers; and Miss Betty Izant for courtesies extended to me. Finally, I wish to thank the libraries of Yale University (in particular Miss Marjorie Wynne), Harvard University, Columbia University, the University of California at Los Angeles, and the public libraries of New York City and of Monterey, Carmel and Santa Monica, California for the use of their facilities.

CHARLES NEIDER

Santa Monica, California
January 1, 1955

OUR SAMOAN
ADVENTURE

A note on pronunciation:

In the Samoan language *g* is pronounced as *ng* in our word *singer*.

1 8 9 0

F A N N Y . SEPTEMBER

Arrived at Vailima on the [blank] day of September. Things rather unsatisfactory, more attention having been paid to the ornamental than the practical side of affairs. A very neat and expensive building, very like a bandstand in a German beer garden, has been built in the corner above the small waterfall. But there was no shelter for the pigs and no chicken house. I set the carpenter to putting up the beds (*not* the sort that had been ordered from Hoffnung's), and Louis gave orders to have the pavilion of the bandstand closed in with boards, so that he could use it to work in.

Just after we had finished breakfast in the morning, the "pantry man" from the *Lübeck,* the steamer we came down in, appeared and asked for work of any kind until Christmas, at which time he expects some trade stuff and intends to open a store. I engaged him on the spot to do anything required. He seems very willing and good-natured but extremely clumsy and not very good at speaking English.

We began opening boxes and getting out a few things for present comfort; but the chicken house seemed more pressing, as the rainy season is just coming on, and my poor Cochins that I brought in a box from Sydney do not seem capable of roughing it, and besides, we can get no eggs while the fowls are laying anywhere in the bush. I found it quite impossible to make Paul (the ex-pantry man is named Paul)[1] understand my directions and was almost in despair. We man-

[1] Paul Einfürer. "Paul—a German—cook and steward—a glutton of work—a splendid fellow; drawbacks, three: (1) no cook; (2) an inveterate bungler, a man with twenty thumbs, continually falling in the dishes, throwing out the dinner, preserving the garbage; (3) a dr——, well, don't let us say that—but we daren't let him go to town, and he—poor, good soul—is afraid to be let go."—RLS.

aged to build a frame of logs left by the carpenter, but it had no slope to the roof, nor could I get Paul to cut the logs to make this slope. Not but what he was most willing, but he could not understand me. Finally, with the utmost difficulty, we got it raised and one side nailed fast to a tree. I suppose it is about twelve feet square.

The next day, to my joy, I discovered a large ball of native cocoanut sennit I had bought in one of the Line Islands. I remember when I was laughed at for buying it. I said, "I feel it in my bones that I shall want that ball of sennit at Vailima." And I packed it in my trunk amid the jeers of my family, who proposed adding to it other building materials, such as branches of cocoanut and pieces of coral rock. I gave my sennit in the morning to Ben[2] (the "boss" of the outdoor "boys") and told him to take his men into the bush and cut saplings to finish the fowl house *faa samoa*.[3] It is now done, and very firm and substantial, and I am beginning to lay up stores of eggs.

While I was in the midst of my building, having the frame just hoisted, the missionary, Mr. Claxton,[4] came riding up to pay us a visit. I was a sorry-looking hostess, covered as I was with mud, my clothes torn, my hair matted with the wind and heat, and one of my bare ankles bleeding where I had scraped the skin off it. I left the guest, who kept saying, "I am not going to stay long, Mr. Stevenson, I am going in a moment," to Louis, while I donned more respectable garments.

After he was gone, my old friend [blank] (meaning "well-doing") came all dressed up to make a first call, a magnificent specimen of manhood. He wore a very scanty lava lava,[5] but its shortcomings were balanced by the size of the garland he wore round his neck. This garland was made of bachelor's-buttons four rows broad and reaching halfway down his thighs. He carried a present of fish and breadfruit,

[2] Spelled by RLS Bene or Peni as well as Ben. "Ben is supposed to be my ganger; the Lord love him! God made a truckling coward, there is his full history. He cannot tell me what he wants; he dares not tell me what is wrong; he dares not transmit my orders or translate my censures. And with all this, honest, sober, industrious, miserably smiling over the miserable issue of his own unmanliness."—RLS.

[3] In the Samoan manner.

[4] Rev. Arthur E. Claxton, of the London Missionary Society.

[5] A sort of kilt.

some of the latter baked and some raw. I had already prepared a fowl
to cook for dinner, with roasted wild bananas, both offerings bought
before we left Apia, so thought we could do no more than invite him
to dine with us, though I knew it was a bad precedent and we should,
in consequence, have an early repetition of the visit.

Sure enough he came the next day with another little basket of
provisions. After much anxious discussion we concluded to say
good-bye to him when dinner was served. It was a most embarrassing
thing to do but positively necessary. When Paul announced dinner
in the room where we sat, Louis rose from his chair, crossed over to
[blank] and, holding out his hand, said, "*Tofa*," the parting saluta-
tion. I did the same and then we sat down to our meal, having committed the meanest action that is possible for a Samoan. "An eater
of private meals" is a reproachful taunt. Our friend retired to the
back porch and we disposed of our private meal, wondering if we
had turned a good friend into an enemy for life. On the contrary,
he returned as soon as we left the table and not only accepted several
cigarettes but before he left begged for a bottle of kerosene, which
I firmly refused.

The next day but one he returned with a basket containing *poli
sami*,[6] breadfruit and a little fish. On this occasion, having already
marked the fact that we did not mean to accept him as one of the
family, we sent him out a well-filled plate of provisions to eat on the
porch.

The day after Mr. Claxton called we had a visit from Père Gavet,
a priest from the Catholic mission. Unfortunately for me he spoke
no English and I could only gather bits of what he said. I was very
sorry, for I wished to talk with him about a great many things. A
very embarrassing and curious thing had happened at the mission.
Père Gavet had just been reading in the newspaper an account of
how some Chinamen in Chicago had been discovered canning for
export the remains of some of their dead countrymen. When remon-
strated with they said that this stuff was for the South Sea trade.
What, therefore, were the Father's emotions when one of his men

---

[6] A native dish of taro tops and cocoanut; a pudding. Sometimes written
palusami by other writers, e.g., Margaret Mead.

came to him with a human tooth they had found in the tinned beef! In vain did he try to prove to them that it was the tooth of a cow —a sheep—any animal but man; they knew better and declared they were not cannibals. All the priest could do was to eat of the dish himself, "with what appetite you may guess," said he.

Besides making the fowl house, Ben and his three boys have been weeding the paddock, where we mean to keep our horse, and we hope a cow. The paddock is at present being fenced round with wire by the carpenter. The grass is propagated by cuttings and is a little difficult to start but when it does grow, grows well, and eats out all weeds. It is an importation from America called "buffalo grass." I am told that though cattle thrive upon it the milk will not be rich nor the butter good; but if the cows have in addition mummy apples[7] and bananas and a scented reed the Samoan women use in their wreaths, the butter will be excellent. I see little mummy apple trees springing up everywhere, so I have given orders to Ben to allow every one to stand.

Last evening I went about and dropped a few seeds of melons, tomatoes and bush lima beans here and there where I thought they might grow, as my garden must wait until the weeding is done, for it would never do to lose the grass just as it is taking a good root hold. I have brought some alfalfa seed to experiment with. Mr. Moors[8] says he tried and failed with it but I think being on the spot makes all the difference in the world. When Père Gavet was here I gave him a packet of the seed to try in his place. There are a good many native watermelons growing here and there but the fruit is poor and the moment it is fit to eat the rats devour all the pulp. A hollow shell was brought in to me yesterday and again this morning. Our only neighbour, Mr. Schmidt, sets out poison for them every night and I suppose I must do the same. I am afraid of Ben's cat eating the poisoned rats but she is as likely to eat Mr. Schmidt's as ours.

For two days an idiot bird has been flying back and forth inside the peak of our roof. It darted in at the open door and I naturally

[7] Papayas.
[8] H. J. Moors, friend of RLS and author of *With Stevenson in Samoa*.

supposed it would leave the way it came; but not it. The wretched creature fluttered back and forth all day, and at night roosted in an inaccessible spot on the mid-rafter. Yesterday I made a pathway of chairs and tried to chase it back and forth by means of a bunch of paper fastened to the point of a long spear, hoping thereby to cause it to take a lower flight and go out at one of the doors or windows which I had set open for the purpose. But though I brandished the spear till my arms were fit to drop with fatigue it kept to the same course, up and down the ridgeway. At present I do not see it, and cannot but hope that it has escaped while I was out directing the building of the pig shed.

We have three pigs, one fine imported white boar and two slab-sided sows. They dwell in a large circular enclosure which, with its stone walls, looks like an ancient fortification. I have another sow on board the *Janet Nichol*, presented to me at Savage Island when a little pig, by the wife of a half-caste named Johnny. It was promised me that the pig should be looked after until the *Janet* touches at Samoa, when she will be landed. I had, also, some sweet cocoanuts for seed in one of the lockers, which I suppose were overlooked when my things were sent ashore. I trust they will turn up with the pig. I had also ordered a black Berkshire sow from a butcher in Sydney but I imagine the butcher doubted the genuineness of my order until it was too late to ship the animal; but as his confidence has been restored by the sight of a very respectable businesslike elderly gentleman, who took a message for me concerning the pig, I feel that I have reason to expect it by the next *Lübeck*.

Of fowls, I brought five Cochin hens and two young cocks, and there are an uncertain number (daily growing less until the fowl house was put up) of black Spanish and mixed native fowls.

The trees that have been left standing in the clearing are of immense size, really majestic trees, creepers winding about their trunks and orchids growing in the forks of their branches. Of the latter, I am told two new specimens have been discovered here lately by a naturalist. Mr. Chalmers (Tamate),[9] the New Guinea missionary,

[9] Rev. James Chalmers of the London Missionary Society. Tamate was his Samoan name.

has promised to send me a lot of different sorts. He and Mrs. Claxton rode out to pay us a visit on Saturday afternoon. They brought the news that the steamer *Richard* had been delayed at Sydney by the strike, so Tamate shall not get away so soon as he expected, which is pleasant news for us, for we love Tamate, and Louis cherishes a hope of accompanying him to the Herveys.

Our great trees are alive with birds who chatter at certain hours of the night and the morning with rich, throaty voices. Though they do not exactly sing, their noise is very musical and pretty. Yesterday being Sunday and a holiday, Ben took his gun and went into the bush to shoot. He returned with a number of small birds, looking like little parrots, almost bursting with fat. I felt some compunction about eating birds that suggested cages and swings and stands but, as we had nothing else to eat, was fain to cook them, and a very excellent dish they made. I have read somewhere that the dodo and a relation of his called the toothbilled pigeon are still to be found on this island. It would be delightful to possess a pet dodo. That is one of my ambitions.

Our house has been a source of much tribulation to us. It is a little cottage, intended to serve in the future for a lodge, containing three rooms on the first floor and two on the ground floor. We live upstairs, one room of about fourteen by sixteen feet being for dining and sitting room; another, much smaller, we have taken for a bedroom. The third, some ten by six, we use as a pantry and provision room generally. Below, the large room is occupied by Ben, his wife, and little girl some two years of age, and the three kanakas[10] who work under Ben. Ben himself comes from the island of [blank], one of the boys from [blank], the third and fourth I believe are Samoans, as is Ben's wife. Mrs. Ben is a fine strapping young woman, with a beautiful figure, a plain face, and a capacity for idleness equalled by none. She generally wears but a single bit of cloth twisted round her waist, but, upon occasions, shows up in a striped cotton saque. The baby is generally quite naked but possesses a garment the size of a handkerchief. It seems a very good quiet little thing but has an unpleasant trick of drinking with its mouth

[10] Natives.

at the faucet of the water tank. The knowledge that Samoan children are liable to a terrible disease called yaws, which is contagious, and incurable in adult whites, does not tend to make this habit exactly acceptable. The small room corresponding to our storeroom is used by Ben for the same purpose. Here he keeps his barrels of salt beef, his tins of kerosene, his rice and ship's biscuit, the provisions for the men; and also a few spades and shovels and axes and knives, all, except the knives, in the most uncared for, dilapidated condition.

I fear I have hurt Ben's feelings this morning. Saturday night an old man, presumably a relation of his wife, arrived and stayed over Sunday. All the Samoans about Apia are inveterate thieves, so I could not but feel rather uncomfortable about a number of boxes that are lying in Ben's premises with the heads loosened. Still I did not want to cut Ben off from his Sunday visitors. But when I found the old man this morning settling himself as a fixture and demanding a native wooden pillow he had discovered on the upper porch, I thought I had better take a defensive policy. "Every man who stays here after his business is done or his visit is over must go to work," I explained, and set the old man to digging stones. He was dismayed at this, and when I went out to see what he was about, he had inveigled the boys away from the pig house to help him. I sent them back to their work and the old man disappeared, but I suspect him of still hanging about somewhere.

But to return to the house. We liked it well enough in any respect but its colour. Our sitting room, open to the iron roof which in itself is an ugly colour, is painted up from the floor four feet high, with a cold black paint. Above that it is a still colder, still more offensive white. The doors are of a chilly lead colour. Altogether the whole place has a chilling, deathlike aspect. We looked over our boxes and unearthed several pieces of tapa, very dark, the ground work being a rich maroon black, and the figures rising through all shades of reddish brown to the lightest coffee-and-milk. There were several pieces that served for bordering, and when they were all nailed up, though only the two principal sides of the room were covered, the whole appearance of the place was changed. Over the door connecting the two rooms we fastened a large flat branch of pink coral from Nanouti,[11] a present given me by Captain Reid[12] when we were on the *Equator*. We have had the carpenter put up shelves in one corner of the room and on two sides of the windows. I also had him nail some pieces of boards together in the form of a couch, upon which I have laid a mattress covered by a shawl. On the wooden table an old pink cloth is spread. When we light the lamp and set the little Japanese box smoking with buhach—for, alas, there *are* mosquitoes—we feel quite snug and homelike. Soon we hope to finish the walls and spread some of our fine mats on the floor.

SEPT. 30TH

The pig house, which was begun yesterday, is finished. I must say it is a very unsightly-looking thing, but a creeper or two will soon turn it into a picturesque object. Tamate came yesterday to say good-bye, as his steamer had arrived unexpectedly. I sent Ben and the rest of the boys down to Apia with the handcart. They came back very late, much too heavily laden, fetching more wine than had been meant they should. The wine we bought in the cask when we were at Noumea,[13] and it has been bottled in Apia. I discovered this morning that all the native chickens had escaped through the interstices of the sides of the fowl house where they join the roof. I should have thought a fly would have been kept captive. Ben has closed up every chink now, so I think we have them safely. While I was superintending the pig house and Louis was down at the pavilion working, the idiot bird managed to escape. I was devoutly thankful to be rid of him, for it tormented me to think of his suffering from thirst and hunger and terror. Louis refused to waste any sympathy on a fool. I have had a milk pan punched with nail holes and sunk into the hole in the water cask where the pipe enters, so I hope now the mosquitoes may become sensibly fewer.

Henry,[14] Louis's former secretary, a full-blooded Samoan from

[11] One of the Gilbert Islands.
[12] Dennis Reid.
[13] A city of New Caledonia.
[14] Henry Simile. "Henry is a chiefling from Savaii; I once loathed, I now like and—pending fresh discoveries—have a kind of respect for Henry. He does

Savaii, came to see us yesterday. When he applied for the position of secretary he said he hoped, in the course of his work, to be able to learn "long expressions." We do not particularly like Henry, who always became lame if I asked any little service from him, such as carrying a chair or going a few steps to the house of the missionary. But still we feel that he ought to be encouraged, as in many ways he is intelligent and a very progressive Samoan. He asked for employment yesterday, and as we had absolutely nothing to do, Louis said he would give him a shilling three times a week if he wished to come out and carry messages for us. As we shall probably have as many visits from him, it was really a shilling to pay a visit. He was on the point of refusing, then became alarmed lest he might lose something better, and accepted.

He brought a curious tale, probably distorted, from Apia. According to his account, some of the black boys on the German plantation got liquor somewhere and while drunk attacked the native police with axes and sticks. The strange part of his tale is that the police were forbidden to follow the black fellows to the German plantation for the purpose of arresting them.

Louis has ridden down to Apia on the good plain little pony that we found among our possessions.

Dr. Stuebel, the German consul-general, came to call just as I was sitting down to my very frugal repast: some very tough stewed mutton, boiled mummy apples, and breadfruit, with a glass of red wine and water. Some strange fatality seems to attend any horse furniture in Samoa: bridles fall apart, saddles dissolve themselves into their primitive elements, and altogether riding is fraught with a somewhat alarming interest. I was, by an accident, able to produce a piece of stout string for the mending of Dr. Stuebel's bridle. I trust it served him well and got him home safely, as I should be loth to have anything happen to a person I like and admire as much as I like and admire Dr. Stuebel.

---

good work for us; goes among the labourers, bossing and watching; helps Fanny; is civil, kindly, thoughtful; O *si sic semper!* But will he be 'his sometime self throughout the year'? Anyway, he has deserved of us, and he must disappoint me sharply ere I give him up."—RLS.

There seem to be a great many mummy apples springing up through the clearing, which I am glad of for the prospective cows. Paul and I have planted out a lot of kidney potatoes, which is an experiment only, as they are not supposed to grow in Samoa. We have filled several boxes with earth and sowed in them seeds of tomatoes, of artichokes, and eggplant. A few days ago Mr. Carruthers[15] sent us half a dozen very fine pineapples, so as fast as we eat them we plant the tops. Mrs. Ben seems to be "on the rampage" today, and poor Ben is having a sad time of it. She goes about tossing her head till the keys she wears hanging over one ear rattle on her cheek bone. She was very much annoyed by Paul's telling her that she should not take her bath under the spout of the water cask. The baby has a very unpleasant habit of sucking the lower end of the spigot. I mean to certainly circumvent her tomorrow by fastening a rough bit of tin round it. I have written a long letter to Lloyd[16] describing our life here and find myself confused, and uncertain whether I am not repeating what I have said already. Mrs. Schmidt sent us a loaf of bread. I know it is ill looking gift bread in the mouth, but I do not like some bread much better than ship's biscuit. I made another attempt at yeast today, having found the proper receipt.

OCT. 6TH

I have been too busy to write a word before. But I have accomplished something, for a good lot of sweet corn is planted, some peas and onions, lettuces and radishes. My lima beans are coming up and some of the cantaloupe melons. Mr. Carruthers has been here, fetching a little root of mint and some more cuttings of the grenadilla, which have been set out along the arbour. He tells us that one of our boys has been offering melons for sale, stolen from our place. It is true they are not fit to eat, but I was properly indignant. I fancy the culprit is a rather glib young man, very handsome, with hair dyed a soft red. I have noticed for some days past that he has been shirking work also. I think an example must soon be made of him.

Ben's wife, Va, is an ill-conditioned creature. A few evenings ago

---

[15] R. Hetherington Carruthers, an Apia solicitor.
[16] Lloyd Osbourne, her son, then in England. *Treasure Island* was dedicated to him, for in a sense it was written for him. In later years he became a writer.

I heard her scolding Ben like a virago. Suddenly she dashed down
the road to the waterfall, screaming as she ran, and after a fine fit
of hysterics returned and joined in family prayers. Upon the next
hysterical outburst an example is to be made of her also. Ben is an
excellent and deserving fellow and it is a pity he is so badly mated.
I was wondering at the poverty, from a Samoan standpoint, of Mrs.
Ben, for I never saw another mat but the one old one she covers
herself with at night, sleeping on some old ones of mine; but Louis
reminded me that Ben was a stranger, without family connexions,
and consequently so bad a match that Va's relations probably refused
to come forward with marriage presents. And that carried us back to
the time at Butaritari,[17] when that most degraded of beachcombers,
Arthur Wise, wishing to insult us, called out as we sat at table, "Do
you know who that is you have got dining with you? *That man
doesn't belong to this island!*" If it came to that, no more did he,
nor did we.

It seems absolutely impossible to get anything sent up to us from
Apia. Lists and notes go flying, but, except from Krause the butcher,
with no results. It seemed an odd thing that there should not be a
spade nor rake for sale in a town where there would be no difficulty
in finding the best quality of champagne, to say nothing of all the
materials for mixed drinks.

It has turned out, sure enough, that Henry brought a garbled
account of the fight between the police and the black boys. The
black boys were drunk and one of their number was put in jail by
the police. His companions broke open the jail and rescued the
prisoner. The police resisted and there was a general row, the black
boys getting the worst of it. Henry came again on the appointed
day and remained for some hours, helping me to unpack boxes. He
asked for employment, and after some haggling it was agreed that
he should come on Monday to help me plant trees and to procure
trees for me, also to ride down to Apia several times a week on errands. Each day he and Louis are to give each other lessons in
Samoan and English. The wages are ten dollars a month and board;

[17] One of the Gilbert Islands.

I am to furnish a blanket and Henry is to sleep below with Ben's family and to eat with Paul.

We have almost starved for want of provisions until yesterday, when Ben killed a couple of fowls, a large piece of meat came from town, Paul bought two pigeons, and Mrs. Blacklock[18] came with fresh tomatoes. Afterwards, my Irish woman turned up, looking thin but very gay, with breadfruit cooked and raw, and poli sami. Afterwards Ben came with more poli sami, and now today comes a young native girl from Mrs. Blacklock with enormous bananas, long green beans, a dozen eggs, and a bunch of flowers. Mrs. Blacklock looked very pretty and very superior yesterday. She made conversation when she could and during the pauses composedly sang in an undertone. She had pulled off a sweet scented creeper as she rode up, and twisted it with much careless grace round her waist so that it fell in two long tendrils almost to her feet. Ben has come in with eight little parrots. It seems either a famine or a feast. Last night we thought we heard a cracking of muskets but it was only Paul failing to make a table in the bandstand. The carpenter, Mr. Willis, husband of Laulii,[19] who wrote the story of her life (very well when she was allowed her own expressions), came with the plans for our house. He is to figure out the cost and let us know. Yesterday morning the woman came with no milk, and this morning brought two bottles, thinking that would do as well.

OCT. 7TH

This has been a day of small events. It rained heavily last night, much to my joy, as my gardens needed the moisture. But when I wanted fair weather it still poured. As our kitchen is some six or eight yards from the house, cooking became a series of adventures. I had set sponge for bread last night and was most anxious to bake the dough early in the day. A black boy came up from the carpenter

[18] A native woman, wife of William Blacklock, a clerk at the American consulate in Samoa, who became vice-consul and then consul, succeeding Harold M. Sewall.

[19] Laulii was a favorite with Louis because of her animation, charm, quaint English, and ability to tell amusing stories. According to Isobel Field, he would interrupt his work when Laulii called at Vailima—which was very unusual for him. Laulii, with the help of her husband, Alex, wrote *The Story of Laulii*, edited by William H. Barnes. San Francisco: J. Winterburn & Co., 1889.

with a moulding board just when I was ready for it, so, placing it on a chair in the back verandah, I knelt on the floor with a shawl over my shoulders to keep the rain off. In making the dough I was successful, but the attempt to bake it almost sent me into hysterics. I ran with the pan of dough, an umbrella over my head, to the kitchen, but to my dismay the wood was all soaked and the wind drove the smoke back into the stove, which belched forth acrid clouds from every opening through which smoke could pour its way. Paul ran down to where the carpenter had been working and returned with a box full of chips, which we dried on top of the stove, swallowing and breathing volumes of smoke as we did so. Then I called Ben and showed him how to nail up half of a tin kerosene can over the outer opening of the pipe to screen it from the wind. That helped a little; but the rain beat in on the stove, and though we consumed immense quantities of chips it still remained cold. Finally I made a barrier of boxes around the stove and that brought a measure of success, so that in about a couple of hours I was able to half bake, half dry a fowl for luncheon. By that time the bread was done for, and I very nearly.

Paul and I held a council of war and concluded to send the boys down to the pavilion to live. We will take their room for a kitchen and dining room, one end serving for the one, the other end for the other. One corner will be reserved for a receptacle for stores, saddles, trunks, etc., and Paul will sleep in the little storeroom. In the meantime Louis had sent off two of the boys to Mr. Carruthers to get the plants and trees he had promised us, and also gave them a small leather bag containing letters for Mr. Carruthers to post. In the midst of my most troublous moments three natives appeared and said they had a bullimakaw for sale. The name seemed very appropriate, for it was very difficult to guess whether the animal was a bull or a cow. There were certainly no indications of an intention to give milk about it. We told the men to take it away—"bullimakaw no good." It was not so easy to take the brute away, however, the fresh young grass being too pleasant to its taste. The men pulled for some time at the end of the long rope; the rope was very long, as they evidently feared to get near the creature, who looked extremely vicious and bore an immense pair of horns. Suddenly the bullimakaw chose to make a start and disappeared, dragging a man after her in a most ludicrous way.

Just after luncheon, Henry made his appearance. Then the black boys returned with the trees and the leather bag. When the latter was opened there lay the most important of the letters sent by Louis. It was most vexing. Instead of handing the bag to Mr. C as they had been told to do they had opened it before their arrival and taken out the letters, leaving the one. Fortunately one of Mr. C's boys came a few moments after upon an errand, so we sent the letter down by him.

I was delighted to find two mango trees among the plants, and wondered to discover also a shrub that is the pest of Tahiti and will soon become the same here if it is planted for an ornamental shrub.

In the afternoon the rain lessened to a little more than a mistiness, so Henry and I began to set out the things. While we were some distance from the house I saw three or four beautiful young men, followed by a troop of dogs, passing along our road towards the bush. I have seldom seen more graceful elegant creatures than these poor fellows, whom I knew it to be my duty to order off the premises. They carried large knives and axes and wore hats of fresh green banana leaves. Their heads were sheltered from the rain by large banana leaves which they carried like umbrellas. Before I could reach them they were out of sight, but Louis sent Ben after them to warn them that the road was taboo. It is supposed that he was afraid to deliver the message, as later in the day the youths came back laden with long withes, singing as they came. Louis went out to meet them and ordered them to throw their bundles to the ground, and Paul to cut the thongs that bound them. By Henry's help it was explained to them that they must in the future keep to the public road, which is only a little way from ours. If they came again, after this warning, they were told that not only their burdens but their knives and axes would be taken from them; in the meantime they might bind up their bundles again and depart. All this interview was conducted by Louis in the sternest voice he could assume, but with a countenance wreathed in smiles. With a friendly *tofa* on both sides, they went on their way, hardly sadder, but I trust wiser than when they came.

After we had planted all the roots and had taken a little rest, Henry and I took a hoe and a pickaxe and finished the afternoon sowing Indian corn. In the meantime the stove had, too late, become so hot that it was difficult to get near it. Ben's wife went away yesterday with the child, ostensibly to stay with a sick father. I told Paul to do the cooking for the boys in her absence. We looked over Ben's stores and found things in a sorry mess. There were bags of beans white and red, but Ben said they were uneatable. It was small wonder, as Va put them on to boil about half an hour before dinner. Paul put a potful on the stove and set some more to soak. When served they were declared to be excellent. A third of a large tin of bread (ship's biscuit) I found to be absolutely unfit for food, crawling with maggots and almost rotten. The floor of the storeroom was soaked with salt drippings from the meat casks, and altogether things were in a most deplorable state. Tomorrow we shall clean it all up and arrange things in a different fashion.

I find Paul an excellent, sterling fellow. I do not see how I should manage without him. Nothing in the way of work seems too much for him and he is good-natured through all our tribulations. Louis gave him a bottle of beer for his luncheon. I think he deserved champagne, though no doubt the beer was more to his taste, as indeed it is to mine. Though he is only intending to remain until Christmas, he takes as much interest in everything as though it were his own home, where he is to live the rest of his life.

I was amused by Henry's adoption of the word "our" as soon as he came to stay. He talks about our house that is to be built, our trees and our affairs generally. Tonight after dinner, as we were enjoying the evening on the front verandah, he asked if we had heard of the war of the spirits. We had been told something that I did not clearly catch, and also that it was feared by the whites to have a sinister political meaning. We were very glad to hear this tale in full from Henry. So well as I can remember, here is the tale.

The spirits of Upolu are at war with the spirits of Savaii. Every night the sound of cannon and musketry and the cries of men fighting

are heard from the two nearest points of Upolu and Savaii. People
have fallen into trances, with stern set countenances like corpses,
and the spirits have talked from their mouths. A woman saw a
strong swimmer coming in from the sea. He leaped to the shore and
ran into the bush, disappearing and appearing as he did so, whereby
the woman knew him to be a spirit. A few evenings ago the missionary at Savaii, who is a doctor and keeps a dispensary, was startled
by two knocks at his window, followed by the cries and groans of
many wounded men. He looked out and beheld a great multitude of
spirits clothed in the bodies of men, all exhibiting dreadful wounds
and all demanding medicine for their hurts. The missionary ran to
call his servant, upon whose arrival the spirits became invisible and
were heard no more.

"In this war of the spirits," we asked, "which was the victor, Upolu
or Savaii?"

"Savaii," was the answer.

"And what," we asked, "is considered to be the meaning of it all
among the Samoans?"

The spirits, we were told, had spoken through the mouths of the
people who go into trances and said that it was the portent of a
coming war in Samoa. The long delay in the coming of the Chief
Justice has unsettled the minds of the Samoans and they seem to
be falling away from Malietoa.[20] Two sections of people who were
before at odds but separately opposed to Malietoa have become
most friendly. When a superstitious people wish to go to war, they
easily find encouraging portents. We possess two pistols and two
boxes of cartridges, a scant armoury for war time.

I asked Henry, when we were planting, which was the best season
for such work, meaning the wet, dry or intermediate time.

"We Samoans," he answered, "always go by the moon; unless we
plant in the time of the big round moon we expect no fruit."

Meanwhile Louis was busily studying the Samoan scene, with his great
curiosity and enthusiam and his constant and inspired scribbling. He
liked the Samoans almost at once. He described them in A Footnote to
History.

[20] Malietoa Laupepa, "king" of Samoa.

They are easy, merry, and pleasure loving; the gayest, though by far from either the most capable or the most beautiful of Polynesians. Fine dress is a passion, and makes a Samoan festival a thing of beauty. Song is almost ceaseless. The boatman sings at the oar, the family at evening worship, the girls at night in the guest house, sometimes the workman at his toil. No occasion is too small for the poets and musicians; a death, a visit, the day's news, the day's pleasantry, will be set to rhyme and harmony. Even half-grown girls, the occasion arising, fashion words and train choruses of children for its celebration. Song, as with all Pacific islanders, goes hand in hand with the dance, and both shade into the drama. Some of the performances are indecent and ugly, some only dull; others are pretty, funny, and attractive. Games are popular. Cricket matches, where a hundred played upon a side, endured at times for weeks, and ate up the country like the presence of an army. Fishing, the daily bath, flirtation; courtship, which is gone upon by proxy; conversation, which is largely political; and the delights of public oratory; fill in the long hours.

But the special delight of the Samoan is the melaga. When people form a party and go from village to village, junketing and gossiping, they are said to go on a melaga. Their songs have announced their approach ere they arrive; the guest house is prepared for their reception; the virgins of the village attend to prepare the kava[21] bowl and entertain them with the dance; time flies in the enjoyment of every pleasure which an islander conceives; and when the melaga sets forth, the same welcome and the same joys expect them beyond the next cape, where the nearest village nestles in its grove of palms.

Enjoying greater health than he had experienced in years, Louis walked about a great deal, always observing, and thinking of what he saw as possible raw material for essays, novels, even political tracts. What he saw fascinated him, and part of it he set down in his *Footnote*.

Apia, the port and mart, is the seat of the political sickness of Samoa. At the foot of a peaked woody mountain, the coast makes

---

[21] A fermented drink made from the root of a pepper plant and widely used on ceremonial occasions.

a deep indent, roughly semicircular. In front the barrier reef is broken by the fresh water of the streams; if the swell be from the north, it enters almost without diminution; and the war-ships roll dizzily at their moorings, and along the fringing coral which follows the configuration of the beach, the surf breaks with a continuous uproar. In wild weather, as the world knows, the roads are untenable. Along the whole shore, which is everywhere green and level and overlooked by inland mountain-tops, the town lies drawn out in strings and clusters. The western horn is Mulinuu, the eastern, Matautu; and from one to the other of these extremes, I ask the reader to walk. He will find more of the history of Samoa spread before his eyes in that excursion, than has yet been collected in the blue-books or the white-books of the world. Mulinuu (where the walk is to begin) is a flat, wind-swept promontory, planted with palms, backed against a swamp of mangroves, and occupied by a rather miserable village. The reader is informed that this is the proper residence of the Samoan kings; he will be the more surprised to observe a board set up, and to read that this historic village is the property of the German firm. But these boards, which are among the commonest features of the landscape, may be rather taken to imply that the claim has been disputed. A little farther east he skirts the stores, offices, and barracks of the firm itself. Thence he will pass through Matafele, the one really town-like portion of this long string of villages, by German bars and stores and the German consulate; and reach the Catholic mission and cathedral standing by the mouth of a small river. The bridge which crosses here (bridge of Mulivai) is a frontier; behind is Matafele; beyond, Apia proper; behind, Germans are supreme; beyond, with few exceptions, all is Anglo-Saxon. Here the reader will go forward past the stores of Mr. Moors (American) and Messrs. MacArthur (English); past the English mission, the office of the English newspaper, the English church, and the old American consulate, till he reaches the mouth of a larger river, the Vaisingano. Beyond, in Matautu, his way takes him in the shade of many trees and by scattered dwellings, and presently brings him beside a great range of offices, the place and the monument of a German who fought the German firm during his life. His house (now he is dead) remains pointed like a discharged cannon at the citadel of his old enemies. Fitly enough, it is at present leased and occupied by Englishmen. A little farther, and the reader gains the eastern flanking angle of the bay, where stands the pilot-house and signal post, and whence he can see, on the line of the main coast of the island, the British and the new American consulates.

The course of his walk will have been enlivened by a considerable to and fro of pleasure and business. He will have encountered many varieties of whites—sailors, merchants, clerks, priests, Protestant missionaries in their pith helmets, and the nondescript hangers-on of any island beach. And the sailors are sometimes in considerable force; but not the residents. He will think at times there are more signboards than men to own them. It may chance it is a full day in the harbour; he will then have seen all manner of ships, from men-of-war and deep-sea packets to the labour-vessels of the German firm and the cockboat island schooner; and if he be of an arithmetical turn, he may calculate that there are more whites afloat in Apia bay than whites ashore in the whole Archipelago. On the other hand, he will have encountered all ranks of natives, chiefs and pastors in their scrupulous white clothes; perhaps the king himself, attended by guards in uniform; smiling policemen with their pewter stars; girls, women, crowds of cheerful children. And he will have asked himself with some surprise where these reside. Here and there, in the back yards of European establishments, he may have had a glimpse of a native house elbowed in a corner; but since he left Mulinuu, none on the beach where islanders prefer to live, scarce one on the line of street. The handful of whites have everything; the natives walk in a foreign town. A year ago, on a knoll behind a bar-room, he might have observed a native house guarded by sentries and flown over by the standard of Samoa. He would then have been told it was the seat of government, driven (as I have to relate) over the Mulivai and from beyond the German town into the Anglo-Saxon. To-day, he will learn it has been carted back again to its old quarters. And he will think it significant that the king of the islands should be thus shuttled to and fro in his chief city at the nod of aliens. And then he will observe a feature more significant still: a house with some concourse of affairs, policemen and idlers hanging by, a man at a bank-counter overhauling manifests, perhaps a trial proceeding in the front verandah, or perhaps the council breaking up in knots after a stormy sitting. And he will remember that he is in the *Eleele Sa*, the "Forbidden Soil" or Neutral Territory of the treaties; that the magistrate whom he has just seen trying native criminals is no officer of the native king's; and that this, the only port and place of business in the kingdom, collects and administers its own revenue for its own behoof by the hands of white councillors and under the supervision of white consuls. Let him go farther afield. He will find the roads almost everywhere to cease or to be made impassable by native pig-fences, bridges to be quite unknown, and houses of the whites to become at once a rare exception. Set aside the German plantations, and the frontier is sharp. At the boundary of the *Eleele Sa*, Europe ends, Samoa begins. Here, then, is a singular state of affairs: all the money, luxury, and business of kingdom centred in one place; that place excepted from the native government and administered by whites for whites; and the whites themselves holding it not in common but in hostile camps, so that it lies between them like a bone between two dogs, each growling, each clutching his own end.

Should Apia ever choose a coat of arms, I have a motto ready: "Enter Rumour painted full of tongues." The majority of the natives do extremely little; the majority of the whites are merchants with some four mails in the month, shopkeepers with some ten or twenty customers a day, and gossip is the common resource of all. The town hums to the day's news, and the bars are crowded with amateur politicians. Some are office-seekers, and earwig king and consul, and compass the fall of officials, with an eye to salary. Some are humourists, delighted with the pleasure of faction for itself. "I never saw so good a place as this Apia," said one of these; "you can be in a new conspiracy every day!" Many, on the other hand, are sincerely concerned for the future of the country. The quarters are so close and the scale is so small, that perhaps not any one can be trusted always to preserve his temper. Every one tells everything he knows; that is our country sickness. Nearly every one has been betrayed at times, and told a trifle more; the way our sickness takes the predisposed. And the news flies, and the tongues wag, and fists are shaken. Pot boil and cauldron bubble!

F A N N Y . OCTOBER 10

After Henry's lesson in English the other evening, he told us that all the talk among the natives is of war. They are tired of waiting for the Chief Justice and believe he is not coming. He asked a good many questions about theology, which rather alarmed me, though Louis was quite ready with answers. I am always fearful of clashing with what the missionaries have taught and thereby unsettling the minds of natives. He particularly wanted to know if it was true that all heathen peoples who have not heard of Christianity are doomed to hell. He understood they were. Certainly Henry is working very well and behaving very well. There has been an undercurrent of feeling on the part of Ben, he *said* because there were too many mosquitoes in the bandstand; but as I knew it was the one spot almost free from those pests I looked for some other clue to his behaviour. It occurred to me that he might infer that the custody of the men's stores had passed out of his hands. Louis immediately went out and told him that Paul had nothing to do with the stores and must always go to Ben if he wished to use anything of the sort. Ben went away smiling and quite happy, apparently, so my guess must have been a right one.

Mr. Carruthers has helped us choose a site for the kitchen garden. It had to be cleared before being dug up. Faliali[22] was set to work on it at once, and Louis, armed with a big forest knife, fell to with him. Louis would be at it still, but the blisters on his hands are very deep and it might not be safe to let them grow worse.[23] The unfortunate thing is that when Louis is not working with F the business grows very slack indeed. A shower came up today and all the fellows, naked but for their breech clouts, ran for shelter. A

[22] A native. Apparently he worked for the Stevensons only a short time.
[23] The Samoan climate had such a remarkably beneficial effect on Louis's health that very often, despite his frailness and his ordinarily precarious health, he worked himself up into a literal sweat of work or play without apparent harm.

couple were discovered in the old cook house, smoking their pipes. Henry, when he saw Ben's gang quit work, ran out and told Ben he must call them, but Ben writhed and didn't dare to. Then Henry took it upon himself to do so, and set to weeding with them to set an example, which was really more than I had thought him capable of. When he spoke of it to me he said that Ben could not order anyone to work, but "My heart," he said, "is strong."

Yesterday Paul asked to go down to Apia to attend to several affairs. "I should like to go today," he said, "and once more on Sunday when the *Lübeck* comes in; and after that, Mrs. Stevenson, don't let me go any more. Don't do it; make me stay here."

I thought there was something ominous in this remark and was not, therefore, greatly surprised when he returned much the worse for drink. We saw him ride up, swaying about in his saddle in a most dangerous way; he took the readiest way of dismounting, for he fell off his horse as soon as it stopped.

He is a very pale and repentant Paul today but nothing has been said to him yet. Louis is going to tell him tomorrow that if he wants to go to Apia to meet the *Lübeck* then they two will go together and return together. He had no proper clothes to go with, so I lent him a hat, a sash, and Louis's only pair of shoes.

I thought one of my yellow hens wanted to sit and that it would be the proper thing to provide her with eggs. To be sure that I should know the eggs I placed in the nest from newly laid ones, I made a black pencil mark quite round each egg. After all was finished I returned from the fowl house and peeped through the palings. Madame hen clucked up to the nest as I had been used to see hens do, but at sight of the marked eggs started back with a sort of cry of surprise and alarm. "What's the matter?" cried the two cocks, stretching wide legs as they hastened to the spot. They, too, started back, just as the hen had done, held a flurried consultation, and finally ventured to touch the eggs with their beaks. By this time all the five yellow hens had gathered round the nest and pretty soon all the other fowls were craning their necks over the yellow ones' back to gaze upon the marvel. After the cocks had both poked the eggs about a little the hens went a little nearer and tried to pick off the black marks. All the time there was a great hubbub of anxious conversation. The next morning more than half the eggs had been destroyed, and to save those left I had to remove them.

Mr. Carruthers and Mr. Maben,[24] the surveyor, have been to the headquarters of one of the streams. They find it flowing from a spring, and the fall, where we shall want to use it, is some two hundred feet. Mr. Carruthers described the source first and took Mr. Maben, who was very incredulous, to the place. He says he has found quite a plantation of bananas, and a lot of taro up one of the streams. As soon as Louis's hand is better he is going to fall to cutting a path to it.

On the path by the stream where the garden is making we find very curious divisions running from the banks of the stream hillward, every few yards, made of stones. I do not know yet whether they are simply surface divisions or real walls, nor how far up the banks they run, but in the working of the garden we shall easily find out. Henry says that before white people came to Samoa the natives all lived inland and not on the beach as is now the case.

It is very difficult to keep these men at work. Both Louis and Henry are after them now. Sarcasm is the only weapon of any use against them and it is difficult to wield that around with no knowledge of Samoan. I have made both Henry and Ben mosquito nets and given Henry a couple of shirts. I am sure he thinks more of these small presents than all the wages he gets. The garden Paul and I made and the one Henry and I made are springing up beautifully, and the peas and sweet corn are beginning to show, while the lima beans are quite robust plants. I am sending for more seeds, particularly of grasses, with which I want to experiment. Two men have been put on to weed a patch of land near the house, where I intend to have maize planted closely to feed a bullimakaw, when we get one, with the green leaves. The butcher, I hear, is expecting a couple of milch cows, and I might have a chance with him.

OCT. 11TH

Dr. Stuebel and Mr. Schmidt came in and interrupted me yesterday. My admiration for Dr. Stuebel is great. They brought the

[24] Thomas Maben, government surveyor, later secretary of state in Samoa.

news that a meeting is to be held today by the native dignitaries to discuss and try to arrive at the meaning of the mysterious portents that have been so alarming and unsettling the native mind. The omens are coming thicker and faster. A fish was caught which Dr. S saw and ate of, all head and no tail, a hideous creature, the prick of whose fins are said to cause certain death, and on its back it was possible to make out a native word that means snapping or biting and betokens war and disaster. A red eel has been caught, and down a river blood was observed to be running, but worst of all a dog has interfered in a kava drinking. When Henry told us of the war of the spirits we were amused that he spoke of only one incident as being doubtful: that of the spirits' call upon the doctor. "Of that," he said, "I cannot be sure."

Ben is evidently on the point of a quarrel with anybody who will take it up. He came to Paul yesterday to complain that the men had meat but once a day, and *that* after the whole business of the commissariat had been placed in his hands alone. He said that black boys must have meat once a day and Samoans twice. It seems an odd distinction when one is aware that the black boys do twice the work the Samoans do. Speaking of work, it is pouring a drenching rain, and in the midst of it I see Henry with an umbrella over his head, and Paul in a mackintosh, both helping the weeders of the corn patch. Louis had a talk with Ben last night which he hopes has been successful, but one can never be sure. If we speak to Ben he crouches into the room and squats on the floor with the humility of a native inferior and giggles a sycophantic assent to everything put forward. If he is told to translate a sharp order to the boys it is just the same, but no order reaches the boys. He is a most invaluable man for us but aggravating beyond description. Louis also had it out with Paul on the subject of his condition when he returned from Apia the other day. Paul wept and gave his word that it should not occur again. The words, "I was ashamed, Paul, when I saw you fall off your horse before the black boys," seemed to have a strong effect.

OCT. 14

Mr. Moors came yesterday morning and stayed all day. In the afternoon Mr. Willis the carpenter rode up: he is the husband of the Samoan girl Laulii, who dictated a very curious book of her reminiscences to her husband and a very stupid American. When Laulii's own words were given, the book was charming, but became vulgar and commonplace as soon as another pen interpreted for her.

I had a couple of chickens for lunch, and potatoes mashed, and pineapple cut up in red wine. As my bread was again a failure I made a panful of American soda biscuits, remembering that Mr. Moors was fond of them. Just as luncheon was well under way and I was congratulating myself that I had at last succeeded in getting the stove hot, I turned to Paul with the remark, "It's all right at last."

"Yes," was his answer, "but I'm not."

I saw then that his face was deathly pale, his features collapsed, while the sweat was dropping from his face. He had changed his clothes to wait on the table, replacing a flannel shirt with a linen one that closed in the back. He said he had a terrible pain under his shoulders. I sent him to his room to put on his flannels again and ran up to tell Louis. Louis took down the dry cupping glass, the application of which drove the pain about his body to different places. I proposed giving him salicylate of soda, which was done. I went on to finish cooking the meal, leaving poor Paul a pallid wreck in bed, with the cupping glass sticking to his back. In the evening the pain was quite gone but the man was very much shaken.

From the balcony we saw the *Lübeck* come in to Apia harbour. Mr. Moors promised to send us our letters. Louis told me that our friend the "bush man" who came in on Saturday with breadfruit and *poli sami* had asked for work, which he saw no way of refusing with decency. It is an embarrassing situation, for F has been very kind, but I do not think he is a hard-working man and I feared he might prove a bad example to the boys, of whom we turned off all on Saturday night except Faliali and Ben, trusting to Henry to get us a new lot. This morning five stalwart fellows turned up, but I know nothing of how they work, for Henry, who was told to send several of them to town with the cart for parcels from the *Lübeck* and elsewhere, sent off the whole five to do the work of three. To our relief, the bush man has not turned up.

After Mr. Moors and Mr. Willis were gone, Louis volunteered to show me the banana patch, carrying a knife with him to clear the path. These explorations on one's own estate are most exciting. For a little way we followed a pretty open path that had been cleared by Louis, but by and by it began to close up and become treacherously boggy under foot. Several times we were ankle deep in mud and water and Louis had to slash down the lianas and tall vegetation that obstructed our way. Before very long Louis cried out, "Behold your banana patch!"

There it was, sure enough, a great number of sturdy thick-set young trees, many with bunches of fruit hanging above the strange purple flower of the plant, choked with a rank undergrowth and set with their roots in sluggishly running water. Here and there the gigantic leaves of the great taro spread out, dark shining green. It was too much for Louis, who fell to clearing on the spot, while I went on to the end of the plantation. Once or twice I was nearly stuck in the bog, but managed to drag myself from the ooze by clutching to a strong plant.

Louis called out to me as though in answer, and I hastened to return to him. When I came he said that he had mistaken the cry of a bird for my voice and supposed I had lost the path. I helped him a little while, pulling up the smaller weeds, for I was in mortal terror of touching a poisonous creeper whose acquaintance I had already made and whose marks I still bear. It went to my heart to drag up and destroy the most lovely specimens of ferns I have ever seen. But I did it bravely, though I determined to return some day and make a collection of them. Some of the more delicate climbing ferns were indescribably beautiful and the tree ferns were magnificent. Occasionally, as I threw out a plant, the air about me was filled with the perfume of its bruised leaves.

It was entrancing work, though we were soaked with mud and water; but before long my head began to swim and I proposed to go back to the house and see about some sort of food. I just managed to get a meal prepared and then gave out utterly; my beautiful banana swamp had given me fever with a most alarming promptitude. I could not sleep all night but kept waking with a start, my heart and pulses pounding and my head aching miserably. This morning

Louis gave me a dose of quinine, which soon helped me, but he took none himself, which he should have done, for he too had a touch of fever, though he did not confess it till long after.

The pigs had to be watered when I came back from the perfidious swamp, but how to manage it I could not see. Paul was too ill, Henry was gone, and I feared it might be dangerous for Louis to lift pails of water. I walked round and round the stone wall, but it seemed unclimbable and impenetrable. I might have got over myself but I could not manage the full pail also. Fortunately, as I thought, one of the Schmidt boys, a lad of some fourteen years, came over to sit with the invalid Paul. I asked him to perform the task for me, to which he readily assented. I went down to the pig yard with him and watched him climb to first one position and then another. Finally, to my surprise he carefully poured the water over the wall, saying, "There, that's all right." And then, "But those pigs won't come to the right place. They've got no sense."

"Oh, they'll come in time," was my reply. But in the night I recalled the curious sound the water made as it was being poured over, so early this morning, before anyone was about, I went down to the place and with some difficulty mounted to the same spot the Schmidt boy had chosen. My suspicions were right; he had emptied the pail into a hole in the ground. I cannot believe those are the sort of sons to help a pioneer.

I fear I have quite ruined my yellow fowls. I saw one today deliberately begin to eat a new-laid egg. She positively stood by the nest and waited while it was being laid. I think I must fill an egg shell for her with cayenne pepper. I had already noticed one of the cocks pecking at an egg. I do not get nearly so many as I should.

Mr. Moors' man came last evening with letters as per *Lübeck*, one charmingly illustrated from Belle,[25] one from Mrs. Stevenson,[26] and one from Mrs. Williams[27] to Belle, and several to Louis.

[25] Mrs. Stevenson's daughter, Mrs. Isobel Osbourne Strong, later Mrs. Isobel Field.

[26] RLS's mother, Mrs. Thomas (Margaret Isabella Balfour) Stevenson.

[27] Possibly Mrs. Virgil (Dora Norton) Williams, a San Francisco painter and close friend of Fanny's who witnessed her marriage to Louis. Louis dedicated *The Silverado Squatters* to Virgil and Dora Norton Williams.

This morning Paul was set upon going to the steamer, and Louis had promised to ride down and dine with Dr. Stuebel. Paul went directly after breakfast, and Louis at about half-past ten. The whole six of the boys set off in a body to catch the pony and were half an hour about the business. In the meantime Louis was having desperate struggles to dress. I was in a dazed state with fever and quinine and could not help him at all. At last he got away, in what sort of garb I tremble to think. He was hardly out of sight before I discovered all the things he had been in search of, in their right places, naturally, just before my eyes.

As all the men were off with the cart, I thought I might as well let Ben plant corn, which he assured me he understood perfectly, for had he not planted all the first lot which had failed through the depredations of the rats? At about three Henry and I went down to the corn patch to put in some pumpkin seeds amongst the corn. To my disgust I saw why the first lot of corn had failed. Ben's idea of planting was to scrape a couple of inches off the ground, drop in a handful of corn, and kick a few leaves over the spot. It is really wonderful that any at all should have germinated. Every grain that Henry and I planted a few days ago is showing above ground already. Ben was given a lesson in planting, and watched to see that he understood what was meant, but the better part of the patch must be set out again.

After the pumpkins were in, Henry and I went to the spot by the bandstand to see how our crop was coming on, examining the potato hills as we went. Many of the potatoes had rotted in the ground, but still a number had sprouted. In the empty hills we dropped pumpkin seed, making excursions off the road to any spear of corn we saw that seemed choked with weeds. We finally gave way altogether to clearing single hills and worked away till nearly dark, when we were interrupted by Sitione,[28] who came laden with pineapple plants, a small boy following him with one of the largest pines I have ever seen. We set out the pineapple on the way back to the house and talked about the chances of war.

Sitione said they were fighting in Tutuila, but he did not think

[28] A chief, later known as Amatua, a name of higher rank.

it would come to war here. I thought, as he is a noted warrior, he might have some influence, and spoke to him of the inevitable consequences of war among the Samoans. German rule: that is their bugbear. I found Sitione quite awake to the facts and most anxious that peace should be kept. His shoulder, in which he was so dreadfully wounded during the last war, seems to be getting really well since Dr. Funk[29] operated on it. The doctor was almost sure that the arm must be eventually amputated, but his skill and Sitione's constitution have saved it. S showed me a large pistol fastened round his waist by a cartridge belt, and tried to shoot a vampire bat with it, but missed. Henry assured me the other day that the vampire bat, or flying fox as they call it here, is very good to eat. I do *not* think I could eat bat.

Paul returned quite sober, but had had a return of pain through the draughts of the *Lübeck*. I gave him another dose of salicylate and in a short time the pain was gone. He received a letter from his father, a well-to-do German, containing the information that goods to stock a store had been sent to him to arrive in February, and there would be money also. Sitione offers me breadfruit trees if I send a man for them. Mrs. Blacklock's mother came today with two noble breadfruits. The boys returned late with a light load for five. My pig from Sydney is at Apia, but as she cost only thirty-seven shillings, I feel doubts as to her quality. Still, in Samoa a pig's a pig.

OCT. 23RD

The pig is a very small, very common pig. I cannot but think it must be the *Janet Nichol* pig, it being spotted in the same fashion as that pleasant animal. She is in the way to have a family very soon, and at present is living in her little sty with three stepchildren sent up from Mr. Moors along with her. I was afraid that the other pigs would annoy her, so had the separate apartment put up with great difficulty, as I could not for a long time get either Beni or Paul to understand about building it. Beni proposed making it of withes propped up by stones, and Paul had some strips of board which he meant to use as posts. Neither plan would answer, I was sure, as a short time ago a couple of the original pigs undermined the heavy

[29] An Apia doctor.

stone wall and escaped. When they understood what I was after they approved highly and worked with a will, as indeed they both always do. I showed them how to plant a couple of posts, a log apart, every ten feet or so. Between these posts we dropped other logs, running round and round the pen, so that the end of one log rested on the end of another. In one corner a sleeping apartment was arranged for Madame Piggie: boards, shingles, bits of boxes, tin kerosene cans beaten out flat, and a few cocoanut leaves from Mr. Schmidt being used in its construction.

Henry has built a fence of withes round the fowl house, but the workings of the gate were too difficult for Paul. Yesterday, therefore, he put on hinges and a catch. Paul, though possessed of many most estimable qualities, is not a dextrous man. He had taken the gate down and it had promptly fallen to pieces in his hands. I saw him with a puzzled, despairing countenance striking at it with a hatchet, one paling bounding off as another was fastened on. I went out to the rescue and showed him how to manage it and held the hinges and catch while he nailed them on. I fortunately escaped without injury, though I am amazed that I should. Every time he raised the hatchet I was in imminent danger of decapitation and whenever the hammer side of the instrument came down I quailed before it, for I was pretty sure of losing a finger or two, if not a hand.

The old cock is really too bad. He follows each hen to her nest, hangs over her, watching for the egg, and the moment it is laid strikes his bill into it, and, throwing it out on the ground, calls his harem to a cannibal feast. We tried clipping his wings and tossing him into the pig sty but he easily climbed out, and marched triumphantly past us on the way to the fowl house.

Something, I cannot make out what, has destroyed almost all the corn planted by Beni and the sweet corn I set out. It lies between the rats and a wild hen. I lay it to the hen and have told Beni to shoot her.

Finding I had chosen a too sunny spot for lettuce, I searched for a better place and found one (I think) up the road Mr. Carruthers made, on its banks, so to speak. When I went out to dig it up, Louis went with me and fell to digging, too, with a sort of dogged fury. I had prepared quite a large place, comparatively, having to stop finally on account of three enormous blisters on my hand, while Louis was sifting and separating from stones and weeds a very small space. I left him there, hard at work, and returned to the house to get lunch. Sitting down for a moment to rest, I fell into a fit of vacancy and forgot all about the cooking for near upon half an hour. When Louis came in, stiff and aching with his long stooping posture, muddy and hungry, the meal was not yet on the table. I felt a very guilty creature.

[30] Louis says that I have the soul of a peasant, not so much that I love working in the earth and with the earth, but because I like to know that it is my own earth that I am delving in. Had I the soul of an artist, the stupidity of possessions would have no power over me. He may be right. I would as soon think of renting a child to love as a piece of land. When I plant a seed or a root, I plant a bit of my heart with it and do not feel that I have finished when I have had my exercise and amusement. But I do feel not so far removed from God when the tender leaves put forth and I know that in a manner I am a creator. My heart melts over a bed of young peas, and a blossom on my rose tree is like a poem written by my son. After I had made a perfect garden and it had been sold and bought several times I beheld it ploughed up, the vines torn down, my trees cut for firewood, the flowers uprooted—planted in potatoes. I could not have felt worse had I seen my favorite riding horse, hock-kneed and ruined, dragging the plough. After all, I believe we present our home the best of it: we possess something deep and strong and never the evanescent sports of the artist. I love the earth not only when she is beautiful but when she is called ugly. I cannot play with her and love her. My things, my house have favored me, and I cannot loosen the strings that bind us without something breaking.*

Last night Louis and I walked up and down the path behind the house. The air was soft and warm, but not too warm, and the most delicious fragrance filled the air. When I am pulling weeds it often happens that a puff of the sweetest scent blows back to me as I cast away a handful of so-called weeds. I have learned to know many of these by sight, now. One, a rough-leafed creature with a strong resistant root, is said to be poisonous. Another, which looks like a lily

[30] The following passage, the conclusion of which is marked by an asterisk, is suppressed in the manuscript.

when growing, though I think it bears no flower, gives out its fragrance only in the shade.

I believe I have discovered the ylang-ylang tree, about which there seems to have been so much mystery. I am told that Dr. Stuebel had the same idea, which makes it in my mind about conclusive. Henry tells me, too, that one of the priests distills a perfume from the same tree. It does not seem to grow very large—at least I have not seen any great trees—and has a peculiarly delicate leaf of a very tender young shade of green. The flowers are in racemes, a greenish white, turning brown on the tree, when they are often used by the natives to mix in their wreaths. I remember at first I thought it was some sort of seaweed. I hardly dare say that it suggests the odor of old boots. That is when it is brown. Another scented tree has something, I cannot tell until I get it in my hand, either flower or fruit, that is dark red, and spicy to the smell. There is one terrible tree in the bush that smells like ordure. We passed one when we first went up Mr. Carruthers' road, and it almost made me sick.

We were driven out of the house last evening to our walk by a tree frog of stentorian voice. He was hidden in a tree near the front verandah and made a noise like a saw being filed, only fifty times louder. It actually shook the drums of my ears—

I had to stop just here to show Paul how to tie a knot that will not slip. The last time Mr. Moors was here he found his horse at the point of strangulation from a slip noose round its neck, as Paul had tethered it out in the grass. I have just tied up one of the cocks by the leg in a proper knot, so I trust the next horse committed to Paul's hands may fare better.

But to return to the tree frog. When we settled ourselves at the table for the evening, what was our horror to hear a second tree frog piping up just over our heads in the eaves of the house. Louis went outside and poked upwards with a stick, while I brushed at him from the table with a broom. A second time he began, and had to be brushed and poked again. I had a horrid feeling that I had done him a mortal injury, but when, after we were in bed, and half-asleep, he started saw filing again, I wished I had. His performance, however, was but a half-hearted one, though he favoured us with two bursts of it, and I believe out of season, for the outdoor frogs had long been silent and there was not an answering note to his.

We have had a very heavy rainstorm, with thunder and lightning. At night the rain fell with such violence that we could not hear each other speak, and it seemed as though the house must be crushed by the weight of the water falling upon it. In the middle of the night Louis arose, made a light, and fell to writing verses. I was troubled about the taller corn, which I feared might be broken down and spoiled. The verses turned out not badly, and the corn stood as straight as I could wish it to do.

Paul just came to me with the other cock to have a string attached to his foot.

"You do it this time, Paul," I said, "and I will see how you mean to tie Mr. Moors' horse."

He made a knot as I had shown him, in the end of the rope, a little further up arranged a slip knot through which the first knot should be thrust. It was as well I let Paul try, for he carefully held the end knot in his fingers, and slipped the noose over the cock's foot.

Yesterday the last of five hundred cocoanuts was brought up by our men from a place where Henry had bought them for five dollars. There is no more Indian corn to be had in Apia, so I must save what little I have left for planting. Mr. Moors sent me a box of horrid rotten potatoes for pig food. Paul and I sorted them over, laying the sound ones aside for our own use, and boiling the rest for the pigs. I could not bear to feed the poor animals on such abominations. Henry, therefore, went on the quest for cocoanuts, which do also for the fowls. Half the number we mean to plant. All our breadfruits are putting forth young leaves. In fact, I think everything we set out is growing, except the corn that has been so mysteriously pulled up. The banana patch is pretty well cleared but it is very difficult to keep men at work there.

"Too many devils, me fraid," explained Lafaele[31] when he came

[31] "Lafaele [Raphael], a strong, dull deprecatory man; splendid with an axe, if watched; the better for rowing, when he calls me 'Papa' in the most wheedling tones; desperately afraid of ghosts, so that he dare not walk alone up in the banana patch."—R. L. S.

back sooner than I had anticipated. There are devils everywhere in the bush, it is believed; creatures who take on the semblance of man and kill those with whom they converse; but our banana patch is exceptionally cursed with the presence of these demons.

Today we should be going to a feast given by a native judge, but it is raining too heavily for the venture. Here is a translation of the invitation. [Not given.]

L O U I S . TUESDAY, 3RD NOVEMBER

All morning I worked at the South Seas, and finished the chapter I had stuck upon on Saturday. Fanny, awfully hove-to with rheumatics and injuries received upon the field of sport and glory, chasing pigs, was unable to go up and down stairs, so she sat upon the back verandah, and my work was chequered by her cries. "Paul, you take a spade to do that—dig a hole first. If you do that, you'll cut your foot off! Here, you boy, what you do there? You no get work? You go find Simile; he give you work. Peni, you tell this boy he go find Simile; suppose Simile no give him work, you tell him go 'way. I no want him here. That boy no good."—*Peni* (from the distance in re-assuring tones), "All right, sir!"—*Fanny* (after along pause), "Peni, you tell that boy go find Simile! I no want him stand here all day. I no pay that boy. I see him all day. He no do nothing."—Luncheon, beef, soda-scones, fried bananas, pineapple in claret, coffee. Try to write a poem; no go. Play the flageolet. Then sneakingly off to farmering and pioneering. Four gangs at work on our place; a lively scene; axes crashing and smoke blowing; all the knives are out. But I rob the garden party of one without a stock, and you should see my hand—cut to ribbons. Now I want to do my path up the Vaituliga single-handed, and I want it to burst on the public complete. Hence, with devilish ingenuity, I begin it at different places; so that if you stumble on one section, you may not even then suspect the fulness of my labours. Accordingly, I started in a new place, below the wire, and hoping to work up to it. It was perhaps lucky I had so bad a cutlass, and my smarting hand bid me stay before I had got up to the wire, but just in season, so that I was only the better of my activity, not dead beat as yesterday.

A strange business it was, and infinitely solitary; away above, the sun was in the high tree-tops; the lianas noosed and sought to hang me; the saplings struggled, and came up with that sob of death that one gets to know so well; great, soft, sappy trees fell at a lick of the cutlass, little tough switches laughed at and dared my best endeavour. Soon, toiling down in that pit of verdure, I heard blows on the far side, and then laughter. I confess a chill settled on my heart. Being so dead alone, in a place where by rights none should be beyond me, I was aware, upon interrogation, if those blows had drawn nearer, I should (of course quite unaffectedly) have executed a strategic movement to the rear; and only the other day I was lamenting my insensibility to superstition! Am I beginning to be sucked in? Shall I become a midnight twitterer like my neighbours? At times I thought the blows were echoes; at times I thought the laughter was from birds. For our birds are strangely human in their calls. Vaea Mountain about sun-down sometimes rings with shrill cries, like the hails of merry, scattered children. As a matter of fact, I believe stealthy wood-cutters from Tanugamanono[32] were above me in the wood and answerable for the blows; as for the laughter, a woman and two children had come and asked Fanny's leave to go up shrimp-fishing in the burn; beyond doubt, it was these I heard. Just at the right time I returned; to wash down, change, and begin this snatch of letter before dinner was ready, and to finish it afterwards, before Henry has yet put in an appearance for his lesson in "long expressions."

Dinner: stewed beef and potatoes, baked bananas, new loaf-bread hot from the oven, pineapple in claret. These are great days; we have been low in the past; but now are we as belly-gods, enjoying all things.

NOVEMBER 4

Fanny was to have rested. Blessed Paul began making a duck-house; she let him be; the duck-house fell down, and she had to set her hand to it. He was then to make a drinking-place for the pigs; she let him be again—he made a stair by which the pigs will probably escape this evening, and was near weeping. Impossible to blame the indefatigable

[32] A native village about a mile from Apia.

fellow; energy is too rare and good-will too noble a thing to discourage; but it's trying when she wants a rest. Then she had to cook the dinner; then, of course—like a fool and a woman—must wait dinner for me, and make a flurry of herself. Her day so far. *Cetera adhunc desunt.*

FANNY . NOV. 5TH

We ourselves became infected with the native fear of *aitus* or spirits. Louis has been cutting a path in the bush. He confesses that the sight of anything like a human figure would send him flying like the wind with his heart in his mouth. One night the world seemed full of strange and supernatural noises. When Louis whispered, "Listen! What's that?" I felt as though cold water had been poured down my back; but it was only the hissing of a fire in the clearing. The same night we were waked by sounds of terror in the hen house. Paul, Louis and I all ran out with one accord, but could see nothing. In the morning we found the body of a pullet with its heart torn out. Henry says the murderer is a small and beautiful bird. But we were quite in the mood to believe it an aitu. We have been greatly annoyed by tree frogs, which come inside the house and make an uproar so incommensurate with their size that it is difficult to believe they are the cause.

Henry has taken a contract to clear the five acres for the house at 20 dollars an acre. He is getting on very well with it, but I think it will cost more than the 100 dollars. He is continually getting new men. The brother of Mataafa (I am not sure of that spelling) came and offered to take the contract off Henry's hands. After much consideration and consultation with us, Henry refused. The gentleman paid Louis and me a formal visit, speaking perfect English with a voice of honey sweetness, and retired, to appear again, after a few days, in the character of a labourer. As I stood in the back doorway I became aware of a very tall, handsome, haughty native advancing up the path. He was clad in a very short lava lava, gracefully kilted up on one side, a shoulder cape of fringed red brown leaves, and a large red hibiscus blossom stuck behind his ear. I was noticing the particularly fine colour of his tattooing—he seemed to be wearing dark blue lace tights from hip to below the knee—when I was entirely taken aback by the man bowing to me in the most approved European fashion and wishing me good morning in correct English. It is needless to say that he was not a success as a labourer. He lounged up hours after the time to begin work, explained to the men that they were fools to work for so low a price, put on all sorts of airs over Henry, and then before the day was done wanted a full day's wages.

Henry came to us afterwards, very anxious to know whether he had behaved as an English chief should have done under the circumstances, explaining that the man was his superior in rank; but when he found that this fine gentleman was trying to swindle him he treated him as he would any other ordinary person and paid him just what he owed him and no more. We thought Henry might have ordered him off the premises but he did not then know that his men had been interfered with.

The last supernatural news is that two [blank] men fishing at midnight in the harbour saw a large war canoe run into Apia, quite up into the land, so they could see the masts through the trees. They made haste to see what this meant. There were four men in the boat, strangers, who demanded that the fishers should help them row. The fishers did so, wondering meanwhile why Apia beach should be filled with dancing people. In the morning they hastened back to have another look at the strange craft, which they had left near the Tivoli,[33] but nothing was there. One of the men took to his bed, or, more properly speaking, his mat, and is now at the point of death. The newspaper says the natives are redeeming the arms they had pledged some time ago, and are using every means to get ammunition. Things look very threatening.

My garden looks quite like a real garden under Lafaele and a very handsome Samoan. It also looks something like a graveyard, the beds being made about the size and shape of graves. Lafaele asks every time I go to the garden if I am *surely* going to plant cabbages. Unless I plant cabbages he will feel that his time has been wasted and he betrayed. Consequently, I am forced to plant cabbages. I have found

[33] An Apia hotel.

a great many lemon trees in full bearing in the further hedge, amongst citron and limes. One day, bent on a voyage of discovery, I lost myself in the bush. To be lost in a tropical bush is a very alarming thing. The vegetation is so dense that there are no shadows, and the whereabouts of the sun are an unsolvable mystery. And yet the terror has an element of pleasure in it, difficult to explain. Had I not feared that Louis would be alarmed at my absence I should have consciously gone deeper into the wood. As it was, I trusted to my instinct, which always betrays me in a town but seldom if ever in the bush, and in a short time found myself in the edge of the clearing.

[34] I am feeling very depressed, for my vanity, like a newly felled tree, lies prone and bleeding. Louis tells me that I am not an artist but a born, natural peasant. I have often thought *that* the happiest life and not one for criticism. I feel most embittered when I am assured that I am really what I had wished to be. Of course, I meant a peasant without aspirations. Perhaps if I had known in time I should have had none of it! I have been brooding on my feelings and holding my head before the glass and now I am ashamed. Louis assures me that the peasant class is a most interesting one, and he admires it hugely.*

I have just read the notice of the death of an Englishwoman. "She," says the journal, "though possessing neither personal charm nor beauty, was a most interesting woman." I wonder how she would like that description could she know of it? Louis says that no one can mind having it said of him that he is not an artist unless he is supporting his family by his work as an artist, in which case it is an insult. Well, I could not support a fly by my sort of work, artistic or otherwise.

[35] I am reminded of a friend of Louis, a poet I think, who, when asked why he looked so gloomy, broke out with, "I want praise and I don't get enough of it!" I am afraid I want no praise for what I do not possess. I so hate being a peasant that I feel a positive pleasure when I fail in peasant occupations.*

[34] The following passage, the conclusion of which is marked by an asterisk, is suppressed in the manuscript.
[35] The following passage, the conclusion of which is marked by an asterisk, is suppressed in the manuscript.

My fowls won't lay eggs, and if they do, the cocks, who are what Louis calls "cril bitens," eat them. The pigs, whom I loathe and fear, are continually climbing out of their sty and doing all sorts of mischief, and my heart sinks when I think of the prospective cow. I love the growing things but the domestic beasts are not to my taste. I have, too, such a guilty feeling towards them, for I know if their murder is not contemplated that at least they will be robbed of their young at my instigation. [About thirty-five words missing.]

Everywhere that the land is cleared I find the mummy apple springing up. There are male and female trees, the male tree bearing a small white blossom and the female a large lilylike flower. I have discovered the wild ginger plant. I had long wondered what it was, for the fragrance of its leaves caught my attention everywhere. Mr. Carruthers tells me that the tumeric looks almost the same, but the root is a vivid yellow. There is another scented plant of the same habit of growth, but very tall, like a small bamboo or sugar cane. In the garden the other day the men turned over a fungus that was enveloped in the most delicate lacelike fabric. I wish I were not so ignorant of these things. And today I found a root or fungus that was new both to Henry and the men.

Louis has gone down to Apia, having received a letter from a man he has but little acquaintance with, asking him to come and visit one who is unhappy. He was not well enough to go, but such an appeal as that could not be refused. Just before he started, a Catholic priest came begging for his church. He spoke English with a strong French accent. He had so many of the native ways that I thought to myself that he must be long in Samoa. And yet I was surprised when he told us that he was a half-caste.

We hear that the *Janet Nichol* was caught in a hurricane and badly damaged, so much so that she was compelled to return to Sydney. I was sorry, for after being so many months aboard I had grown fond of even the "Jumping Jenny."[36]

Paul has been working all day repairing the tumble-down native hut on the Schmidts' place for a temporary shelter for the two draught horses expected by the *Richmond*. I went over to see how

[36] The Stevensons cruised on the *Janet Nichol* April 11–July 25, 1890.

he was coming on. He had an elaborate partition put up between the stalls, but unfortunately I laid my hand on it and the whole structure collapsed under its weight, five posts coming down with a crash and very nearly crushing me. Paul was away at the time, so I hastened to get Lafaele who, under my instructions, set up one of the posts, removing the other four, and we had the whole thing on a substantial basis before Paul turned up. Since then he has been mending the roof with tin kerosene cans, but I have not seen his work yet. In fact, I fear to. My own wounded vanity smarts too much for me to be insensible to Paul's disappointments. He works so hard and continuously, poor fellow, and the results are so deplorable.

I have just been out on the verandah to speak to Paul. It is now half-past eight and very dark, for the moon is not yet up and the sky is overcast. The air is fresh, and sweetly damp and redolent of many scented leaves and flowers. I can hear the sea on the Apia beach. The sound of it is regular, like hoarse breathing; or more like, still, to the rhythmic purring of a gigantic cat. Crickets and tree frogs and innumerable other insects and small beasts are chirping and pecking with various noises that mingle together harmoniously. Occasionally a bird calls with a startling cry, perhaps the very bird who murdered my poor pullet.

When I stood in the doorway and looked in, the room seemed glowing with colour, glowing and melting. And yet there is nothing to go upon but the tapa on the walls (which is really very fine), the coral, the pink and maroon window curtains of the coarsest cotton print, a ragged old ink-spotted pink table cover, a few print covered pillows, and the pandanus mats on the floor. Louis's books, with their bindings, blue, red and green, to say nothing of gold lettering, help greatly on their six shelves; and the two kava bowls that I have worked as hard to colour as a young man with his meerschaum have taken a fine opalescent coating. I can drink my own kava with pleasure but when I offered it to a real kava drinker he did not take to it so kindly as I hoped he might. Another failure; but perhaps an artistic one, which would not be to my mind [?].

Henry has a bad foot. He and Paul were in the fowl house with the hatchet and nails. Paul laid the hatchet sharp edge up on the ground and stood upon it with one foot. Henry, not to be outdone, followed suit, but as he was barefooted, while Paul wore heavy boots, the result was disastrous.

L o u i s . NOV. 7TH

I am very tired, and rest off to-day from all but letters. Fanny is quite done up; she could not sleep last night, something it seemed like asthma—I trust not. . . .

F a n n y . NOV. 15TH

We could not go to the English consul's ball, to which Louis had rashly accepted an invitation, as it was pouring rain. On Saturday there were to have been races and games, but the weather being so bad, the festivities, except the ball, were postponed. Henry went down to Apia on Saturday morning, mounted on a horse, or rather pony colt, of a very ratlike aspect. He borrowed a bridle of me and has lost the chin strap, but rode on his own saddle, if such a conglomeration of bits of broken wood, rags, and the smell of old leather could be called a saddle at all.

The cart horses have arrived from Auckland, a couple of large, mild-eyed, gentle, dappled greys. It was pleasant to see them fall upon the grass after their tedious sea voyage, and amusing to watch Jack's[37] reception of them. He gazed at them in surprise at first, apparently thunderstruck at the great size of the two chiefs (for so he evidently regarded them) from the colonies. Then he began to show off before them, dancing and prancing and galloping around them in circles. The two big chiefs looked at him with mild curiosity. One said to the other, "That, I presume, is what is called a kanaka. Odd creature." And then they both returned to their luncheon and quite ignored poor Jack and his advances.

Just as we were thinking about going to bed, an alarming noise was heard from the stable. It had been raining hard all day and

[37] RLS's horse.

was still drizzling; the weeds on the way to the stable were up to my waist and dripping with water. The prospect was not inviting but we nobly marched out with the lantern and an umbrella. As we entered the enclosure where the stable stands, or rather, stood— we became aware of two large white objects shining indistinctly through the darkness. A little nearer and our two horses were looking us in the face. They had eaten the sides and end of their house quite away. They must have thought it very odd to find themselves housed in an edible stable. When we entered, they received us with every sign of welcome. But we were dismayed to find them entangled with each other and the wreck of the partition, of which nothing was left standing but Lafaele's post. Louis crawled in under their big hairy feet and after a long and patient struggle got the knot of one wet rope untied, the horses meanwhile smelling and nosing about the top of his head. He said he expected every moment to have it bitten off, for, he argued, if the horses find a stable edible in these outlandish parts, they might easily conceive the idea of sampling the ostler.

The next morning Beni called me to come to the fowl house. There he had discovered our best cock fastened under a native basket in the outside enclosure, where he had been lying all night in the drenching rain. No doubt we had disturbed a thief in the very act of making away with him.

According to advice from Mr. Moors we sent the two chiefs down to Apia yesterday to bring up the cart. When the man engaged as carter turned up, he was drunk and manifestly incapable when sober. He was turned off on the spot, and Henry, who had never in his life driven, or I suppose mounted anything on wheels, was sent to drive the thing up to Vailima. Mr. Moors, feeling alarmed at the rate he was going, started after him in hot haste. The wagon, however, had been here some twenty-one minutes before he arrived, breathless, and dripping with sweat as though he had been through a river. A nice pickle he found us in. Henry must have come up that terrible, really almost impassable road with some 13 hundred pounds weight altogether in about twenty minutes, or even less. One of the poor chiefs looked ready to die and I thought he would. Sweat ran off him by the bucketful as he stood with heaving sides and hanging head and, most horrid of all, blood running from his nose. I told Paul to get the blankets off my bed but he got his own and they were thrown over the animals. The only thing I could get hold of to rub them down with was a couple of chemises of mine. Louis with one and Paul with the other rubbed the bleeding horse and then all hands set to work to get them out of their harness. Not one of the whole lot of us had any idea how to accomplish this feat, so everyone who could find a buckle unfastened it, and finally the chiefs were led out of the tangle.

Louis sent Henry and Lafaele, who were in a miserable state of alarm and despair, to walk them slowly up and down the road to the woods, as it didn't seem safe to let them stand still in such a state, lest they should get chilled. They went further than Louis had meant, disappearing in the trees, so he finally went after them and found them all standing still in the damp, cold, windy woods, the boys supposing they were sent there because it was cooler.

At that point Mr. Moors appeared. He immediately discovered that the wagon was badly dilapidated, one of the forward wheels leaning at a very dangerous angle. Why Henry was not thrown off the thing I can't conceive, nor why it did not come down with everything. The wagon was to be of American make and what is called "an American lumber wagon," but the one sent us is what is known in New England as a carryall, generally used for carrying small parcels, but more particularly used for picnics. It is absolutely useless to us, and cost 125 dollars. I am sure the wrong directions were sent to the agent, for I remember saying several times "You are sending for a 'spring wagon' (another name for the carryall), not for a lumber wagon." But nobody would listen to me. They might have trusted the peasant woman when it came to wagons. This tragic affair of the first drive from Apia made Henry look quite haggard and old. I was very sorry for him, but not a word of fault finding was said to him, for we knew he was not to blame.

NOV. 20TH

Louis went down last evening to see the carpenter and to spend the night, that he might be on hand for the feast of S [blank],[38] given on the birthday of his daughter. The adopted daughter of S[39] has lately (?) been elected maid of the village. It is to be a very grand affair and doubtless many hen houses and pig sties have suffered in consequence, for every guest must carry a present. At the last great feast one man had ten pigs stolen. Jack, whom Louis rode, was sent back for me this morning, but I had a headache and was altogether too tired to go.

I felt very doubtful about our own fowls, having discovered a large native basket carefully stowed away out of sight, so when I heard a commotion amongst the fowls a little after midnight I wasted no time in hastening to the spot. Paul followed me, for I waked him by calling Pussy as I passed his door, for I wished to clear poor Puss of the dreadful charge of chicken murder that has been hanging over her for some time. Sure enough, Puss was innocently asleep with Paul, but an almost grown chicken lay on the floor dead, its throat torn open. I saw a rat run away as I approached, which places the matter beyond a doubt.

In the early part of the evening, as I sat alone (Paul being gone to the Schmidts) I was startled by a strange, ghostly sound between a cough and a groan. I knew all the pigs were in their sty; the moon gave light enough for me to see all round the place, but nothing was in sight. I then remembered Lafaele's tale of a devil he had seen and heard. I had sent him a little way into the bush to fetch back several banana cuttings I had left there. To my indignation I beheld him returning with his friend Maya.

"Don't you want me to help you?" I asked.

"Me 'fraid," was Lafaele's reply, "too many devil up there."

He then went on to say that he had actually seen one in the guise of a black fellow and had heard others making a terrible noise, "like this," and then he made exactly the sound I heard last night.

We have had the most wretched time with the two native sows. Nothing made by human hands will keep them within any enclosure. They are out now, ravaging the premises, while Henry, Lafaele and

[38] Seumanutafa, chief of Apia.
[39] Fanua.

Maya plant taro. Day before yesterday Paul, with all the men he could muster, went over to the German plantation and got roots of orange, breadfruit and mango, also more seed of the cacao. The same day my plants from Sydney came to hand: a Chinese persimmon, raisin tree, pomegranate, eleven navel oranges, and a lot of strawberries, the latter almost, if not quite, rotten. Paul and I planted out the Sydney things while Henry and a friend of his attended to the rest. In the evening and all that night we had wild weather.

I am interrupted here for a moment by Henry to ask some questions about planting pineapples. I wish I could take his photograph as he stands at the door with the steady eyes of a capable man of affairs but the dress of an houri: about his loins he has twisted a piece of white cotton; a broad garland of drooping ferns passes over his forehead, crosses at the back of his head and, coming forward round his neck, is fastened in a sort of knot of greenery on his breast. Henry is rather a plain young man but he looks really lovely just now and the incongruous expression of his eyes heightens the effect.

The storm of which I was speaking was quite alarming to people living in such a vulnerable abode. The house shakes as though it would fall if anyone comes upstairs rapidly when the weather is fair, and the slight iron roof is entirely open at the eaves, ready to catch any wind that blows. We could not keep a lamp burning and Paul having broken the lantern kept for such emergencies, we were in semidarkness. Late in the afternoon a cloud enveloped us, so that we could see no farther than in a London fog. From that the gale increased, lashing the branches of trees together and in some instances twisting their trunks and throwing them to the ground. We could see the rain through the window driving in layers, one sheet above another. Occasionally there was an ominous thrashing on our iron roof as though the great hardwood tree alongside of the house meant to do us a mischief. I have studied him since and there is no doubt but it was this tree, an immense fellow with a girth of some six feet at our upper story. Water poured in under our ill-fitting doors, the matches were too damp to light, and the general discomfort and sloppiness gave me quite the feeling of being at sea. I wished we might reef in one or two of our green sails, which reminded me of Ah Fu's[40] terror of the land and longing to be at sea in bad weather.—Am interrupted by a young Scotchman come to beg for a place as general servant. He is only twenty-three and has a sick wife and a young baby.

L o u i s . TUESDAY, NOVEMBER 25TH

Fanny's time, in this interval, has been largely occupied in contending publicly with wild swine. We have a black sow; we call her Jack Sheppard; impossible to confine her—impossible also for her to be confined! To my sure knowledge she has been in an interesting condition for longer than any other sow in story; else she had long died the death; as soon as she is brought to bed, she shall count her days. I suppose that sow has cost us in days' labour from thirty to fifty dollars; as many as eight boys (at a dollar a day) have been twelve hours in chase of her. Now it is supposed that Fanny has outwitted her; she grins behind broad planks in what was once the cookhouse. She is a wild pig; far handsomer than any tame; and when she found the cook-house was too much for her methods of evasion, she lay down on the floor and refused food and drink for a whole Sunday. On Monday morning, she relapsed, and now eats and drinks like a little man. I am reminded of an incident. Two Sundays ago, the sad word was brought that the sow was out again; this time she had carried another in her flight. Moors and I and Fanny were strolling up to the garden, and there by the waterside we saw the

[40] A Chinese cook whom the Stevensons picked up in the Marquesas. He stayed with them about two years. Ah Fu had been abducted to the Marquesas as a child laborer. He abandoned the queue and did not look much like a Chinese. Fanny later wrote of him: "Ah Fu had as strong a sense of romance as Louis himself. He returned to China with a belt of gold around his waist, a ninety dollar breech loader given him by Louis, and a boxful of belongings. His intention was to leave these great riches with a member of his family who lived outside the village, dress himself in beggar's rags, and then go to his mother's house to solicit alms. He would draw from her the account of the son who had been lost when he was a little child, and, at the psychological moment, when the poor lady was weeping, Ah Fu would cry out, 'Behold your son returned to you, not a beggar, as I appear, but a man of wealth!' "—Nellie Van de Grift Sanchez, *The Life of Mrs. Robert Louis Stevenson,* p. 139.

black sow, looking guilty. It seemed to me beyond words; but Fanny's
cri du coeur was delicious: "G-r-r-r!" she cried; "nobody loves you!"

F A N N Y . DEC. 2ND

Louis has gone down to Apia, hoping to get the mail from a cutter
which runs over to Tutuila to catch the mail boat for San Francisco.
Henry and I are each filling out our respective diaries at the only
table the house possesses. Poor Henry has gone through many tribulations lately. First of all he was the attempted victim of a forgery. One
of his boys brought a letter purporting to be from a man to whom
he owed, I think, six dollars. Henry got an order for the amount from
Louis and, enclosing it in an envelope, gave it to the messenger. By
an accident he happened to be in the road a short time afterwards
and saw the messenger calmly tear open the letter and abstract the
order. He fell upon the miscreant and recovered the order. It appeared that there was a confederate waiting down the road, but at
Henry's onslaught he fled and has not been seen since. It turned out
afterwards that the letter itself was forged. Henry promptly lodged
his man in prison and this morning appeared against him before the
native judge. The crime was a new one to his honour and he hardly
knew how to meet it. I am sorry to say that the rascal got off with
a fine of ten dollars.

I am reminded of a bill sent in to the consuls the other day. It
seems that they are responsible for the maintenance of Malietoa. "To
so much per week for board of 1 king."

Henry had another story of seeing the devil when he came last
back from Apia, but I could not clearly understand it. "Two young
ladies, very *fine* young ladies, *very* fine young ladies," seemed to be
taking a walk. They were "very *finely* dressed," being clad in "*fine*
lava lavas of *very* fine ti leaves," with garlands of scented berries and
leaves round their necks. Then followed something about a chief
with whom they apparently thought of dining, but finally declined
because one of them said in a squeaking treble (carefully imitated
by Henry) that she smelled fish cooking, but she preferred that
dainty raw. Again I do not follow, but late that night a man's voice

was heard crying out (very agonized, as given by Henry), "Oh, my God! Save me! Save me!" And "then they saw the birth of a spirit on the water."

But I have wandered off from Henry's troubles. Today he had to go before the judge to lay his complaint against the forger. His horse was left tied by permission to a tree. When he went to get it the horse was turned loose and he had to run after it for a quarter of a mile. I suppose he must have returned to the tree and upbraided the woman, for she struck him across the face with a horsewhip. He instantly and unchivalrously returned the blow and, as he said, "for every time she gave me one, I gave her one." The unfortunate woman must have got it very hot, for the whip (my whip) was broken and threshed to strings.

Louis said, "You should know, Henry, that we do not strike women. If they strike us, we do nothing."

Henry looked nonplussed at this revelation but brightened up again and said proudly that when a white man ran up and took the woman's part he did not strike him.

I have just discovered a bit of Samoan manners. You must not ask the name of any person directly. I fear I have often offended, for I generally ask to look at the arm of any person I take a liking to, that I may read her name, which is generally tattooed between the wrist and elbow.

Yesterday one of the chiefs fell in the cart and for some time Mr. Hay[41] held her up by main force, since if she had gone quite over there were stakes in the way that would have horribly killed her. He shouted for Henry and his men, who came running from the bush where they were burning logs. After the cart was away, Louis and I remained and showed the men how to raze the stakes to the ground. We were much amused to find them not only garlanded with ferns and flowers as usual, but each man with an immense pair of black moustaches painted upon his face.

I once came upon Lafaele with his head coated with lime, and

[41] A white employee at Vailima. In the beginning the Stevensons hired white help. The story goes that these people were troublesome and expensive. For whatever reasons, the Stevensons soon staffed Vailima almost exclusively with natives.

white as Father William's, and mutton chop whiskers, and a small, neat moustache done in black. I had to ask his name, to his intense amusement. Both Lafaele and Monga live in the midst of alarms.

Word has gone out that I am dissatisfied with both men. Monga confines himself to divining my wishes and languishing with his beautiful eyes. I never heard anything more "fetching" than the way he said to me today, "Here is a little small one." He is very clever, Monga, for he does not overdo the business. Today, however, for the first time really, I caught him shirking. He had sneaked away from the garden work, leaving Lafaele to face devils alone, and was hanging about the cook and dinner preparations. He was abashed only for the part of a moment and then snatched a brand from the fire, as though in extreme haste, and started up the path to Lafaele, pretending to carry a light for burning the brush there. But as an immense blaze had been showing for the last hour, I advised him to give up the scheme.

Lafaele is much coarser in his tactics than Monga. When positively brought to book his voice bleats like a lamb and every other word, if addressed to Louis, is "Papa," or if to me, "Mama." "Papa, I work like hell," is a common remark. But generally it is one word for himself and two against Monga. "He no work, that fellow," and "That fellow he no good" or "That fellow he talk very bad."

But whenever there is a showy service to be done it is the handsome Monga who is to the fore. A few evenings ago I saw him beating in an idiotic way upon a tin cup with a spoon.

"What *are* you doing?" I asked.

"Call him those men come in," was the reply.

I then became aware of a swarm of bees settling upon a mummy apple branch. Monga got a box and, walking fearlessly up to the buzzing mass, shook them into their extemporized hive and set the box triumphantly up against a tree, meanwhile his naked body being black with the insects, not one of which stung him. The other men were either terrified or filled with wonder, very few, not even our Henry, having seen bees before. Monga looked rather foolish, however, when detected in the mistake of attempting to feed his new pets on cold rice.

Three eggs were lost today, apparently at three different times, first by Miss Schmidt, then by Paul and lastly by Henry's cook. Monga was charged with having abstracted them and proof was brought that he was seen having to do, so to speak, with eggs. But as I was with him at the time (we were hunting hens' nests, finding two in the grass) I would not allow that evidence to go against him. If Monga was the thief then it was clear I was a confederate. We found seven eggs all together in the two nests, and all the eggs are mine, anyway.

I have been quite ill and am still pretty weak. The last time Louis was in Apia he was asked to dine with the American consul, Mr. Sewall.[42] A note was sent up begging me to join the party and I foolishly went, never thinking that the river was too high to ford. It was, however, and I had to walk a long wearisome distance and arrived more dead than alive. I could not walk back, so Mr. Sewall sent us to Mr. Moors in a boat. The town and harbour were inconceivably lovely by night. The next day we returned to Vailima and, as usual when overtired, I fell very ill and kept poor Louis up all night giving me laudanum, which for the first time failed to lull the pains. Today Mr. Sewall came, walking up, complaining of approaching paralysis but looking fresh as a rose, to help me out in his consular capacity with a law paper. I couldn't find it till he was gone, which was very annoying.

I had just come in from the garden, where I have been lying on newly dug ground, planting celery. In planting the celery I stabbed my hand with the trowel, making a very painful wound. Lafaele saw his chance and flew to a plant nearby, calling meanwhile to one of Henry's men, from whose lava lava he tore off a strip to serve as a bandage. He bruised the leaf between his fingers, warmed it at the fire, and laid it upon the smarting cut. The pain ceased like magic and has never returned. This is the second time I have been indebted to Lafaele's skill as a medicine man. I had meant to turn him away today, both him and Monga, but after the leaf treatment I hadn't the heart, and I could not send off Monga just when unjustly accused of purloining eggs in my company. So they are both still with us.

[42] Harold M. Sewall, U.S. consul in Samoa.

I fear the Schmidts are going downhill very rapidly. When we first came we interchanged little presents, I fine eggs for setting and occasional small quantities of sugar, etc., they bananas from their garden, a few green oranges, and green mummy apples, both of which I took only for civility. Today comes a bill for a little work Mr. Schmidt has done for me, the presents included.

Henry seems to have discovered a plantation of *Puas*.[43] He brought down all his men could carry to plant out by the river. A truly beneficent rain has been falling, soft and warm, and not as usual blustering like a northern squall. We are very glad of it, both for my garden and because of the tank having gone dry. Paul has sore feet, from mosquito bites. I must leave this and get him some drugs.

DEC. ? (FRIDAY)

Paul's feet nearly well, cured by boracic acid dusted on the sores. Boracic acid is an indispensable drug in the tropics. Louis came back from Apia with the startling intelligence that it was a white woman, Mrs. Bell, to whom Henry applied his horsewhip. All Apia was ringing with the tale and prognosticating all sorts of evil to come to us through Henry. One says, "He comes of a bad lot," another, "I do not like his face." Mr. Carruthers broke out against the cowardliness of his having struck a woman. But one should bear in mind the difference in customs between us and Samoans. A woman here, if she strikes, is struck in return the same as though she were a man, and no disgrace is attached to the act. I am glad it was Mrs. Bell and no other, though I do not believe that there is a white woman in Apia other than Mrs. B who would have opened the attack in such a fashion. I am sure I hope not. The Bell family are considered *the* Apia nuisance. They beg, and then bite the hand that feeds them.

A gentleman who was annoyed by Bell's pertinacious and insolent begging held up a golden sovereign between finger and thumb.

"I'll give you that," said he, "if you will promise never to come near me nor speak to me again."

I must mention that he prefaced this insulting offer by a very plain-spoken criticism of the man's character and behaviour.

[43] *Pua*, the frangipani tree.

"I'll take the sovereign," was Bell's eager answer.

Not long ago Mrs. B suddenly appeared in the only sitting room we possess, which is sacred to Louis and his work throughout the day. He explained this to the lady, very coldly, who, nothing daunted, took a seat on the verandah with her daughter, remarking, "Oh, that makes no difference." Apparently tiring of the dreariness of this position, she soon followed after me—I had gone to the banana patch in the bush—so far as the path was pleasant walking. Then the two seated themselves comfortably on a log to await my return. I discerned them from afar, but to make sure that I was not mistaken, asked the young lady her name as she advanced towards me.

"Miss Bell," was the smiling answer. "Allow me to introduce my mother."

I stopped short and looked at the woman still seated on the log, with eyes as hard as nails.

"I fear I am introoden," she remarked, apparently a little abashed.

I looked at her steadily for a few moments longer and then said, "Yes, I am very busy."

I am not at all sure that is not one of her reasons for the spirited attack upon Henry. She would have liked to lay that whip across my face. Well, poor soul, I bear her no ill will, and am extremely sorry for the daughter, but I will not be annoyed by such a person as the mother. Yesterday Henry went before the native magistrate and was fined five dollars, reduced to four by Mr. Bell's having to pay one dollar for tearing his coat in the melee.

The mail cutter has just come in with a letter from Mrs. Stevenson, in which she casually mentions Lloyd, the first news we have had of him. *What* has become of our letters that we should have received from him? There is something terribly amiss in the colonial post office; no one seems to get letters except by way of San Francisco. A letter also came from Nelly,[44] giving me the news that my house that was soon to be torn down is burned; and even the hedge around it, which was a long way off, is burned also. I had left two boxes there containing things of no great value to anyone else but of great

[44] Her sister, Mrs. Nellie Van de Grift Sanchez, living in Monterey, California.

value to me. I fear they are all gone, a portrait of my great-grand-father amongst the rest.

I have turned away Monga, to the inexpressible joy of Lafaele. This morning I spent in the garden, thinning out and transplanting turnips. I have put out a trial row of celery, which looks most lively. Different kinds of beans are up but the last heavy rain destroyed my peas. In my baskets the cacao seeds are breaking through the earth, and many other seeds are already showing green.

Yesterday I sent Lafaele part of the time to work on Mr. Schmidt's fence, as reparation for the damage done to their garden by the two white chiefs, who broke through their paddock hedge. Since then every night Mr. Moors' horses have come into our place, trampling about, waking me up, eating my corn, and finally walking over and killing Paul's duck, which was fast by a string in the grass. A note was sent to Mr. Moors, and his fence is being mended, for which I am very glad, as Louis was determined to shoot them if they did a third night's damage. I was so disgusted by the loss of my corn (I had planted it myself) that I felt a positive personal hatred for the horses and should not have minded in the least to have them shot dead; but to have a wounded horse running about the premises I fear would be too much for even my vengeance, and Louis is not a dead shot.

DEC. 13TH

Sunday was a regular field day for the horses, since which they have behaved themselves quite properly. Mrs. Schmidt had told me the day before that the two chiefs had been seen leaping the big gate. It seemed impossible that great cart horses could make such a jump; but the Schmidt story was corroborated by Lafaele, who declared that he, too, had seen the "girl horse go right over." Paul and I hastened to nail a board over both gates, hoping the chiefs might be so unintelligent as to imagine it to be a barrier. Louis went down to Apia (where he is just now) and I remained home. At about 11 Mr. Maben, the surveyor, and Mr. Blacklock, the American vice-consul, came up on foot. We were sitting on the front verandah, where I had just been telling the woeful tale of the horses.

"Look at the two big greys," said Mr. Blacklock; "they mean mischief sure as you're born."

I looked, but only saw the two chiefs standing placidly under a tree.

"I tell you they are plotting mischief," continued Mr. Blacklock. "Look at the sly, confidential way they are putting their heads together; they're not eating grass, they are hatching a conspiracy."

We had hardly turned our heads before we were startled by the dreadful screams of horses in pain and anger.

"Run, Paul, run!" I shouted, though what poor Paul could have done had he arrived in time, except to offer himself a voluntary sacrifice, is a mystery. But long before he could reach the spot, it was over. The first thing I saw was a horse of Mr. Moors in a corner of the paddock where the lime hedge and the barbed fence meet. He was lashing out with his heels at the two greys, who were calmly and deliberately crowding him closer and closer into the corner. When he was quite incapable of turning, they both reversed positions and let fly at him. Quicker than I am writing these words they kicked the unfortunate creature through the barbed fence, which fortunately was not well built and gave way under the strain. Three posts were down and the wires torn out from their staples. I examined the barbs with fear and trembling; to my horror there was blood upon them here and there. The Moors horse was found afterwards, very little the worse for his encounter with the chiefs, in his own paddock. He had some hair bitten off his hind quarters and a long scratch or two from the wires. Horses seem to be almost as much trouble as pigs.

Speaking of pigs, the lady pig from Sydney has at last produced a family, originally seven, but by accident reduced to six. She was very genteel, receiving us with the most affected grunt. Some straw and dried cocoanut leaves had been thrown in to her and these she had arranged in a circular bed, so that it looked just like an immense bird's nest. The next day a very heavy shower fell, and remembering that the nest was outside the protection of the roof, I was curious enough to go down and inspect her ladyship's proceedings. The selfish thing had retired to the dais Paul had built for her, leaving, quite contentedly, her babes to perish in the cold rain. Henry happened to come running past, clad in nothing but a kilted lava lava. He leaped the fence and indignantly tore the dais from under the fine lady, tossing the pigs and nest into the dry corner.

The wild black sow is a beautiful animal. Her bright intelligent eye is large and of a lovely soft brown. Her long nose is perfectly straight and her legs are like a deer's. Not exactly the style for bacon, but beautiful to contemplate when safely imprisoned. She never ceases her endeavours to escape. I can hear her at it every time I wake in the night. I could soon learn to like her but, as Louis justly says, "Once form an intimacy with a pig and eating pork partakes of the nature of cannibalism."

The *Archer* has come and gone. She brought letters for us, drenched by a sea she had taken on board in heavy weather. A bit of edging I had sent for was almost rotten. Captain Henry[45] and Mr. Hird[46] came up to see us, both looking very well. They were confused when the Savage Island pig was mentioned, and pretended not to know what had become of her. Finally the captain said, "Well, I spent a day trying to get that pig off the *Janet*, but the last I saw of her she was in irons on the deck, and that's all I know of the pig." Certainly I do not regret the Savage Islander.

They brought sad news concerning Penrhyn.[47] Leprosy, which was just beginning to show itself when we were there, has broken out with great virulence, so much so that the people themselves became alarmed and segregated the unclean. A Hawaiian woman is said to be very bad with leprosy down in Apia. Today Seumanu[48] came to see us, or rather, as he said, he wanted to borrow some money, "And that is the reason why I came." Louis had a very serious talk with him on the subject of leprosy and the dreadful danger that menaced Samoa. Seumanu has a fine intelligent face and smiles a little like our dear Tembinoka.[49] His wife, who is a "big chief woman," is Henry's aunt.

[45] Sailing-master of the *Janet Nichol*.
[46] Ben Hird, supercargo on the *Nichol*. *Island Nights' Entertainment* was partially dedicated to him.
[47] Penrhyn Island, of the Manihiki group in the south Pacific.
[48] Seumanutafa.
[49] King of Apemama, one of the Gilbert Islands.

The latest Henry has brought us from the spirit world is a little more intelligible than the last. It seems there is an evil female spirit whose name means "come to me, thousands." She sometimes appears in the guise of an ill-mannered old crone and demands small services of women who are alone. It may be a drink of water she rudely asks for. If she is answered in chief's language and the water is politely brought to her, no harm ensues. If the contrary, she waits till the victim is asleep, when she enters the unconscious body and spends the night racing over the mountains or in carousing. The doomed person, never properly resting, and quite unconscious of the reason why, gradually wastes away and finally dies. Upon occasion she takes the form of a man. If, in this guise, she fancies a girl, the unfortunate is done to death that the demon may have her spirit. It is very common for her to fall in love with beautiful young men, who may then consider themselves lost. In one of the neighbouring villages lived a young man, an acquaintance of Henry's. He was very beautiful, very clever and very good, and occupied a corresponding position to that of "the maid of the village"[50] in consequence. This was the first I had heard of a young man of the village, but Henry says it is common. The *aitu fafine* (female spirit or devil) found this good and clever and beautiful youth so irresistible that she first took his life and then his spirit. Her mode of procedure, or rather, the signs of it, are well known. The person becomes first a beautiful ruddy hue all over his body, and feels very lightheaded. Then the blood begins to show through the skin and the flesh becomes transparent, "like that," said Henry, holding his closed fingers up beside the lamp. Very soon after that the end comes, and the *aitu fafine* is away with her new bridegroom. Henry's acquaintance had the symptoms very clearly marked, so there can be no doubt about it.

Louis says he does not wonder that the Samoans are afraid to be out in the bush after dark. When he came home from Apia the last time there was no moon and it was very dark; before him and around him and all through the bush a phosphorescent light, due to decaying wood, spread over the ground. He said he seemed to be picking his way over the mouth of hell. That same night a drunken

---

[50] *Taupo-sa*, or sacred maid.

man from the *Sperber* was thrown from his horse and lay insensible on the road for several hours.

The Chief Justice is expected here now in less than a fortnight. In spite of all remonstrances the king has ordered in all the chiefs to do him honour. It will be like locusts passing over a field of corn. The question is: how are they to be fed? I fear a good deal on other people's pigs and fowls. I do not believe the missionaries will approve of my means of protection. I could think of nothing else so sure. I took the round top of a small meat cask and painted upon it a hideous head with great eyes and a wide, open mouth displaying a double row of pointed teeth. Instead of hair, flames radiate out from the head. These flames, the iris of the eyes, and the pointed teeth I have painted in luminous paint. It almost frightens me. The *aitu fafine*, I may add, has red hair that rises from her head very high, and a beautiful figure. The breasts are [not?] very well formed, which is one of the weaknesses of the Samoan female figure.

DEC. 15TH

Henry has discovered that we have an *aitu fafine* of our own. She lives in the spring from which our main stream rises. She moves with a rushing wind. It is she of whom Lafaele is so much afraid. He told Henry that when he was working in the garden one day he heard a strange noise in the bush behind him and became aware of a wind dashing through the trees, which rustled and swayed in a most alarming manner.

The young man who committed the forgery and opened Henry's letter, and received in consequence a fine of ten dollars, has been fined again by the chief of his own village to the extent of six barrels of salt beef, each barrel costing five dollars. Three of these "evil young men," according to Henry, are in league together, though they have been known to rob each other.

Not long ago the American consul-general, intending to give a feast, found he could not hoist his flag, as the halyards were stolen. Being a sentimentalist, and a fervid champion of the Samoan race, he meant to keep his loss a secret; but Mataafa, coming to the house, learned of the affair and was exceedingly angry. The next morning when the consul opened his door he stumbled over something lying on the threshold, which upon examination proved to be the culprit, bound hand and foot. There was nothing for it but to let him go to trial, the matter now having become too public to be hushed up. The sentence, to the horror of Mr. Sewall, was sixty lashes and six months' hard labour. Of course the sentimentalist begged the thief off and his sentence was lowered to three months' hard labour. A short time after this occurred, a lady visiting at the consulate passed a young man who was sunning himself and smoking in great content. He saluted her with easy grace as an old friend. She looked again and could hardly believe her eyes when she recognized the man just condemned to hard labour. Since which the saucy rascal has taken up his position in front of the consulate, where he receives his friends and passes the time in smoking and gossip.

The carpenter is hard at work on the stable, which is already roofed in. Henry and his boys are building, or rather excavating, a hurricane refuge. I went to see it yesterday, a big mud hole with immense boulders of volcanic rock heaving up from the bottom. I advised the instant digging of a ditch unless they wished to use it for a bathing pool, but I do not believe they have begun the ditch yet. The hole must be, today, pretty well filled up, as last night the rain came down in awful torrents.

For the last two days the evening light has been very strange and disquieting. A whitish glare in the sky, the trees and bare ground a burnt sienna red, lighter and darker, and the vegetation a strong, crude green, with a delicate white bloom. The rain is still pouring and the whole world is damp and uncomfortable.

Three of the best yellow hens are sitting in the grass. One I have brought in to the kitchen with her eggs. If we can induce her to remain, the others shall come too.

At last the Schmidts have received a cow and calf by the *Richmond*. It came yesterday. During a torrent of rain the calf strayed, but no one dared wake up the son, Gustav, to fetch it in; it was about eight o'clock. Their money seems to be done, for they have accepted a tin of flour from us with thanks.

Henry wishes an advance on his wages of 120 dollars to buy a piece of land in partnership with his cousin; it is under consideration. Paul, who is alarmed by the thought of approaching changes, asks that a contract be made with him. He also anxiously begs to know what his work will be. Lafaele, whose wife ran away from him a short time ago, is to be, or is already, married again, this time before the consul. He tells me that he really cannot stop any longer in Apia, but must attach himself permanently to our establishment. He and his wife will sleep anywhere and both will "work like hell." If the new wife does not suit me in any way I am to just kill her and Lafaele will bear no ill feeling but keep on working like hell.

Yesterday afternoon a large strange vessel was to be seen lying just outside Apia, where she still remains. She was signalling and receiving signals from the *Sperber*. We cannot make out what she is or what she means. A letter came by the *Richmond* from Tamate. We have been reading his books with ever-increasing admiration for Tamate.

L o u i s .   MONDAY, TWENTY-SOMETHINGTH OF DECEMBER

I do not say my Jack is anything extraordinary; he is only an island horse; and the profane might call him a Punch; and his face is like a donkey's; and natives have ridden him, and he has no mouth in consequence, and occasionally shies. But his merits are equally surprising; and I don't think I should ever have known Jack's merits if I had not been riding of late on moonless nights. Jack is a bit of a dandy; he loves to misbehave in a gallant manner, above all on Apia Street, and when I stop to speak to people, they say (Dr. Stuebel the German consul said about three days ago), "Oh, what a wild horse! it cannot be safe to ride him." Such a remark is Jack's reward, and represents his ideal of fame. Now when I start out of Apia on a dark night, you should see my changed horse; at a fast steady walk, with his head down, and sometimes his nose to the ground—when he wants to do that he asks for his head with a little eloquent polite movement indescribable—he climbs the long ascent and threads the darkest of the wood. The first night I came it was starry; and it was singular to see the starlight drip down into the crypt of the wood, and shine in the open end of the road, as bright as moonlight at home; but the crypt itself was proof, blackness lived in it. The next night it was raining. We left the lights of Apia and passed into limbo. Jack finds a way for himself, but he does not calculate for my height above the saddle; and I am directed forward, all braced up for a crouch and holding my switch upright in front of me. It is curiously interesting. In the forest, the dead wood is phosphorescent; some nights the whole ground is strewn with it, so that it seems like a grating over a pale hell; doubtless this is one of the things that feed the night fears of the natives; and I am free to confess that in a night of trackless darkness where all else is void, these pallid *ignes suppositi* have a fantastic appearance, rather bogey even. One night, when it was very dark, a man had put out a little lantern by the wayside to show the entrance to his ground. I saw the light, as I thought, far ahead, and supposed it was a pedestrian coming to meet me; I was quite taken by surprise when it struck in my face and passed behind me. Jack saw it, and he was appalled; do you think he thought of shying? No, sir, not in the dark; in the dark Jack knows he is on duty; and he went past that lantern steady and swift; only, as he went, he groaned and shuddered. For about 2500 of Jack's steps we only pass one house—that where the lantern was; and about 1500 of these are in the darkness of the pit. But now the moon is on tap again, and the roads lighted. . . .

Fanny has been quite ill with ear-ache. She won't go,[51] hating the sea at this wild season; I don't like to leave her; so it drones on, steamer after steamer, and I guess it'll end by no one going at all. She is in a dreadful misfortune at this hour; a case of kerosene having burst in the kitchen. A little while ago it was the carpenter's horse that trod in a nest of fourteen eggs, and made an omelette of our hopes. The farmer's lot is not a happy one. And it looks like some real uncompromising bad weather too. I wish Fanny's ear were well. Think of parties in Monuments! think of me in Skerryvore, and now of this. It don't look like a part of the same universe to me. Work is quite laid aside; I have worked myself right out.

CHRISTMAS EVE

Yesterday, who could write? My wife near crazy with ear-ache; the

[51] On a projected expedition to Sydney.

rain descending in white crystal rods and playing hell's tattoo, like a *tutti* of battering rams, on our sheet-iron roof; the wind passing high overhead with a strange dumb mutter, or striking us full, so that all the huge trees in the paddock cried aloud, and wrung their hands, and brandished their vast arms. The horses stood in the shed like things stupid. The sea and the flagship lying on the jaws of the bay vanished in sheer rain. All day it lasted; I locked up my papers in the iron box, in case it was a hurricane, and the house might go. We went to bed with mighty uncertain feelings; far more than on shipboard, where you have only drowning ahead—whereas here you have a smash of beams, a shower of sheet-iron, and a blind race in the dark and through a whirlwind for the shelter of an unfinished stable —and my wife with ear-ache! Well, well, this morning, we had word from Apia; a hurricane was looked for, the ships were to leave the bay by 10 A.M.; it is now 3:30, and the flagship is still a fixture, and the wind round in the blessed east, so I suppose the danger is over. But heaven is still laden; the day dim, with frequent rattling bucketfuls of rain; and just this moment (as I write) a squall went overhead, scarce striking us, with that singular, solemn noise of its passage, which is to me dreadful. I have always feared the sound of wind beyond everything. In my hell it would always blow a gale.

SATURDAY, 27TH DECEMBER

It cleared up suddenly after dinner, and my wife and I saddled up and off to Apia, whence we did not return till yesterday morning. Christmas Day I wish you could have seen our party at table. H. J. Moors at one end with my wife, I at the other with Mrs. M; between us two native women, Carruthers the lawyer, Moors' two shop-boys— Walters and A. M. the quadroon—and the guests of the evening, Shirley Baker, the defamed and much-accused man of Tonga, and his son, with the artificial joint to his arm—where the assassins shot him in shooting at his father. Baker's appearance is not unlike John Bull on a cartoon; he is highly interesting to speak to, as I had expected; I found he and I had many common interests, and were engaged in puzzling over many of the same difficulties. After dinner it was quite pretty to see our Christmas party, it was so easily pleased and prettily behaved. . . .

Ah, my wicked Jack! on Christmas Eve, as I was taking the saddle bag off, he kicked at me, and fetched me too, right on the shin. On Friday, being annoyed at the carpenter's horse having a longer trot, he uttered a shrill cry and tried to bite him! Alas, alas, these are like old days; my dear Jack is a Bogue,[52] but I cannot strangle Jack into submission.

DECEMBER 29TH[53]

We are in the midst of the rainy season, and dwell among alarms of hurricanes, in a very unsafe little two-storied wooden box 650 feet above and about three miles from the sea-beach. Behind us, till the other slope of the island, desert forest, peaks, and loud torrents; in front green slopes to the sea, some fifty miles of which we dominate. We see the ships as they go out and in to the dangerous roadstead of Apia; and if they lie far out, we can even see their topmasts while they are at anchor. Of sounds of men, beyond those of our own labourers, there reach us, at very long intervals, salutes from the warships in harbour, the bell of the cathedral church, and the low of the conch-shell calling the labour boys on the German plantations. Yesterday, which was Sunday—the *quantième* is most likely erroneous; you can now correct it—we had a visitor—Baker[54] of Tonga. Heard you ever of him? He is a great man here: he is accused of theft, rape, judicial murder, private poisoning, abortion, misappropriation of public moneys—oddly enough, not forgery, nor arson; you would be amused if you knew how thick the accusations fly in this South Sea world. I make no doubt my own character is something illustrious; or if not yet, there is a good time coming.

But all our resources have not of late been Pacific. We have had enlightened society: La Farge[55] the painter, and your friend Henry Adams: a great privilege—would it might endure. I would go oftener to see them, but the place is awkward to reach on horseback. I had to swim my horse the last time I went to dinner; and as I have not

[52] The Skye-terrier of Bournemouth days, celebrated in RLS's essay "The Character of Dogs."

[53] To Henry James.

[54] Shirley Baker, like Bully Hayes, enjoyed a dubious reputation in the South Seas. A missionary on the island of Tonga, he was accused of ruling despotically and of maltreating natives.

[55] John La Farge, American painter.

yet returned the clothes I had to borrow, I dare not return in the same plight: it seems inevitable—as soon as the wash comes in, I plump straight into the American consul's shirt or trousers! They, I believe, would come oftener to see me but for the horrid doubt that weighs upon our commissariat department; we have *often* almost nothing to eat; a guest would simply break the bank; my wife and I have dined on one avocado pear; I have several times dined on hard bread and onions. What would you do with a guest at such narrow seasons?—eat him? or serve up a labour boy fricasseed? . . .

Kipling is by far the most promising young man who has appeared since—ahem—I appeared. He amazes me by his precocity and various endowment. But he alarms me by his copiousness and haste. He should shield his fire with both hands "and draw up all his strength and sweetness in one ball." ("Draw all his strength and all His sweetness into one ball"? I cannot remember Marvell's words.) So the critics have been saying to me; but I was never capable of— and surely never guilty of—such a debauch of production. At this rate his works will soon fill the habitable globe; and surely he was armed for better conflicts than these succinct sketches and flying leaves of verse? I look on, I admire, I rejoice for myself; but in a kind of ambition we all have for our tongue and literature I am wounded. If I had this man's fertility and courage, it seems to me I could heave a pyramid.

Well, we begin to be the old fogies now; and it was high time *something* rose to take our places. Certainly Kipling has the gifts; the fairy godmothers were all tipsy at his christening: what will he do with them?

Louis was one of the most charming geniuses of English letters. When he died he was mourned by his friends around the world and by many admirers who knew him only by his books and gossip. He had the ability to project himself into his style with a vivacity and a naturalness which are beyond imitation. Not the least unusual of his qualities are his optimism and courage. Although in ill health since an early age, he rarely faltered—and he wrote incessantly and under all conditions. It is regrettable that he is currently out of fashion, for his spirit and style are an ornament in any time.

Compared with his rich rhetoric Fanny's is almost dry and matter-of-fact. She writes as a gifted amateur, allowing her material to stand in the foreground while she herself retires modestly. She does not, like Louis, consciously or professionally write in a personal vein and yet the effect of her diary is to personalize her very well. Like her husband she wrote copiously, and many of her letters—which Henry James exclaimed over, urging that they be collected and published—survive.

They were indeed a remarkable pair. It is well to recall that Fanny—so energetic and seemingly so tireless—was a woman of fifty at this time, a grandmother, with a daughter only some eight years Louis's junior. It is easy to imagine that Louis saw in her more of a mother than a mate and yet this assumption will not quite do, for there is much evidence to the contrary. But one wonders about their conjugal relations. There is hardly any mention anywhere of open tenderness between them. At Vailima they had separate bedrooms, which may have been only a luxurious arrangement. On the other hand it is more than possible that the conjugal role was largely proscribed for Louis because of the nature of his illness. Whatever their relations, they lived their lives at Vailima energetically, not unaware that they played interesting roles on the literary stage.

1891

F A N N Y . JAN. 12TH

It is a long time since I have written in my diary. First I had a very painful abscess in my ear, and afterwards Louis went to Sydney and I had no time. On Christmas eve we went down to Mr. Moors'. We had been told that the barometer had fallen and a hurricane was expected. I did not notice that the wind had changed and the sky had cleared before we started, but Louis had. As he wished to go to Apia, he did not call my attention to the fact that there was no more fear of a storm. I was glad I went, however. We stayed over Christmas, as Mr. Moors made a little impromptu party at which the notorious Mr. Baker was the chief guest. A young Mr. Baker was with his father. He also had had an abscess in his ear, as had several other people. I did not particularly like Mr. Baker, though I could not help being interested in a person who had a career so singular and eventful. He was very stout and smug, with a honey sweet voice and a honey sweet smile. I was the only white woman present. Besides myself there were two Samoan ladies and one very charming half-caste. The latter sat down to the piano like a little child and played easy exercises and bits of "Yankee Doodle" for, I should say, a full hour.

One day last week a cow was brought over to me from the German plantation. I thought, from a distance (I did not see her near), that she looked ominously like a bullimakaw. A whole drove of kine were brought up to induce the chosen one to come this way.

"Had she not better be tied up at first?" I asked the white man who had ridden up to the house.

"By *no* means," was his emphatic answer. "You must *never* put a rope on her."

"I'm afraid that doesn't sound like a very gentle animal," said I.

"Gentle!" protested the man. "Why, she is my own cow, my own family cow, and I'm very sorry to part with her. She is as gentle as a cow can be."

"And how much milk does she give?" I asked.

"Oh, about three bottles, I should say."

"Three bottles! Why, that's only six a day!" cried I.

"Oh, no," was the rejoinder, "*three* bottles a *day* was what I said."

"Oh," said I, "that will never do. It isn't worth the trouble of milking to only get three bottles a day."

"Well," said the man, doubtfully, "she may give more. You see, I've only had this cow two days now, so I really don't know how much she really might give after she is used to a place."

I did not ask him upon what she based her claim to be a family cow, and his own attached family cow at that. The animal was somehow inveigled into the paddock, upon which she galloped like a mad creature, her tail sticking out perfectly stiff behind her. With a parting admonition to drive the beast into a yoke, which must be locked over her head before milking, the man rode away and left me face to face (at a little distance, to be sure) with the cow. I appealed to the carpenter about the yoke. He said he could make one, but in the meantime he meant to tie up the cow, no matter what instructions had been given.

"If I don't," he said, "she will be over the fence in five minutes."

And over the fence she was in five minutes or less, sure enough.

Early the next morning, Mr. Hay, who sleeps in the new stable (just finished), heard a great racket of dogs and pigs. Three dogs from Mr. Trood's place, used for wild-pig hunting, were worrying my three poor half-grown pigs. Before they could be chased off, one pig was very badly wounded. It crawled into the bush, covered with blood, and could not be found. The principal offender was said to be a large well-known brown dog. A little later, while I was at breakfast, I heard a plaintive whining at the foot of the stairs. There lay Mr. Brown Dog, his two hind paws bound together and the two front. He had been captured and carried up to me swinging from a pole, and was awaiting his sentence. Of course it should have been instant execution but I hadn't the heart, and sent him back to his master with a caution against bringing his dogs this way.

Yesterday the dismal cow was found in Trood's place, where she had destroyed a lot of bananas. A man came and demanded damages.

"You had 'em in advance," I said, "in the shape of a pig."

Paul and Mr. Hay and Lafaele went after the cow. They had to hire another man to help them, and then Mr. Hay hardly thought they could get the creature home alive, she fought so viciously. I mean home with her own family, for I would not have her for my family cow.

Today I had meant to write at a story begun long ago, but instead have spent nearly the whole time sitting in front of the bees. They were making a most portentous buzzing and hissing inside the box, and the carpenter, to whom I appealed for advice, said they were surely going to swarm at once. I never saw anything so aggravating. There would be a sudden hurrahing and shouting, "Here she comes!" Bees would rush in every direction in frantic excitement—it was a false alarm. I remember the same sort of thing going on once when Queen Victoria was expected. Bees and people seem very much the same. They certainly seem very gentle bees. The carpenter said I would know the queen by her corpulency, so I sat with my nose almost in their doorway, watching lest I should miss Her Majesty, but not a sting did I get. Mr. Hay says there is no doubt but I am one of those people that bees do not attack. I think these bees are the kind that do not attack.

It is strange that each night has its separate plague of insects. The mosquito, of course, is always with us; but one night it is moths we breathe and are generally tormented by; at another time it will be small black beetles, myriads of them. At another the creatures may be mostly of a large cockchafer sort, or a dreadful square-tailed thing that is especially obnoxious. Tonight I have had, for the first time, two sets of tormentors. The first, small burnished beetles of the most lovely colours imaginable. A pink bronze fellow lies on my paper as I write; at least his body. He kept standing on his head until he died in a fit. It seems a colour night, for I now have small silver moths, all of a size, but with different lovely markings.

Last Thursday evening I was invited to dine at the American consul's to meet the Chief Justice.[1] I was very tired and not particularly well, but as both Mr. Sewall and Mr. Clarke[2] (the latter wrote to ask me to sleep at the mission house) pathetically mentioned that the other ladies would be Mrs. Cusack-Smith,[3] Mrs. Clarke and Mrs. Claxton, I felt that I had to go. So many men, and only three ladies besides myself—I really would fill a much-needed if not "long felt" want. And then, besides, I must show respect to the new Chief Justice, to say nothing of my own consul.

The old mare did *not* go fast, and I had to speak to Mr. Moors on business before I went to the Clarkes. Certainly the Clarke clock must have been fast. Mrs. Claxton says it was very fast. At any rate, they were all gone. A beautiful young half-caste girl with lovely manners got a man to lead my horse through the river. She and I started over the bridge. Alas, the stream was too deep to get the horse across! I found Henry, who tried in vain to get me a boat. The end of it was that I had to go down to Mr. Moors and beg a little food, after which I returned to the Clarkes.

I had been shown into a bedroom when I first arrived. On my return a lamp was burning in this room but no one was visible. I knew my horse wanted water, so finally, anxious about the creature, I looked through the house. I found a room full of women but no mode of communication with them. I had to give it up, as one of the young women showed signs of being on the point of preparing a meal for me. It seemed then a good plan to go to bed. I was almost asleep when I was startled broad awake by the thought that I had perhaps only been shown into this particular room to take my things off; that this was Mr. and Mrs. Clarke's room, and the light had been left for them to go to bed by. I had put the light out, and didn't know where the matches were.

[1] A Swede, Konrad Cedarcrantz.
[2] Rev. W. E. Clarke of the London Missionary Society. Louis was extremely fond of Clarke, often saying that he was one of the finest men he had ever met.
[3] Wife of Thomas (later Sir Thomas) Cusack-Smith, British consul in Samoa.

[JANUARY] 13TH

This afternoon I felt two distinct shocks of an earthquake. I fancied the first was accompanied by a rumbling sound like thunder. The second and sharper shock, following quickly after the first, certainly was. Mr. Hay was drawing water from the tank for the horses. He did not feel the earthquake but heard the noise.

"I heard thunder," said he.

"But look at the sky," I said. There was nothing to be seen there to account for thunder.

The bees did not swarm, so Mr. Baker[4] and I, assisted by Lafaele, in a blue fright, turned up the box and looked at them. There were an immense number of bees hanging to the sides and top of the box and to some very nice looking pieces of comb, but no signs of swarming. Mr. Baker has made a stand for them and I shall change them tomorrow night.

The pig supposed to be killed has been seen by Paul, very lame and looking badly. It crawled out of the bush and then back again. Of course Paul came back to tell the news without following it up, and it could not again be found. Louis calls Paul "Handy Andy."

A short time ago I made a little movable coop for the hen with chicks and put it, with the hen inside, on a dry spot of ground, for at this time of the year the grass is very wet. Two more hens brought out broods and Paul, having watched me, volunteered to make the coops for them. He came to tell me they were finished. They were very well done, exact counterparts of mine. I expressed my approval and said, "Take them out now with the hens and chicks, and be sure you put the coops in a dry place." Pretty soon I became aware of a couple of hens and a number of chicks running about in the wet grass. I called Paul.

"Oh, yes, Madame," he said, "those are the hens. I put them out, as you told me."

"But why are they not in the coops?" I asked.

"You told me to put them out with the hens and the chicks," was Paul's exasperating answer, "but you didn't tell me to put the hens inside the coops."

[4] Not to be confused with Shirley Baker.

And sure enough, there were the two coops carefully placed in dry places, food and water under them, just as I had arranged mine, and the fowls, for whom all this trouble had been taken, wandering about catching roup and pip and gapes, and whatever else chickens do catch from dampness. Last night the hens were removed to the new hen house with great trouble by Paul, who locked the door and brought the key up to me but did not mention that he had left two large windows open, out of which the fowls all made their way at the first peep of dawn.

JAN.

Louis has been gone about a fortnight to the colonies for a change of air. He was very much averse to leaving me, lest I should be ill while he was gone. I have been very ill, indeed. This attack has lasted longer than usual. I had quite a fright the other night, when I felt that my head was going wrong under stress of pain, there being no one in the house but Paul, asleep downstairs. To have him upstairs would be worse than being alone. The day that Louis left here, intending to stay the night in Apia, Paul behaved very badly. He asked to go down to the town to see to his "soft goods," that should have arrived by the *Lübeck*. In the afternoon three men from the *Lübeck* came up to the house, very drunk and noisy, and, upon my telling them to go away, used the foulest language, and one of them tried to ride Henry down with his horse. They went away once and returned, behaving in such a manner that I had to send Henry down for the police. Towards evening Paul returned, a spectacle for the gods, fetching back with him for the third time one of his drunken comrades, who absolutely supposed that I would be willing to let him stay the night in the house. Paul is in great disfavour since, and Henry comes flying back to me if he meets or hears of Paul on the road, refusing to leave until he sees in what condition Paul returns.

Paul and Lafaele have planted out all the cacao, only unfortunately Paul placed the most of his in the tops of rubbish heaps, left by Lafaele until he could find time to cart them away. Those properly planted look very well.

All our fruit trees are growing and the cocoanuts are coming up finely. Our new house is going on apace, and tomorrow it is expected the frame will go up. Someone has given Paul a small starveling of a kitten. It is crawling all over me as I write. Last night a dog attacked the cats, and old Putch drove him off like a tiger; his cries were heart-rending. Henry ran to the door just in time to see his retreat, followed by both cats at a hard gallop. Heard that Beni was very ill. Henry went to see him with a message from me that if he were ill he was to come up here, not to work, but to rest and kai kai.[5] However, he, like Louis, was away for a change of air. I trust that no alarming accidents may take place while Louis is away.

Everybody, white, brown or black, comes to me with apparently full confidence that I am able to cure any wound or disease. I heard a loud weeping as of some person in great pain. Before I could get to the door, the carpenter was there to ask for remedies for a man who had just had two fingers dreadfully crushed. I really didn't know what to do, except to go to the doctor; but as the wound was bleeding a good deal, I mixed up some crystals of iron in water and his hand was washed with that. To my surprise his cries instantly ceased and he declares that he has had no more pain since. It was only for the effect on his mind that I gave the iron, which so far as I knew was a styptic only. I always think I had better give something. I have cured both Paul and the carpenter of violent lumbago. But then I had a little knowledge to go upon. Today a man came to me with the sole of his foot very much inflamed. He had run a nail into it the day before yesterday. I bound a bit of fat bacon on his foot, an old Negro remedy which was the only one I could think of.

I do not think it occurred to me at the time to mention a very mad act of mine. I came in from the bush with the inside unrolled fronds of a great number of ferns. I boiled them like asparagus, and for dinner served them with lime juice and butter. Louis began eating them, then stopped and asked me what certainty I had that the things were edible and not poisonous. I had either been told or had read that they made an excellent vegetable. But Louis persisted: how did I know what variety to gather? I didn't know, so gathered every kind that grew. Louis ate no more, but to find out whether they were poisonous or not I ate the whole dishful with an effort.

[5] Take food.

I waked up in the night with a pain in my stomach and a most deathly feeling altogether. I began to think the question was settled, especially after I remembered the chemist at Hyères telling us of the death of a man caused by an overdose of extract of fern seed. It seemed to me that in eating the very heart of the plant I had got a good deal of the extract of every part of it. However, I tried a little whiskey before waking the household, and soon fell asleep, waking the next morning none the worse for my foolish experiment.

Lafaele has had a quarrel with his wife and her father and mother. He came in to me looking very dangerous and not at all a person to trifle with. He had freshly dyed his hair with lime, was scented and oiled, and had a wreath round his neck and a flower on the side of his head. He knelt down with unusual dignity and poured out his sorrows. He did not belong to this island, he said. When he was "a *lee*-tle small boy" a whaler stole him and kept him a slave on board his ship for a long time; and finally, when he was tired of the boy, dropped him at Apia.

"Three time," said Lafaele, "I marry Samoa girl. Samoa girl no good."

He was twice married "faa Samoa," both wives leaving him for other men. This last and third time, to make sure, he was married before the consul, "allee same white man."

He announced his intention to stop with me now.

"Me no got father," he said, "no got mother, no got brother, no got sister, no got friend, neither. Wife she no like me, she like Samoa man. Me alle same one fellow."

He said that I was "allee same" his mother. This I denied, but he waved me lightly aside, saying if I didn't like him I could kill him, and from that moment I could count him as a member of the family.

Henry came in, heard the tale, looked very wise, and acted with still greater wisdom. The wife, the father and the mother were sent for, witnesses were examined by Henry, who with a few shrewd questions got the true story of his own misconduct from each member of the party, Lafaele himself proving to be more in the wrong than any of the others. Mutual apologies were made, and after a lecture from the young Solomon on the duties of man and wife, and father and mother-in-law, and son-in-law, there was a general reconciliation; so I have not yet become "allee same Lafaele's mother." I am sure, though, that day will yet dawn.

The weather has been exceptionally good, though this is the season for hurricanes. Henry's "hurricane cellar" has become a great mud hole and a fertile breeding place for mosquitoes, having been abandoned as a bad job. When the cellar was dug for the new house, seven feet deep, they were still in fine rich loam at the bottom. A pineapple brought by Mr. Carruthers, a very odd variegated variety, has begun to fruit. It is bending to the ground under the weight of a very large vivid red pineapple encircled by bristling young plants. Henry is sure that it will not be good to eat, but it looks delicious. I have had quite a number of ripe tomatoes and a few beans from the garden. The "long-podded" beans are most flourishing. Today I planted out, with much misgiving, one of my precious rhubarb plants. The globe artichokes, with one accord, after a fine start have withered and perished. The onions I cannot account for. They come up most luxuriantly and then disappear entirely in a single night. I think some insect must eat them. As soon as I can get a brood of young chicks I shall put the mother's coop into the garden and see what the effect will be. The boys brought up two big iron tanks for rainwater today. The big tree leaning over the house where we live rains leaves upon the roof, and so spoils the water. Paul has actually invented a dish that is good, yams made into a sort of cake, seasoned with nutmeg.

My bedroom presents a most extraordinary aspect. Whenever a thing is twice lost downstairs I order it up to my room, so that it cannot be taken out without my knowledge. Amongst my dresses are hanging bridles, straps and horse ropes. On the camphor wood trunk which serves as my dressing table, beside my comb and tooth brush, is a collection of tools, chisels, pincers, and the like. Leather straps and parts of harness hang from nails on the wall. There are, besides, other incongruous articles, a Kingsmill bucket, a long carved spear, a pistol and boxes of cartridges, strings of teeth (fish, human and beast), necklaces of shells, and quantities of hats, fans, fine mats and tapas piled up in heaps. My little cot bed seems to have got into its place by mistake.

I find that Paul was, in spite of my orders to the contrary, lighting the fire with kerosene. "Fetch the can upstairs," said I.

Paul started to my bedroom with the can, but I draw the line at kerosene. I forgot to mention that in every available space bottles of red and white wine are piled in tiers; also a large quantity of smoking tobacco in tins, neither of which are safe anywhere else. There are besides an easel and two cameras in one corner. Indeed it is difficult to say what is not to be found in that very small and crowded apartment. When Mr. Moors was here last, the door was open. I became aware that he was gazing with a fixed stare at the strange conglomeration of articles thus betrayed to view. "Call *this* a lady's chamber!" was the expression of his countenance.

FEB. 15

Lloyd and Mr. King[6] arrived about ten days ago, quite unexpectedly. The *Lübeck* broke down on the voyage up to Sydney and had to be laid up for repairs, another vessel being sent down in her place. They arrived with tons of stuff, mostly mistakes. I had written in my list two black sows, one of them for Mr. Moors. I received two crosscut saws, one of which Mr. Moors naturally refuses to accept. Any number of things they thought it a good plan to duplicate, so that I have among other things two wire stretchers for fencing. One lasts forever, and but one can be used at a time. I put Mr. King at once to making the pig fence. What he wanted was the tool box, so I have hung the tool box before him as a reward for the finishing of the pig fence.

The brother of Seumanu's wife has been eaten by black boys. They are trying to hush it up but I think there is no doubt about the business. At the plantation, where it occurred, they say that they only ate one of themselves, as though the fact of cannibalism going on at our door is of no moment unless some of ourselves are eaten. A number of black boys have been caught already. There are supposed to be a great many in our bush. Near the garden I sometimes hear a strange subterranean rumbling. It may be that a cave

[6] An employee.

is thereabouts, in which blacks are living. All those caught are armed with knives.

It is also possible that there may be what I would consider a more alarming reason for the rumbling: it may be volcanic. Not long since, just about midnight, I felt a very sharp shock of an earthquake, and once before, in the daytime, another was accompanied by a long rolling sound like a continuous peal of thunder. Many times, in the garden, I have smelled, when no bush fires were alight, smoke and sulphurous fumes; a chemical sort of odour.

Henry has brought an old ambrotype of his father to get advice about having an enlarged copy made. The father has a plain sensible face, very like Henry's own, but his costume is very amusing; apparently a white lava lava worn with a lady's old-fashioned basque trimmed with guimpe, and *bretelles* running over the shoulder, the collar being fastened with a gold brooch. The arrangement of darts for the bust looks very comical. On the head is a wreath of flowers done in the natural colours; the brooch is carefully gilded.

We have had Lafaele's wife up for a trial. She was not of the slightest use, and Henry suspected her of pilfering sugar and biscuits.

A very pleasing old lady came up from Lesher and asked to be taken as a general servant. I jumped at the offer but Lesher couldn't let her go. She had all the manners of a stage duchess and I never saw anyone get more expression into a countenance than she did. She complained of a want of food, pressing her hands upon the pit of her stomach to emphasize her statement that it was always empty. There was nothing in the place but grass, she said, and she was left there alone without provisions; all of which I had been told before.

"Look at me!" she cried; "I no got belly allee same bullimakaw!" I wish I could have caught her photograph at this moment. She threw out both hands with all the fingers outspread, protruded her eyeballs, and, allowing her jaw to drop like a dead person's, the lower lip falling away from it, sat a few moments as though petrified with the horror of her position.

The day before yesterday she came to visit me when I was weeding, in company with her sister. They both promptly joined in the work, and she never stopped till dinner time. The sister fled about an hour before, with some weak excuse. If she stopped in the weeding to take breath, she was hounded back to it instantly by the old woman.

Mr. Hay, who solemnly promised Louis that he would not use the horses for carrying his own down-loads, has been doing so every time the steamer came in. I also know that he used the horses in Apia an entire day, hauling stuff of his own between the steamer and the German firms, telling me that the horses were being shod. Just before the steamer comes in, he goes about to all the places where he has bought produce and gathers it in and makes our poor tired chiefs haul it down to Apia. I saw cases of a thousand oranges being slyly carried from Schmidt's one day. Now I find that a few days longer and I shall be able to do without the honest farmer. On Saturday the *Warrior* comes in, therefore on Friday my gentleman will begin hauling down the produce he is at present buying. I mean to turn him off on Thursday night so he will be left with all the stuff he has been buying, and no way to carry it down.

Lloyd brought with him several of the Strong cats from Sydney. One, a kitten, was crushed and killed in bad weather; another, Maude, escaped, but the captain thinks she is still on the ship and he is to try and catch her and send her back by the next *Lübeck*. So only two, Mother and Henry, have arrived. Putch, our own cat has been reared here, alone, with no cat society. I thought he would be pleased to have company but he is very inhospitable, and Henry and Mother are in much dread of him.

Lafaele comes in to report a serious outrage by an American sailor. Mr. Willis, our consulting carpenter, and Lloyd have just gone down with him to lay the case before the American consul.

Mr. King, who seems to have a predilection for spirits, after trying various methods to effect his purpose, was taken last night with a severe stomach ache. To his disappointment he got only a few drops of laudanum. I don't know how much of it was genuine, but he resolutely refused to deny himself green beans, etc., today, and recoiled aghast when I proposed administering a dose of sulphuric acid. He had an ill-founded belief that a bottle of brandy would stand on the table for anyone to put his lips to it when so disposed. But, as Henry says, this is a gentle house and not a beachcomber's store. I see that our young friend will need a good deal of training. His whole object seems to be to prepare to get ready for work, and he is most ready and willing to order all sorts of the most expensive tools for the purpose. I fear we have made a mistake in taking him. However, we were so agreeably disappointed in our now dear Henry that I shall suspend judgment yet awhile. He proposes that I send the money for his cousin to buy an "outfit" and pay her passage, and that he marry her when she arrives. He says she will be most useful, as she would be able to serve as a companion to Mrs. Stevenson, of course with the understanding that no menial duties will be required of her.

I hope to be Mrs. Stevenson's companion myself, so far as she requires services for her. I don't know what menial services would be in a place like this. I blacked my own shoes this morning, as I could do it very well, and it saved Paul a little work, and I am quite ready to black the shoes of everybody in the house if they are busy and it is better the shoes should be blacked. The bush is no place for fine lady companions. At least I do not imagine that I shall advance any money for the purpose of fetching one here, though of course Mr. King may bring a palaceful with his own money.

Louis fell ill with fever in Sydney and was nursed by his mother. When he was partly recovered they sailed on the *Lübeck* for Samoa. The elder Mrs. Stevenson received her first views of Upolu and Apia and Vailima the early part of March. She found Fanny looking very well, and busy with gardening, as usual. The hours kept at Vailima struck her as primitive: breakfast at 6, lunch at 11, dinner at 5:30. At about 9 in the evening Louis would take a biscuit and some whiskey and water and go off to bed. In more ways than one she felt uncomfortable at Vailima, and it was decided to have her return to Sydney and wait there until affairs at Vailima were in better order. Meanwhile Louis recovered rapidly.

L o u i s . MARCH 19TH

Before the sun rises, at 5:45 or 5:50, Paul brings me tea, bread, and a couple of eggs; and by about six I am at work. I work in bed —my bed is of mats, no mattress, sheets, or filth—mats, a pillow,

and a blanket—and put in some three hours. It was 9:05 this morning when I set off to the stream-side to my weeding; where I toiled,
manuring the ground with the best enricher, human sweat, till the
conch-shell was blown from our verandah at 10:30. At eleven we
dine; about half-past twelve I tried (by exception) to work again,
could make nothing on't, and by one was on my way to the weeding,
where I wrought till three. Half-past five is our next meal, and I
read Flaubert's *Letters* till the hour came round; dined, and then,
Fanny having a cold, and I being tired, came over to my den in the
unfinished house, where I now write to you, to the tune of the
carpenters' voices, and by the light—I crave your pardon—by the
twilight of three vile candles filtered through the medium of my
mosquito bar. Bad ink being of the party, I write quite blindfold,
and can only hope you may be granted to read that which I am
unable to see while writing.

I said I was tired; it is a mild phrase; my back aches like toothache; when I shut my eyes to sleep, I know I shall see before them
—a phenomenon to which both Fanny and I are quite accustomed
—endless vivid deeps of grass and weed, each plant particular and
distinct, so that I shall lie inert in body, and transact for hours the
mental part of my daily business, choosing the noxious from the
useful. And in my dreams I shall be hauling on recalcitrants, and
suffering stings from nettles, stabs from citron thorns, fiery bites
from ants, sickening resistances of mud and slime, evasions of slimy
roots, dead weight of heat, sudden puffs of air, sudden starts from
bird-calls in the contiguous forest—some mimicking my name, some
laughter, some the signal of a whistle, and living over again at large
the business of my day.

Though I write so little, I pass all my hours of field-work in continual converse and imaginary correspondence. I scarce pull up a
weed, but I invent a sentence on the matter to yourself; it does
not get written; *autant en emportent les vents;* but the intent is
there, and for me (in some sort) the companionship. To-day, for
instance, we had a great talk. I was toiling, the sweat dripping from
my nose, in the hot fit after a squall of rain: methought you asked
me—frankly, was I happy. Happy (said I); I was only happy once;

that was at Hyères; it came to an end from a variety of reasons,
decline of health, change of place, increase of money, age with his
stealing steps; since then, as before then, I know not what it means.
But I know pleasure still; pleasure with a thousand faces, and none
perfect, a thousand tongues all broken, a thousand hands, and all
of them with scratching nails. High among these I place this delight
of weeding out here alone by the garrulous water, under the silence
of the high wood, broken by incongruous sounds of birds. And take
my life all through, look at it fore and back, and upside down—
though I would very fain change myself—I would not change my
circumstances, unless it were to bring you here.

F A N N Y . MARCH 28TH

It is a long time since I have written in my diary, and there has
been much to write. First we had what some called a stiff blow and
others a hurricane. It blew very heavily up here. For several days
squall succeeded squall without intermission. One afternoon the
barometer (I had borrowed one from Mr. Moors to frighten myself
with) seemed very low, and the wind was steadily increasing. I
thought it a good plan to be ready for emergencies, so had bedding,
candles, etc., taken to the stable, and mosquito nets put up. Unfortunately, in the midst of the preparations I stepped on a nail,
which ran far into my instep. I limped up to the house in the most
excruciating pain. Lloyd had some cocaine, a very small bottle, which
I applied to the injury. The agony was less intense, but that was all.
Every moment the wind was rising, and the rain poured down in
torrents. It is a miserable sensation to sit helpless when any moment
you may need to run for your life. The house was rocking and groan-
ing in the most alarming way. With one gust of wind it swung over
so far that I thought it was gone.

"I can't stand it, Lloyd," I cried, "you've got to carry me down
to the stable."

By this time it was dark, though not very late. Lloyd carried me
halfway down the road, when he said he must rest, so I was put down
in a puddle of water, standing like a crane on one leg while Lloyd

took breath. He had been carrying me in his arms like a baby, which, in the darkness, and with the uncertain road, made it very difficult work. He therefore proposed that I should sit upon his back, and stooped down that I might mount. I tried to obey his instructions and thought I had managed very cleverly, but "Good heavens," he cried, "I didn't think you would leap upon me like that." For a few awful moments we swayed back and forth, very nearly going over head first into the horrid mud.

Arrived at the stable door, behold it was locked, and Mr. King gone to the pavilion with the key. I was left on a doorstep, shaking with cold and almost suffocated with the rain. I could hear trees crashing about me on all sides; one swung so near my head that, alarmed, I crawled on my hands and knees through the mud to a more sheltered door. It seemed a long time before Lloyd returned with the key and a lantern.

The first night I slept in a little harness room, but the rain beat in and it was soon swimming in water, so the next night I joined Lloyd and Mr. King in the stable and took possession of a stall. Paul resolutely refused to leave the house. "If anything happens I ought to be there," said he. Poor Lafaele, quite grey with fright, was taunted by Paul until he, too, agreed to stop at the post of danger. His position was none the more honourable, however, as he constantly dilated upon his terrors.

"Me too muchee 'fraid," said he, "no sleep, no can, too muchee 'fraid. Alleetime allee same cold, like dis"—shivering to show how his nerves were affected by his fears.

For several days we lived in the stable, sweeping out the water continually and lying in wet beds, and worst of all simply devoured by mosquitoes. When at last, after several days of the most miserable existence, the storm abated and I managed to hobble up to the house, everything there was wet and mildewed and the house had taken a decided cant over. The most distressing incident was a dreadful injury to the white horse. The last I had noticed of the horses they were all rushing about like mad things, kicking, leaping and rearing. Apparently a heavy branch of a tree had been blown down, striking the barbed wire fence and our poor chief at the same time. In his terror the horse had entangled himself amongst the wires and then kicked himself free.

It was twenty-four hours before Mr. Hay put in an appearance, and we did not know what to do. Paul, who was nearly dead with fatigue, went to bed, but could not go to sleep for thinking of the horse. Finally he got up and dressed and came out to me. I mixed some styptic to stop the bleeding, which Paul went out and applied, binding up the wound with a piece of my underclothing, the only thing I could get at in a hurry. It was twenty-four hours before Mr. Hay came, and the wound by that time was very badly inflamed.

Shortly after the storm the *Lübeck* came in, with Louis very ill, and his mother to nurse him. It is plain that he [must] stay in the South Seas; no other climate suits him. Mrs. S brought with her a sofa for her own use, which showed plainly that she had meant to stay; but the close quarters, continuous rain, and general discomfort were too much for her. She only stayed over until the *Lübeck* left. So fixed was she in her determination to leave, that when I accidentally waked her up in the night, the poor lady sat up in bed and demanded her horse. I was very sorry she saw the place in its rough state. It will be very different when she comes back, for the house is almost finished and the furniture is on the way.

APRIL 2ND

We have an additional member of the family, perhaps two. "Emma," a strapping, rather sullen-looking native woman, recommended by Melana, is helping Paul in the kitchen, and if all goes well, will in time become our laundress. The other is a small, grey-haired Malay, whom I call "Mat." He appeared at the kitchen door one day, wreathed in insinuating smiles, and begged for work of any description.

"What wages do you want?" I asked.

"What you like," said he. "I no got Papa, I no got Mama, you allee same my Mama."

I seem to be "allee same Mama" to a great many people.

Emma was both embarrassed and shocked when I touched upon the question of wages with her; at the same time she made private inquiry of Paul as to what she was likely to get. I have asked in town, and they say eight dollars a month for her, and also for Mat.

One of the carpenters was attacked day before yesterday with *fe fe.*[7] It is strange that no doctor has taken up the study of a disease so prevalent in all the South Seas, and I believe in most tropical places. Years ago I knew an elderly woman in Indiana who had elephantiasis of the leg. It evidently has to do with malaria. And yet I have never seen a case that did not begin with a sore on the leg or foot. The carpenter took a dose of Epsom salts last night and has just told me that he is much better in consequence. The person affected has attacks of fever at intervals of months. During each attack of fever the part affected swells, and that swelling never goes down again, remaining in the same state, to be augmented by the next attack of fever. I believe I will write to the *Lancet*[8] on the subject.

Mrs. Stevenson sent me by the last steamer some Brazil nuts and dried dates. I am going to try and grow them. According to instructions from Kew Gardens, I have broken open the nuts, extracting the meat whole. Emma has been making baskets of cocoanut leaves to plant them in, as is the custom with cacao. The whole thing may then be put into the earth without disturbing the roots. My kitchen garden is in a sad state with weeds, but a few spots where plants are growing I have managed to keep clear. There are large green peppers in full bearing, a few long pod beans, some tomatoes, and egg plants coming on, also a few sticks of celery that will do to season soup, and my asparagus, which seems to be doing very well indeed. The avocado pears I planted some time ago are growing in the most exhausting manner, also all the cocoanuts.

Lafaele gave us a most interesting account of the government of his native island, Fatuna. (I have just asked him the name, as I had forgotten it. He was too polite, in the native fashion, to say it was absolutely Fatuna, in case I had other views. "Call him name Fatuna—I *think*," said he.) In this well-governed land each man is compelled on pain of punishment to own fifty pigs, a certain num-

---

[7] Filariasis, the usual cause of elephantiasis.
[8] A leading British medical journal.

ber of fowls, and to gather in the season a fixed amount of taro, bananas to feed the pigs, and cocoanuts. In the planting season he plants the amount of everything as fixed by law. Trespassing is punished, also stealing, very severely, and most wisely of all, the breaking of an appointment. In Fatuna it costs you five dollars to break an appointment; in default of payment the delinquent must work for the king.

Our own government moves very slowly. The chiefs of Manono have not behaved well. They came to give presents to the Chief Justice, with a following of some three thousand men, very elaborately gotten up. It was said to be the finest procession ever seen in Samoa. But the speaking men were very insulting, giving the title of king to Mataafa. The Chief Justice attempted to stop their seditious talk but they would not be silenced, and it ended by both Malietoa and the Chief Justice leaving the premises while the speaking men were still talking. I think they should have done something more decided.

Lloyd and Louis have gone to Tutuila with Mr. Sewall (the American consul-general) and are to make a melaga round the island. I never thought of their taking presents until this moment.

I sent by the last *Warrior* to New Zealand for a Jersey cow. The Schmidts are going to give up their place very soon, so there will be no more milk unless we have a cow of our own.

APRIL 8TH

Yesterday Lloyd's birthday.[9] Had a letter to say he and Louis would be gone another three weeks. I spent the greater part of the day going down to Apia on a horse I had for trial. It turned out to be some fourteen years of age, with damaged knees; the sort of horse thought suitable for a woman. I send it back today.

I have engaged a carpenter named Skelton to work by the day to move the small house, enlarge it, and make it generally more habitable; also to build a cook house, with bedroom attached, for Paul. Mr. King, at present engaged in painting the pavilion, and Lafaele will help. The new house is almost done. One of the German prison overseers has been to see me about taking him on to work the

[9] He was twenty-three.

plantation. He wants to plant—that to me objectionable crop—cotton. I did not tell him what was in my mind: to make scent from the mussaoi and ylang-ylang. Mr. Skelton tells me there is a tree growing in the bush from which a perfumed gum exudes. I shall see what may be done with that also.

One of our little pigs suddenly died. Someone suggested that there might be something poisonous to pigs growing in the piggery. Henry went to look, and found two poison trees. He and his boys took them out by the roots. The wood of this tree makes a brilliant red dye.

My asparagus is growing finely. I am going to make another bed of it, as I have plenty of roots. Mr. King and I tried eating the pitch of a palm called the wild cocoanut. It was very good and would make a pleasant salad. Henry is planting yams or, as Paul calls them, "jams." Jam he calls yam.

Lloyd was greatly amused, when he first came, by Paul's appearance when waiting at table. A plump little German with a bald head, clothed in a flannel shirt thrown open over his breast; a pair of ragged trousers, particularly dilapidated in the seat, held up by a leather strap round the waist, a sheath knife thrust through the belt; barefoot; and most likely offering the information in a polite voice that "the meat is tough, by God." I am sure he takes "by God" to be the English equivalent of *mon Dieu*, as Valentine,[10] a former French maid of mine, did when she first came to England.

I have just begun Stanley's book[11] and am much struck by the many points of similarity between some of the people he speaks of and the Pacific islanders. One that I remember just now is the use of cicatrices for adornment. He speaks of eating grubs and beetles. Henry one day brought me an immense, horrid-looking grub, which he said was much relished by the Samoans. One evening a beetle over two inches in length suddenly dropped on the book I was reading. Lafaele sprang forward and caught it, crying out "Him bite, him bite!" The creature had a pair of most formidable-looking nippers,

[10] Valentine Roch, a Swiss-French girl who remained with the Stevensons about six years and of whom they were very fond. She married and settled in California.
[11] Henry Morton Stanley's *In Darkest Africa*, published in 1890.

with which he clutched the table cloth when Lafaele picked him up. It took several moments to loosen his hold. I felt the thing had better be killed, but there was so much body to dispose of that I was embarrassed as to the form of execution. Lafaele proposed cutting off his head, which he did with a table knife.

"Samoa man like eat him too much," he said.

"You like?" I asked.

"Oh, no," returned Lafaele in answer to the expression of disgust he saw on my face.

Yet I noticed that he carefully dismembered and diswinged the beetle by the lamp light before carrying it out, and that he remained on the verandah for some time, quite long enough to devour it himself.

There is a great scare in Vailima on the subject of ghosts, or "devils," as the Samoans call them. The stable seems to be the particular abiding place of the devils. I certainly heard very strange noises there at night during the storm, and was waked in the dark hours of the morning by the smell of tinned salmon being cooked. There was a great noise, apparently under our feet, as of horses stamping, and great stones being hauled about. I thought at first it must be the noise of a subterranean stream, but the salmon caused me to take another view: that the noise might be caused by black fellows hiding in a cave just under the stable. A long time ago Mr. Carruthers told me that he suspected the existence of a cave in the neighbourhood of the stable. Mr. King and Lafaele slept there for some time, but Lafaele has been frightened out, and Mr. K himself was getting a little nervous. Last night Mr. Skelton took up his quarters with Mr. King. Paul comes to me to say that dreadful sounds were heard by them last night, talking and laughing and women's screams. Emma says the kitchen is as bad as the stable, and worse, for the devils openly appear to her. Every night at about four o'clock a woman with two children comes in to her, demands a cigarette, and then the three intruders lie down beside her and apparently go to sleep. She says too many people have been slain here, too many heads cut off, and that the whole place is thronged with devils.

APRIL 12TH

Mr. Skelton, who has been here for thirty years, says that at one time two chiefs lived on this land. It was from the son of one of them that he got the following information. Both of these chiefs were cannibals, and lay in wait to catch each other's men, who were killed and eaten. The chief who abode on Vaea Mountain[12] (the father of Skelton's informant) used to stretch a rope across a path leading in this direction, and all who reached the rope he claimed for his table. Remorse, however, harried him in his old age, and he vowed that he would kill no more people, but set them instead to work upon a road that should cross the island. This is the road passing our house. Before it was finished the repentant chief died and the road remains as he left it. The ghosts of his victims, however, not having received proper burial, walk to this day. Emma declares that a man and woman were murdered by the chief's orders just where the small house stands, and it must be the spirit of the woman and her children who appear nightly.

I have been reading Stanley's book to the end now. He speaks of the same trees we have here. One of the very hard yellow ones lies now in front of the house, where it was chopped down. It went to my heart to lose a tree so majestic in size and symmetrical in form, but all said it was unsafe. Ants, white and black, abound here also, but I find that a medium solution of carbolic acid cures all their bites, even that of the fire ant. I have just had five of those unpleasant ulcers, and wonder whether my remedy would have been useful to Stanley. The sores were very painful, and spreading with great rapidity. I tried carbolic lotion, carbolic oil and carbolic soap. Then [blank] and [blank], but they steadily got worse. It occurred to me that I had once cured a horse of obstinate saddle sores with calomel. If a horse, why not a human being? Twice I rubbed calomel into the ulcers, and from the first application they began healing, and I have needed to do nothing since the second.

Fortunately there seem to be no fleas here, so *that* nuisance we have not to contend with; but the mosquitoes are a dreadful pest.

[12] Mt. Vaea, behind Vailima, on the summit of which first Louis, in 1894, then Fanny, in 1914, were buried.

It is not possible to write without burning buhach powder. I use a pretty little incense burner that I bought in a Chinese shop. In that way a very little of the powder is effective. Before I had the incense burner I used to fill a dish with sand, and mark the sand in a spiral with my finger; into the dent made I dropped buhach and lighted it at one end. That was a clumsy affair compared with the incense burner, and very wasteful besides.

Lafaele put one of the bones of his arm out of joint yesterday while planting out my asparagus seedlings. I can't think how he did it, for he was doing very easy work. He has gone down to Apia to have it set.

Mr. Carruthers and Mr. Moors have just been here. They think I do not look well, and advise me to go to Sydney for a change. I have not felt well for a long time but I do not think a change will make any difference.

L O U I S . SATURDAY, APRIL 18TH

I got back on Monday night, after twenty-three hours in an open boat; the keys were lost; the Consul (who had promised us a bottle of Burgundy) nobly broke open his store-room, and we got to bed about midnight. Next morning the blessed Consul promised us horses for the daybreak; forgot all about it, worthy man; set us off at last in the heat of the day, and by a short cut which caused infinite trouble, and we were not home till dinner. I was extenuated, and have had a high fever since, or should have been writing before. To-day for the first time, I risk it. Tuesday I was pretty bad; Wednesday had a fever to kill a horse; Thursday I was better, but still out of ability to do ought but read awful trash. This is the time one misses civilisation; I wished to send out for some police novels; Montépin would have about suited my frozen brain. It is a bother when all one's thought turns on one's work in some sense or other; I could not even think yesterday; I took to inventing dishes by way of entertainment.

FANNY . APRIL 23RD

Louis and Lloyd returned, the one brown and fat, the other (Louis, of course) very ill with fever. They had come over in an open boat, a great risk in every way. I got frightened about Louis, and as he said he felt too ill to see the doctor (a boisterous surgeon named Funk), I sent instead for Mr. Clarke, the missionary, whose very presence seemed to do him good. This was several days ago; he is now much better, but still has fever at night. I think he has recoiled from Dr. F since the day of Capt. Hamilton's burial. There seemed to be some doubt as to whether Hamilton were really dead, so before the coffin was finally closed, the doctor came in to have a final look at the body. Louis had been there for some time and was talking in subdued tones to the widow and friends of the deceased man, when a loud cheery voice was heard, that of Dr. Funk. The gentleman (?) came pounding in with a lighted cigar in his mouth, and filling the room with his strident voice.

While Louis and Lloyd were away they stopped at an island quite near here, which Louis thinks of getting instead of either of the others we had thought of. He and I shall soon make a melaga that way. I have been feeling rather better again and have about made up my mind not to go to Sydney just yet. The new cook house is not yet finished. Day before yesterday there was almost no work done by either Skelton or King. An ice machine had been set up in the stable, where King amused Skelton by making ice, never dreaming of asking permission. In the afternoon a long time was spent by Skelton in proving to King that the horizon was level with his eyes. They were doing it with the spirit level. Other odd moments were filled up by King in skylarking with Emma and watching Innes unload the wagon and contemplating Lloyd at work with the type-writer. Louis had a short and sharp interview with both. Skelton was inclined to be impertinent but, having slept over it, apparently came to the conclusion that civility was the best policy, and promised me there should be no more cause for complaint. King, much less wisely, said that he had done no harm to the ice machine, etc., and the next morning informed Lloyd that he was not a slave. Louis now thinks Captain Otis'[13] plan a good one to follow. When Otis found a man not to his taste he proceeded to "make his ship a hell," and the man was soon glad to leave. I am curious to see Louis taking King through this process.

We have given the horses in charge of Innes, who is getting more work out of them with less fatigue (at least the mare, as the horse is not fit yet to work) than Hay ever did. Innes came home on Saturday with a message from Mataafa to this effect. The public road across the island which we have just made for the third time was diverted from its former straight course during the last war and now runs across some land just bought from Mataafa. Mataafa, to show the natives that the road must go back to its former place, proposes to block up the road some time this week, so that only a single horseman may be able to pass. He wished Innes to say to Louis that in doing this there was nothing meant against him, and "it in no way referred to the affair of the window." The window, he also said, had now been converted into a door, so that question might be considered ended. Louis sent word back that he could not and would not allow himself to be cut off from his base of supplies; and that if the road were blocked, without any reference to the window, our people would promptly tear it down.

Something very like an open attempt at swindling on the part of Hay has just turned up. Lloyd has gone down to get Carruthers' advice on the subject. It looks very much as though he had been buying things, charging them to me, and then selling them to me on his own account. The new stove has arrived from San Francisco.

L o u i s . april 29th

News: Our old house is now half demolished; it is to be rebuilt on a new site; now we look down upon and through the open posts of it like a bird-cage, to the woods beyond. My poor Paulo has lost his father and succeeded to thirty thousand thalers (I think); he

---

[13] A. H. Otis, captain of the *Casco*, on which the Stevensons sailed from San Francisco to the South Seas.

had to go down to the Consulate yesterday to send a legal paper; got drunk, of course, and is still this morning in so bemused a condition that our breakfasts all went wrong. Lafaele is absent at the deathbed of his fair spouse; fair she was, but not in deed, acting as harlot to the wreckers at work on the warships, to which society she probably owes her end, having fallen off a cliff, or been thrust off it—*inter pocula*. Henry is the same, our stand-by. In this transition stage he has been living in Apia; but the other night he stayed up, and sat with us about the chimney in my room. It was the first time he had seen a fire in a hearth; he could not look at it without smiles, and was always anxious to put on another stick. We entertained him with the fairy tales of civilisation—theatres, London, blocks in the street, Universities, the Underground, newspapers, etc., and projected once more his visit to Sydney. If we can manage, it will be next Christmas.

On May 15th Louis's mother arrived at Vailima, and Fanny was exhausted by the preparations for her arrival. In "Aunt Maggie" 's opinion, the house now looked very nice indeed. The outside was painted a peacock blue, and the roof and verandahs red. The inside walls were hung with tapa, and there were large sliding doors, more than half glass, opening on to the verandah overlooking the harbor. There were an American stove, and quite adequate provisions. "Aunt Maggie" 's room rather pleased her, with its view of the sea, its floor covered with white Samoan mats, soft and thick to the tread, and its walls painted pale green and hung with tapa and the flags brought from the *Casco*.

Toward the end of May, Fanny's daughter and the latter's husband and child arrived to stay, and were met grandly at the harbor. Meantime Fanny was busy planting orange trees that had come by the *Lübeck*. When Lafaele complained that he was afraid of devils, Fanny took him in hand with one of her deft tricks. Assuring him that her devils were stronger than any in Samoa, she pressed a finger of each hand on his closed eyes, then shifted them slyly so that she touched his eyes with two fingers of one hand only, and ended by slapping his cheek sharply with the free hand. He was convinced, and thereafter was willing to work in distant patches of the garden.

In June Fanny was busily making perfume out of a blossom called mussaoi, which was very fragrant. Then the china arrived, and there was excitement to see the "home things" so far from home. A new cook

was taken on, named Ratke, a German, and Louis was having his breakfast at 4:30 A.M. and begging for mercy.

JUNE 21ST

I cannot stand 4:30; I am a mere fevered wreck; it is now half-
past eight, and I can no more, and four hours divide me from lunch,
the devil take the man! Yesterday it was about 5:30, which I can
stand; day before 5, which is bad enough; today, I give out. It is like a
London season, and as I do not take a siesta once a month, and
then only five minutes, I am being worn to the bones, and look
aged and anxious.

F A N N Y . JUNE 30TH

My diary has been lost since the last entry. Many things have
happened since. Paul's father is dead, and has left only a small sum
of ready money, his mother getting a life interest in all the rest of
the property. It will be another three months yet before Paul receives
his inheritance; in the meantime he stays on here with uncertain
wages. We are afraid to give him too much money, and limit him to
his necessities, with which he is perfectly content, working harder
than any other man on the place. When his money was quite done,
just before he learned of his father's death, all his boon companions
turned against him and showed their true characters, an excellent
thing for poor Paul. I have not seen him once since the worse for
drink.

Lafaele's pretty wife, who caused him so much trouble and anxiety,
is dead, poor soul. She fell ill, and when Lafaele went down to see
her, at his request swore a solemn oath on the Bible that she had
always been a true and faithful wife, asking that God might strike
her a mortal illness if she swore falsely. According to the native
account, her tongue immediately swelled to a great size, protruding
from her mouth, and she never spoke sensibly again. When word
came that she was in the last agony I went to find Lafaele to tell
him to make haste. He was discovered with the focussing cloth of
the camera in his hands, which he begged for a mourning garment.

As soon as the burial was over Lafaele announced that that chapter in his life was closed and he was about to begin another with a new wife, at that moment concealed on the premises. I very reluctantly consented to keep her a week on trial, but we have now all become so much attached to the pretty young creature that we could not part with her on any account.

The whole family are now with us, the Strongs[14] living in the cottage, which has been rebuilt on a larger and better plan, and eating and spending the evenings in the large house. Joe has charge of the fowls, showing great interest in his department. In the kitchen we have a German chef, named Robert Ratke, Paul, who has become a planter, and is now busy with coffee trees, Mr. King (doing very well at present), Henry, who spends his evenings with us, Emma, and her assistant, Java, a magnificent young woman who leads the singing at family worship, Harry, the man from the low islands who assisted Mr. Hay, Lafaele and his wife Faauma; and, finally, a person who is growing to be a fixture, only known as the "yam man." Louis and I have a few moments' special delight every morning when Emma and Java come to our respective rooms to fetch fresh water, etc. Emma stalks in with a sturdy appearance of one who does her duty; but Java is as good as a play: she lifts one long shapely brown leg high in the air, looks for a suitable resting spot for her foot, comes down light as a feather on one toe, lifting the other leg with the same slow and graceful sweep; and so she moves about all her work. Her body she holds reverently bent forward, following the catlike movements of her leg with a corresponding swing of the arm. Upon her face, all the while, is a bright set smile, like that of an acrobat. Louis says the strange thing is that she really, with all this dramatic display of carefulness, does not make a noise.

JULY 1ST

The furniture is now all in the house, the piano, the last piece, coming today. The dining room we have hung with a yellowish terracotta tapa, the window casings and door being a strong peacock blue, and the ceiling a sort of cream colour. With the chairs and

---

[14] Joe and Isobel (Belle) Strong and their son, Austin. A painting of RLS by Strong hangs in Stevenson House in Monterey.

pictures, the colours make a most delightful harmony. At the double window I have put a curtain of Indian gauze, cream-white and silver, lined with soft orange-coloured silk and edged with lace. My own room is beginning to have the softly jewelled look that I am so fond of. Louis's room is still in a state of ferment, the last books having arrived only two days ago. I find it more difficult to manage with his colours, the room being two shades of pale blue, not colours I am on any degree of intimacy with. I feel them chilly and repellent. Black, white and light blue always puzzle me; I don't know how to manage them. In my room the ceiling and walls are natural California redwood, varnished (I couldn't afford polishing, which would be lovely). The edges of the floor are stained with a native dye and waxed. The furniture is old mahogany, with a little brass. I had a rather raw Turkey carpet, very deep in the pile and delicious to the bare feet. Now that it is spread on the floor with a border of native mats (Tembinoka's farewell present)[15] it looks quite subdued, and harmonizes very well. The window and door casings are very dark peacock green.

We have had one luncheon party, at which Louis declared that he was swollen with pride. Mary,[16] the maid Mrs. Stevenson brought with her from the colonies, has taught Faauma to wait at table very prettily. For the occasion she was provided with a couple of yards of red Turkey cotton for a waist cloth, and a couple of blue and red bandana handkerchiefs for a bodice. The handkerchiefs were tied together at the four corners, the knots lying on each shoulder, and a handkerchief hanging down over her breast, the other down her back.

The war has very nearly begun several times, but now it seems fairly on its feet. Which reminds me that I have to look up our cartridges so soon as I stop writing. There has been a good deal of vague talk about a massacre of all the whites, and it is as well to be prepared, though nothing of the kind is really anticipated. Mataafa has declared himself king and has made a stand with an immense number of followers. For the last two nights Henry has had to take part

[15] That is, when the Stevensons left Apemama in the Gilberts.
[16] Mary Carter, whom Fanny disliked.

in standing guard over Malietoa, who fears assassination. The guards
spend the night in singing and dancing. When news came that the
war had really begun, Lafaele immediately blacked his face in the
manner of a warrior.

"Why do you do that?" I asked. "You are not going down to
fight, are you?"

But it was, he assured me, to emphasize the fact that he was prepared to protect "the place" and us, and not that he had any
political bias, that he had striped his face with black. It happened
that very afternoon that the doctor came up to see Louis, and as
Lafaele had a bad toe, I sent for him. The doctor said the nail must
be pulled out. Poor Lafaele, with his warrior's face, had to be held
forcibly while the operation was performed.

We have rented the Schmidt place for eight years and bought a
young cow from them. Some time ago I sent to Sydney for a cow
warranted of a lamblike disposition, choosing the Jersey breed as
being the most likely to be amiable. The cow is here, a pretty little
thing that gives very good milk, but with an eye filled with hell fire,
and the temper of a fiend. A musician, Louis's flageolet teacher,
named Watts,[17] is stopping with us. The other day the terrible cow
barred his path and I had to engage her attention at the peril of
my life, as I believed, till Mr. Watts got safely past.

[JULY] 10TH

The war news continues disquieting. Emma has been sent away
for attempting to take Faauma to Apia for the fourth of July
against Lafaele's wish and without permission. I had a long talk with
her before she left. She says the natives are "no flend white man
now," and that they mean to fire the town of Apia beginning at the
German end, and massacre all the whites. There has been, absolutely,
talk of deporting Mataafa, which would be a terrible mistake.
Mataafa seems to be behaving extremely well. His people are trying
to force his hand and he is resisting all he dares. Yesterday there was
a fono at Malie. Mataafa (who has himself paid his taxes) begged
the people to return to their homes, pay their taxes, and remain in
peace. He nearly succeeded, and the people even promised, but after-

[17] Harold Watts.

wards went back on their word and now remain in Malie. When the chiefs announced their refusal to go home, Mataafa, in public as he was, burst into tears. The three consuls have issued a proclamation to the effect that they, in union, and representing the three powers, will resist any attempt to put Mataafa on the throne. The captain of the *Sperber* is ready to help in case of necessity, and the king's ammunition has all been brought in to MacArthur's store, a wooden building that could be rifled with no difficulty. Louis said to Mr. Carruthers (who thinks the situation of the whites a very serious one), "We shall be in a bad box if there is an outbreak in Apia."

"It will be worse for us," returned Mr. C. "Think of the spirits in Apia."

"At least," said Louis, "you've men enough to make a fight for it."

But that idea Mr. C scouted. There were no more than ten men in town that could be counted on, he said, and assured Louis that when there was a scare once, but no real danger, men fell off the pier into the sea in their haste to get into boats to make for the man-of-war.

Mr. Moors has come back to find his trusted manager, who called himself Walters, decamped with a thousand dollars. Sophia he found in a bad condition. The two Jennings had a fight, one being beaten. The four natives immediately fell upon the victor and beat him, and announced the fact that they threw off allegiance to either, and would obey them no longer. Mrs. Moors (a native woman of Samoa) took charge of affairs, and when her husband arrived at the island she not only had her cargo ready, but a new baby besides.

Lafaele has a very sore toe. He now thinks it is bewitched, or that a devil has entered it. Today Faauma was sent for a Samoan doctor; or, as I believe, a warlock to counteract the charm. Emma being gone, Henry produced a minister's family, two very respectable-looking women, but they can't wash like Emma. They were engaged to come up and wash, and when the work was done, to return again to Apia. One seems to wish to stop, so she might as well.

Ratke and Mary have been quarrelling, and we have been compelled to hire a boy to act as a buffer between them. They will not receive anything from each other. I had thought Mary a more sensible girl. Paul has been all day at Captain Hufnagel's[18] to get coffee trees. He has brought home some very fine ones. The captain sent some flowers to Mrs. Stevenson and a lot of trees and roses to me. I have planted them all out. He also sent some Indian beans, which I had been wanting very much indeed. The hens are hatching out a good many young ones, though several have died. Joe feeds them lime at once, which I think kills them. He has read that fowls *must* have lime, and jumps to the conclusion that newly-hatched chicks have the same tastes or requirements as their elders. Austin has had a very bad foot; it is better now. I wished to send for the doctor when I saw it, but it got better so rapidly under my treatment that we waited, and are still waiting. For a whole day I had the child's mother drip over the sore warm water rather strong with permanganate of potash; after that it was covered with dry calomel. In the meantime, he took internally sulphide of calcium.

JULY 12TH

Yesterday Ratke killed a pig. He found in its body a spear thrust; evidently black boys. As he very pertinently remarked, had it been Samoans, they would have cleared the run. Lafaele sent for a Samoan, skilled in the caring of wounds, to examine his foot. I said I must be present at the examination of the toe, so when the doctor came I was sent for. I found him, a grave, middle-aged man, sitting on a mat in the laundry, where the minister's family were busy with the ironing. Lafaele's countenance became more and more downcast as he was plied with questions. I could make out that I was often referred to by both of the men. I took advantage of a pause in the conversation to ask that Lafaele should translate to me the wise man's opinion of the foot.

"Mrs. Stevenson! Madame! I tell you true," began Lafaele.

It seems that a devil, instigated by some Samoan enemy, had entered the toe and was now on the point of travelling up the leg, and unless he was checked in time would soon have possession of Lafaele's entire body.

[18] Manager of the German plantation, Vailele.

"But that is nonsense," I said. "You know, Lafaele, that no Samoan devil can do harm to a man that belongs to me."

Lafaele admitted the truth of what I said, and had already talked it over with the wise man, who said, certainly, there was no doubt of that; but Lafaele, a year ago, did not know of my existence, nor I of him, and it was at that time the devil had entered the toe at the lower inside corner of the nail. The obnoxious thing had now shifted his position to the opposite corner of the nail and was plainly on the move. I could say no more except that I trusted Lafaele had no more dormant devils concealed about his person and would soon be rid of this one. He wished to "mak siccar" [German: *mache sicher*, make certain] and proposed to use both my medicine and the wise man's, but I told him to trust all or nothing to the Samoan. He assured me with great earnestness that he was not afraid of devils since I had promised to protect him, and it is quite true he shows no evidence of fear other than to sing very loudly when he is alone.

Mr. Gurr,[19] his wife, and his newly arrived sister came to see us last evening. They are going to be our nearest neighbours, at Lesher's former place. We are much pleased with that idea. It is dark and lowering today, so that Mrs. Stevenson does not care to go to church. Ratke has asked to go home for the night, as he had a presentiment something was wrong there. He was quite pale and trembling when he started. I have just learned more about the medicine man. Belle had him to look at Austin's foot, which was in a fair way to get well. It now seems much worse.

Lafaele's foot is better, but I think that is owing to the calomel I had put on it. The worst thing is that the medicine man declares that this place is rampant with the worst form of devils and that they have a particular animus against Lafaele. All the cleared land about the two houses has been exorcised but Lafaele is warned not to go outside of certain limits alone, lest he meet with some terrible fate. I must somehow show that I am stronger than the medicine man, or Lafaele will be of no use to me. I wish I knew some conjuring tricks. There is no use in trying to laugh him out of the superstition. I know natives too well for that.

[19] E. W. Gurr.

Mr. King has just returned from Apia. He says that the natives are all steadily buying ammunition and trooping away from Apia.

AUGUST 12TH

This entry is written in Suva, Fiji. For a long time I had not been well, and when we found that the *Warrior* was going to Fiji I had not enough energy to object to being sent off in her, though I went with a heavy heart, for I did not think Louis looked right. I have been here a couple of days, and already feel the benefit of the change. I am stopping at a place called, I think, "The Club House," kept by people named Sturt. It is very cold today; at least it seems so to me. There is but one other boarder of my own sex, a Mrs. Phillipi, a simple, pleasant young woman with dyed hair. She is here for her health. Next me at the table sits a rather handsome dark young man who looks as though he might possess a drop or two of Indian blood, though perhaps not. He is going to get me an Indian cook to send to Samoa. I offered one pound a week, which he says is wealth incredible to an Indian. I could not give less (I thought of doing so) with the other wages in Vailima. It would be neither politic nor fair. I have been to the acclimatization gardens. I find little to interest me, and am to go again and see what I can get for Vailima, both in the way of information and plants, with a Mr. Moore, who is something of the Agricultural Society. The dark young man has also told me of many plants that grow in India that should do well in Samoa, and is to give me an address to write to.

I have found the place where the travelling dentist stops and shall call upon him this afternoon and lay the case of Apia before him. Yesterday I had a strong desire to drink kava. In one shop I bought a little bag of ground kava and in another a small bowl of wood. The latter, the shop woman assured me, was a "real brain bowl" in which the natives used to eat the brains of their enemies. Beside it, in the shop, there hung a "cannibal fork." Both it and the bowl had been made, apparently, a few days since. I refused the cannibal fork (when I wish to eat cannibals I can make one for myself if that particular sort of fork is a necessary adjunct) but bought the "brain bowl" to make my kava in. I also found a kava strainer in a shop. My whole kava "outfit" came to just four shillings.

It amuses me to hear our landlady lay down the law concerning the natives. "Ours are bad enough," she says, "but those Samoans of yours beat everything. Why, they seem to want to put themselves on an equality with the whites! It fairly makes me sick to see them walk along the road, holding up their heads so impudent!" And then she goes on to tell ("I know it seems incredible," says she) how at some public gathering, races, or something of the sort, some Samoans who were here were absolutely helping themselves to seats. "And I believe if they had been allowed, they would have taken the front seats too. Now what do you think of that for impudence!" I didn't ask—what's the use with people like that—whether the modest whites were monopolizing the back seats or not.

The woman from whom I bought the "brain bowl" poured out her whole history while I was buying it. She was married to a bad man, she said, who had deserted her, leaving her penniless. She has since got hold of some letters of his which seem to be from a former wife and her family. They proposed following him to Fiji. Now he has sent for this wife to come to Africa with her two children (eight have died, mercifully).

"Surely you'll not go," said I.

"I think I shall," she replied. "I have heard through reliable sources that he has made a lot of money there." And she added, thoughtfully, "He's an old man now." Her youngest child came in just then, poor creature—an idiot.

[AUGUST] 22ND

I left Suva and came over to Levuka, a much pleasanter, more picturesque town than Suva. Mrs. Phillipi came also, the next day. We neither of us could stand the noise at night of the hotel in Suva. While there I made the acquaintance of a Mr. Moore, an extremely handsome man of forty-nine, with snow-white hair. One of his daughters is on the stage. They seem altogether a very talented family. Mr. M, who is something of an agriculturist, took me to the botanical gardens, recently put under the charge of a pleasant, simple young fellow from Kew. I saw everything there and was told to mention what plants and trees I should like to carry away with me.

I mentioned a great many—fruits, nuts and flowery trees and plants. I am, to my great delight, to have them all.

It was a most exciting day for me. The young man from Kew told me a trade secret: if cauliflowers get an occasional watering with sea water they will hold up in any climate. I was told of seeds that produce a radish which, when older, may be used as a turnip. I shall probably get a few. An Indian in a shop divided some Indian melon seeds with me and told me how to plant them. At the table, a very good-looking young man named Davidson, evidently with a little Indian blood, sat next me. He is trying to get me an Indian cook. One was produced just before I left. He had an excellent written character for six years' service from a former master, but he had been dismissed from his last place in Suva and I wish to know why before I engage him definitely. The captain of the steamer which brought me here, Capt. Saunders (he brought Louis from Noumea[20] to Sydney), knew the cook and thought well of him. He offered to see the last master and write me particulars here.

Opposite me at table in Suva was a man of middle age named Harvey, a university man, he said, and I saw no reason to doubt it. He went, he told me, to Fatuna, stayed there alone for eight months to get matter for a book on the history of the island, and especially concerning the Chinese who once landed there. He put his manuscript on board a ship, having copied it out and destroyed his notes. Mr. George Smith, Mrs. Stevenson's cousin, was the person responsible for it. That was five months ago and it has never been heard of since.

Just after I was told this story four or five young men of common appearance and vulgar manners came to the hotel. Unfortunately for me, two of them had the room next to mine. None of the partitions of the bedrooms went up to the roof. I could hear the person next me throw his sheet off or pull it up as the case might be. For three nights these young men came to the room next mine at midnight, all roaring drunk. There was no sleep for poor Mrs. Phillipi, who was on the other side of me, or for myself. On the third night their conduct was abominable. The whole house was awake all night with

[20] City in New Caledonia.

their uproar. I was really alarmed when they began throwing articles at each other over the partitions, lest I should have my brains dashed out. In the midst of the uproar I heard one man struggling to speak as though a hand were over his mouth. What was my surprise to hear him suddenly shout out, "I *will* call you by your name, Harvey." In the morning Mrs. Phillipi and I made up our minds to leave. Mr. Harvey came to her and apologized, but did not apologize to me. I pretended to be quite unaware of his existence. Before Mrs. P left, one of the rowdy lads, a miserable, hollow-chested, consumptive young fellow, came to her and apologized also. In the midst of the noise I could hear his sweet musical laughter choke into a desperate fit of coughing. He is whipping up the black horses, poor fool.

This hotel is the same as that in Suva, only more homelike and with inferior food. The master: an ex-labour captain named Robbie, and the second husband of his wife, the latter a simple, ignorant, kind little dumpling of a woman, with a passion for flowers. I forgot to say that opposite me at the Suva table, next to Harvey, sat a man named Coates. I know something about Coates, but what, I have forgotten; but I should imagine no good. He has eyes like Basett Coloni and a nasty dour look and sneering smile. He differed with everybody on any subject. Mr. Moore said one day that he had just been present at a bad carriage accident and mentioned some of the details.

"It took place at the other bridge," said Coates.

"Were you there?" asked Moore.

"No, I wasn't there, but it was at the other bridge it happened."

"Well, I *was* there and it *didn't* happen at the other bridge."

"It *did* happen at the other bridge, though," persisted Coates, making boiled gooseberry eyes at his plate, with his usual smile.

One day I ventured to put him right about Apiang, which he said belonged to the Caroline group; he smiled into his plate and said I was quite mistaken. Like Mr. Moore I asked "Have you ever stopped at Apiang?" No, he had not, but he knew where it was— another gooseberry-eyed smile into his plate.

"I *have* been there," I said, "and at that time it was one of the Gilberts."

"Well, I haven't been there, but I happen to know that it belongs to the Carolines."

A most disagreeable-looking, exasperating man, with an annoying little tuft of hair parted into two prim curls over his forehead in front of his baldness.

The second day I was here an old man came up to me on the verandah and said, "I am glad to meet you, Mrs. Stevenson. Welcome to Levuka."

I said, "Um—aw," the sort of inarticulate noises one makes under such circumstances.

"I am glad," continued the man, with a hideous, Yankee nasal drawl, "I am glad to meet the wife of my distinguished countryman."

"Then I'm not the person you take me for," said I, "unless you are a Scotchman, which doesn't seem likely."

Oh, no, it was the distinguished author he meant, but he was surprised to learn that he was a Scotchman.

"You can't have read any of his books," said I, "or you would have known that much."

"No, can't say I have," said he cheerfully, "don't think I ever saw 'em. But I'm the very man for you. I'm the oldest resident in Fiji and I can give you all the information you want about the islands. I can give you the whole inside history of the government."

In vain I laboured to explain that I wanted no information on any subject. If he sees me on the balcony he darts after me like lightning and proceeds to pour information into my ear.

"Now you tell your husband that this place is a blot upon civilisation."

"I couldn't really."

"Just tell him from me, a man forty years in the group, that the government is rotten, rotten, I say—" etc.

I am bound to say the feeling seems general about the government. I never heard a more general shout of laughter than when I said that our Chief Justice very nearly came over to study the form of government.

"Sir John Thurston[21] is the typical self-made man," said a Mr.

[21] High Commissioner for the Western Pacific.

Sketchly to me today. "We are on bad terms because I called him to his face an ignorant, arrogant, swindling humbug."

I should think they would be on bad terms. When I go back to Suva I shall call at Government House and see what I think of the other side. There are generally two sides to a question.

This Mr. Sketchly is experimenting with tobacco. He is planting several thousand acres and seems confident of success. It was he who brought the ostriches to California. He gave me a lot of valuable information about cacao and India rubber planting and also told me something about scent making. He seemed shrewd, clever, very energetic, a gentleman, and I should say the stuff of which soldiers of fortune are made. I was very thankful at lunch to find that he had ousted the dismal old American who sat at my elbow and drenched me with historical information. The poor old man watched me with a burning eye over intervening heads. I believe he had an awful fear that I was imbibing untrustworthy information from a stranger.

Yesterday the American consul, Mr. St. John, called, a superior article, of the same sort as my old man of the sea.

And that carries me back again to Suva. I was leaning over the balcony one day and there was old Tony, with his pith helmet and umbrella. My heart warmed to the dreary old wanderer; I called to him and said, "How d'ye do." The next afternoon he appeared at my door. He said it was really so extraordinary we should meet everywhere that he felt he must make me a little visit. He hemmed and hawed awhile, informed me that the world was tottering on her last legs, and disappeared to turn up again in the next most unlikely place.

I heard them speaking at Suva about the *Cordelia* and I must say was not much surprised to find out that the members of the Fiji Club, after asking the officers to join, had to ask them again to leave. "But the captain had some good points," said our landlord's kindly wife. "He was very nice to his men. Why, his favorite amusement was to get one of his sailors up on the quarter deck and have a boxing match with him. There was no stiffness about him, oh dear no."

SEPT. 23RD

At home again. I was very ill during the latter part of my stay in Fiji, with an ulcerated sore throat. I brought with me four boxes of plants, some from the botanical gardens and some gathered by Mrs. Robbie of Levuka. I also brought an Indian cook named Abdul Razzuk. Lloyd and the Strongs have, in the meantime, been teaching a native boy called Talolo to cook, with the best results, so my fine cook is a fifth wheel in the house. Mr. Haggard[22] has agreed to take him, but poor Abdul is loath to leave Vailima, where he says he is happy, his fellow servants are gentle and kind, and his master and mistress all that could be desired. Talolo is a fine, stout, smiling lad, very like a Hawaiian, and skips joyfully whenever he is spoken to. I am glad to see that Henry has given up European clothes and dresses now like a Samoan gentleman in lava lava and coat, the latter a shell jacket for the evening.

The day I left Suva, the Chief Justice of Samoa arrived. Truly I was sorry to see him, for I think his place is at home just now. Still, I may be wrong, as he is the only reticent man on the beach and no one knows exactly what his business is in Fiji. Some say that he is afraid and has run away, others that he has gone to try and borrow a gun boat from Sir John Thurston. He told me that he was constantly threatened with assassination, but took no steps to guard himself. He also told me how a great body of men came over to Apia to be tried for sedition (I *suppose*, as the wording of the charge was not given me). They were apparently unarmed except for their staves of office. It was demanded that their arms should be given up, when it was discovered that each man had a hatchet concealed in his lava lava. These were removed, and five big chiefs chosen to represent the party.

The five chiefs were condemned to several months' imprisonment in the common jail. The C J said it was a most dramatic scene when, with one movement, the five chiefs raised their staves and flung them onto the house. Afterwards they wept bitterly, saying that they were disgraced. According to the wording of the sentence, they were

[22] Bazett M. Haggard, British land commissioner in Samoa, and brother of H. Rider Haggard, the writer.

Fanny Stevenson

Fanny Stevenson

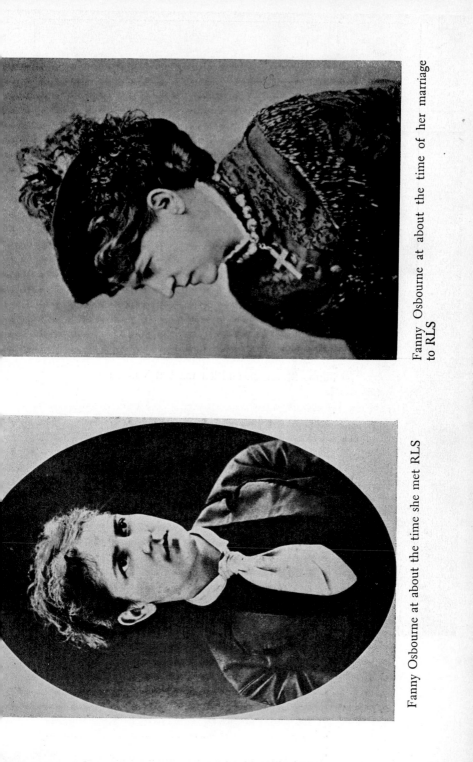

Fanny Osbourne at about the time she met RLS

Fanny Osbourne at about the time of her marriage to RLS

Fanny Stevenson and her maid at Vailima

Outer cover of Fanny Stevenson's diary

Arrived at Vailima on the ___ day of September. This is rather unsatisfactory more attention having been paid to the ornamental than the practical side of affairs. A very neat and expensive building very like a band stand in a German beer garden has been built in the corner above the small waterfall; but there was no shelter for the pigs, and no chicken house. I set the carpenter to putty up the beds (not the sort that had been ordered from Hoffmungs) and Lou gave orders to have the pavillion of the bandstand closed in with boards so that he could use it to work in. Just after we had finished breakfast in the morning the "pantry-man" from the Lubeck, the steamer we came down in, appeared and asked for work of any kind until Christmas at which time he expects some trade stuff and intends to open a store. I engaged him on the spot to do anything required. He seems very willing and good natured, but extremely clumsy, and not very good at speaking English. We began opening boxes, and getting out a few things for present comfort; but the chicken house seemed more pressing, as the rainy season is just coming on, and my poor cocking that I brought in a box from Sydney do not seem capable of enjoying it, and besides we can get no eggs while the fowls are laying anywhere in the bush. I find it quite impossible to make Paul, ~~understand~~ (the ex pantry man is named Paul) understand my directions, and was almost in despair. We managed to build a frame of boxes left by the carpenter, but it had no slope to the roof, nor could I get Paul to cut the boxes to make the slope. Not but what he was most willing, but he could not understand me. Finally, with the utmost difficulty we got it raised and one side nailed fast to a tree. I suppose it is about twelve feet square. The next day, to my joy, I discovered a large ball of native cocoanut sennet I had brought in one of the Line Islands. I remember when I was laughed at for buying it, I said "I feel it in my bones that I shall want that ball of sennet at Vailima," and I packed it in my trunk amid the gircs of my family, who proposed adding to it other building materials, to ends as branches of cocoanut, and pieces of coral rock. I gave my sennet in the morning to Ben of the "boss" of the out door "boys", and told him to take his men into the bush and cut saplings to finish the fowl house faa Samoa. It is now done, and very firm and substantial, and I am beginning to lay up stores of eggs. While I was in the midst of my building, having the frame just hoisted, the missionary, Mr Clax---

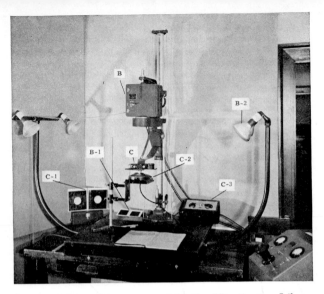

Photographic equipment used by the Huntington Library to reveal the suppressed portions of Fanny Stevenson's diary:

B	Recordak camera, used with infrared film
B-1	Selected filters, used with infrared film
B-2	Light source for Recordak camera
C	Leica camera, used with positive film
C-1	Selected filters, used with ultraviolet lamp
C-2	Ultraviolet lamp
C-3	Transformer for the ultraviolet lamp

Print A. Part of page 90 of Fanny Stevenson's diary, photographed by ordinary light and showing the heavy cancellations

Print B.   The same passage as photographed with the use of infrared film, showing some of the underlying writing

Print C.   The same passage as photographed by ultraviolet light, revealing much of the original writing

Part of page 27 of Fanny Stevenson's diary, photographed by ordinary light

The same canceled passage on page 27, enlarged, as photographed by ultraviolet light

Young Stevenson and his mother

FIG. 1.

Stevenson on his horse Jack

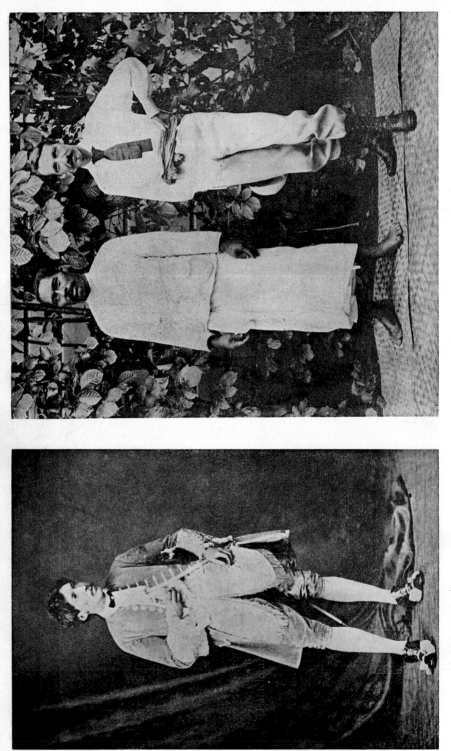

Stevenson and a Samoan chief, taken at Vailima

Stevenson in fancy dress

Family and servants on the steps of the house at Vailima

Left to right: Joe Strong, Auvea (a plantation hand), Mary Carter (maid to Mrs. M. I. Stevenson), Mrs. M. I. Stevenson, Elena, Lloyd Osbourne, Arrick, Talolo, RLS, Austin Strong, Fanny Stevenson, Isobel Strong, Simi (butler), Lafaele and Tomasi

The band of H.M.S. *Katoomba* after attending a feast at Vailima

Standing, left to right: Isobel Strong, Bazett Haggard (with beard), Stevenson, Graham Balfour and Fanny Stevenson

Family group at Vailima

Left to right: Mary Carter, Lloyd Osbourne, Mrs. M. I. Stevenson, Isobel Strong, RLS, Austin Strong, Fanny Stevenson and Joe Strong

Left to right: Lloyd Osbourne, RLS, Joe Strong, Auvea and Lafaele

The first house built at Vailima
Left to right: RLS, Tin Jack, Fanny and H. J. Moors

Seated, left to right: Mrs. M. I. Stevenson, RLS, an unidentified friend. Isobel Strong is standing on RLS's left. The man in the large hat is Graham Balfour

The house at Vailima before additions, with Mt. Vaea in the background. The figure in white on the upper porch is RLS

The house at Vailima. RLS is on the upper porch. Below are Mary Carter, RLS's mother, and a family group

The house at Vailima after the additions

Vailima: a view of the grounds

Vailima: down by the river

Vailima: the falls

Vailima: above the falls

A Samoan scene

Mataafa

Malietoa Laupepa

Tamasese

Seumanutafa, chief of Apia

lex Willis at the age of fourteen

Laulii, wife of Alex Willis, at the age of fourteen

Fatulia, Seumanutafa's wife

Mataafa's hut

Stevenson lying in state, December 4, 1894

The tomb of the Stevensons on Mt. Vaea

to be treated "in a gentlemanly manner" and allowed to walk about
as they liked, but attended by guards. It seems the president, Baron
von Pilsach,[23] feared an attempt at rescue. The story runs that he
threatened to blow up the jail containing the prisoners with dynamite, and had actually engaged one of the wreckers to do the job.
The wrecker, to nerve himself up for his work, took a great many
drinks and, becoming loquacious in his cups, divulged the plot. All
the people living near, or owning property in the vicinity of the jail,
were furiously angry, and many others savagely indignant at the
treacherous barbarity of the president. They say now, but it is perhaps not true, that the imprisoned chiefs were brought in under an
intentional false impression. The chiefs, who were to receive "gentlemanly treatment," have all been deported, it is supposed to the
Tokelaus. That was not in their sentence.

Yesterday we were told that the *Ebon* had been over to Mataafa,
carrying him 40,000 cartridges, and that Mr. Moors was suspected
to have sent them. While I was away, Lloyd accompanied Mrs.
Moors to Malie on a visit to Mataafa. The consuls tried hard to
prevent Lloyd going. He was charmed with Mataafa, as everyone but
his political enemies seems to be. He saw a German stopped by one
of Mataafa's sentries. The German, who was riding, raised his whip,
but lowered it again, fortunately, as there was an instant flurry of
rifles.

Louis has written out a paper which is being signed by a number
of serious men, asking the president about the dynamite. If he refuses
to answer, or confesses to the truth of the report, then I think Louis
should openly declare his position. I also think, if it is settled that
he is to try and oust the president, that Mataafa should be told and
asked to hold his hand in case the affair may be settled peaceably
by the pen.

My poor horse, given me by the consul (I call him Harold for the
consul), has been badly hurt on the barbed wire fence. Harry had
a stallion in the paddock. I ordered him out the moment I came
back, but it was too late for Harold, who had been bitten by the
brute, and in trying to escape had been torn by the wires. A Mr.

---

[23] Baron Senfft von Pilsach, president of the Municipal Council of Apia.

Davis came up and sewed up the wound and we hope it may come all right in time.

On Sunday Paul Leonard, "the passenger from Mariki," came to see us. He is now settled permanently in Samoa and is going to join Freis in making soda water, and possibly in ice making. Belle and Lloyd went down to the Gurrs the other evening. Fanua talked more than usual, and very well. She told how she went to the fighting place with her father to load his gun, and how, peeping through the bushes, she saw the German heads cut off. The pallor of the dead white face she thought most horrible, as indeed it is. At some of the islands the first white men were thought to be walking corpses, and the sight of them terrified the natives.

Three days before I arrived, the *Archer* came in to Apia. Mr. Hird and Tin Jack[24] visited our people, carrying presents in the island fashion. For Louis a fine London hat of white felt, with a twist of silk around the crown. For Lloyd an anvil, and for me a frying pan and a fine young boar. I find everything growing well— the oranges, cocoanuts and cacao, and my asparagus great green bushes. The rhubarb is alive and looks well and the custard squashes in full bearing. The cows, unfortunately, have damaged our best breadfruit, but it is not dead. I have had beds made on each side of the house, where I have put out the flowering plants.

Paul looks pale and thin but says he has quite recovered from the severe illness (inflammation of the lungs) he was suffering from when I left. He has an offer as assistant overseer on one of the German plantations: fifty dollars a month and a house and black boy. He is to take Putch with him, as Joe has sworn vengeance against that fine cat. He bit off one of Henry's (the cat Henry) toes and now keeps the poor fellow in a chronic state of lameness, having discovered his weak point. I have seen poor Henry with three feet bitten and swollen so that he could hardly walk.

A short time before I left, Mr. King came to Lloyd, saying that Johnny Skelton had offered him three dollars a day to do "fancy work, and no manual labour," and if we would give him ten pounds,

---

[24] (Tin being the island equivalent of Mr.); a trader who sailed with the Stevensons on the *Janet Nichol*.

he would leave us and accept Johnny's offer. We hastened to give him the ten pounds, though I feared the effect on our other men. However, when he went out to boast that we had been forced to buy him off for ten pounds he was met with jeers and laughter. We discovered afterwards that Johnny had made him no offer at all, but that a white man had given him his half-caste daughter in marriage, with a dowry variously stated to be 2,000 dollars and 4,000 dollars. "He's got 200 dollars and a half-caste wife with a big leg," said Paul with a scornful laugh. I believe it is quite true that she has elephantiasis.

Tomorrow there is to be a meeting of the council, when the letter prepared by Louis is to be publicly presented to the president and an answer insisted on. I am afraid Louis is not well enough to be there. No one has ventured to tell Louis's mother about the affair. She has been greatly worried lest we should lower our "social status" by quarrelling on political subjects with the government officials. I feel, on the contrary, that it is *their* social status which is lowered by our breaking with them. They have all but Mr. Blacklock been invited here to luncheon or dinner parties, and I refused to invite him until I know what part he took in the dynamite business. I will not associate with people who are capable of such things.

[25] There is a big row on hand concerning—prayer! It seems that Lafaele had to be with the wounded horse at prayer time and Joe, having scalded his right hand very badly, took Austin away to help him with the fowls. All this work *must* be done before the sun gets too hot, and it could not be helped. Unfortunately Belle was caught prowling like a cat, with no ostensible—and I fear no real—business on hand, and then there was an explosion. Mrs. S considers that she has received a personal insult from them all, and when Austin came to her for his lessons he was sent flying.

A fight about prayers is really enough to bring a cynical smile to the lips of a bishop. Mrs. S says she will not be left to pray with only servants. I am afraid that distinction is not made in other quarters. I see again she dislikes the life here which we find so enchanting and

[25] The following passage, the conclusion of which is marked by an asterisk, is suppressed in the manuscript.

is disappointed and soured that she is not able to persuade us to throw it all up and go to the colonies. We have given the colonies a fair trial and they mean death to Louis, whereas this is life and reasonable health.

I think she could be happier if she had some occupation, but I can't think of anything she would like. All the rest of us have every moment accounted for and are all enthusiastic in our different departments. It is very difficult for me to understand that anyone can prefer a life of calls, leaving and receiving cards, with a proper church and invested meals and a nap on Sundays, to this open air paradise where one feels so near to heaven that to believe ill is almost impossible.*

SEPT. 24TH

Henry, who had taken the wagon down to Apia, came back last evening with a box of presents for me, brought by the *Archer* from the Gallecros, six egg cups carved from very small cocoanut shells, six necklaces of white shells and beads, two cigarette ash holders of small cocoanut shells swinging on rings of tortoise shell, two whole cocoanuts, also very small, on rings, and two large beautiful mats. With them was a characteristic South Sea letter from Mr. V, complaining of the longest taboo that had ever been imposed on a white man, and attributing it to the influence of the Samoan teachers, of whom there are three resident on the island.

OCT. 23RD

Many exciting events have taken place since last I wrote. The president resigned as president of the council, but when he found out that by so doing he also resigned his salary and position as adviser of the king, tried a masterly retreat and now hangs in the balance. To the letter of Louis, Mr. Gurr, and the other gentlemen, asking about the dynamite, he wrote an insolent quibbling reply, referring them to the consuls for protection. Then they wrote one other letter, receiving a reply, no longer insolent, but weak and feebler quibbling. Louis sent the whole correspondence to the *Times*[26] with a letter of explanation; and upon hearing of the resignation, the signers of the letters called upon the king to congratulate him on the event. They were received very coolly, the king at first pleading "chief's" illness,

[26] Of London.

but they insisted on waiting and his majesty finally appeared. According to Samoan etiquette, their reception was almost an insult; no kava was offered nor excuse made for its lack.

Louis had been trying in vain to get hold of the letter sent to the chiefs on the subject of the dynamite. A wild Irishman, a most delicious creature, offered to fetch it in the face of the king's having proclaimed Mataafa and other high chiefs rebels, declaring their lands confiscated. The letter was retrieved and is now safe. In it dynamite was not mentioned, but the threat was made that upon any attempt to rescue the imprisoned chiefs DEATH would be their portion. The Irishman, named Dowdney, was informed by Mr. Blacklock that he had better look out or he would be deported.

Last Sunday Mr. Claxton came up plainly from the president, who has at last awakened to his danger. He tried every way to induce Louis to agree to meet the president and have an explanation; the offer came too late. We learned afterwards that at the same time Mr. Rose,[27] a horribly low, vulgar fellow, the president's secretary, had spent the day with Mr. Gurr, intent on the same errand. Neither was successful. The same ludicrous scene took place at both houses. Here, the American men-of-war officers dropped in, followed by Mr. Moors and Mr. Dowdney. The unfortunate missionary had to remain upstairs alone, in hiding for the better part of the afternoon, being at daggers drawn with Dowdney. After leaving us the party stopped at Gurr's, and the unfortunate Rose had to go into retirement.

Mrs. Stevenson has bought a pinto horse from the circus.[28] At one of the performances a Mr. Parker horsewhipped his wife in public and in the presence of Mr. Eggert,[29] the land commissioner, with whom she had gone on the trained horses. Mr. Eggert, on one side of the lady, and Captain Reid, who accompanied them, witnessed the brutal scene without a word or act of protest.

One *might* forgive Reid, but Eggert—? He does not seem fitted for the position of gay Lothario.

This morning Gurr came with another letter for Louis to sign, asking the three powers to abolish the office of president. Louis re-

[27] The next five words are suppressed in the manuscript.
[28] Called Circus Jack, or Tifaga Jack.
[29] German land commissioner in Samoa.

fused to sign, and showed Mr. Gurr the utter folly of the step, so I trust it may be dropped. The day after the visit of the missionary the president sent Louis a *resumé* of [blank]

28TH OCT.

Paul left us some time ago, having an offer from the German firm as assistant overseer on a plantation. He only stayed a few days, not being able, he said, to witness and join in with the barbarous treatment of the black boys.

"Why, Mr. Stevenson," said he, "all the overseeing I had to do was to follow the black boys with a whip, and that's no employment for a man."

We heard of him as barkeeper in one of the Apia hotels, and then as doing copying for the president. I am sorry to say that he borrowed thirty dollars from Mary some time before he left, and has not yet paid her. Mary should have asked us first whether she was doing right, as she well knew, so I am not very sorry for her. When I came back from Fiji I did not like Paul's appearance, which I attributed to the illness he had had, but now suspect to be the fruits of Mary's foolishness in providing him with money for drink. Mary says that Mr. King also supplied poor Paul with spirits.

Wishing to do all he could for me before he left, he has, with immense misdirected energy, worked fearful havoc among my plants. A Japanese persimmon just about to bear has been torn up and destroyed. A row of beautiful flowering trees that bordered the stream at the side of my garden is gone. In making a bed for planting in the new garden place, he ruthlessly pulled up finely growing coffee trees that he had planted out himself last season, and the vanilla beans that he has always had a perfect mania for transplanting have disappeared entirely. He paid us a visit last week, and just as he was leaving I asked him where he had put the vanillas. After a moment's thought he said he must come back and dig them up again, as at present they were planted among rocks quite inaccessible to me. It is lucky the vanilla is so tough a vegetable, though they may be quite worn out by now through these constant removals. I felt sorry to see the last of Paul, for with all his mistakes his heart was in the right place and I had grown quite fond of him.

But much more distressing is the fact that our dear Henry is also gone. He wept very much when leaving, saying that his "poor old family" in Savaii required his presence. We were told since, by a member of his family, "Jack," a capable, impudent, fighting cock of a young fellow, that Henry had in reality eloped with a young lady of his family, which I fear may be the truth of the matter. We really can do pretty well without him just now, as we have a good set of men that Lloyd and I can oversee very well.

We have given Yoseppi to Talolo in the kitchen, while Lafaele takes charge of all the animals. Among the outside workers is a large, serious, very villainous, one-eyed Tongan[30] boy called the "Tongan-hearted" (a term of reproach, equivalent to black-hearted) but now come to be "Pussy Wilson." He has married a Samoan wife, and confided to me yesterday when weeding coffee that his ambition was to fetch his wife to Vailima and become one of the family.

We are amused by the exclusiveness of the house people, who keep themselves to themselves most particularly. They may pay a visit to the stable, where the out boys sleep, in the evening, but that is all. When they were given a pig the house people sat round it by themselves, sending to the others a basket of the cooked meat. I find that Talolo is the boy that I noticed when we first came here, working quite alone, and separate from the others. Henry said it was so arranged that Talolo should not be contaminated by the "evil talk" of the others. Lloyd has promised a pig to the out boys so soon as a certain piece of work is finished. Lafaele is now shutting up the pig to fatten him.

We were invited for today, I believe, to lunch on board the American man-of-war, and told we were to meet Captain Foss of the German *Sperber*. Captain Foss is a most charming person, and we hold him in much esteem, so it was with sorrow we read a letter yesterday from him, bidding us farewell, as he could not meet us again as friends after the attack on the president, who, by the way, is said to be leaving in January. A proclamation has been issued by the king to the effect that all visitors to his majesty must apply two days beforehand for permission to the consuls. No doubt the presi-

[30] Referring to the Tonga Islands in the South Pacific.

dent's last childish attempt at reprisals. We are all very sorry for both him and his wife, but more sorry for Samoa.

Lafaele wants to go to Tonga to see his son. I tell him his son may come here and visit him, as I am afraid to trust him to go so far away; he is almost certain not to come back. It is the first I ever heard of the son, though that might mean a brother's child. Lafaele offered to leave Faauma in pledge. "But," I said, "that will be of no use; I shall only have the trouble of finding another husband for Faauma," of which he had no notion, being of a naturally jealous disposition.

I am in a horrid state from the drug given me by Uncle George's[31] advice for what is supposed to be an aneurysm inside my head. The beating in my head is already much less distressing, but my eyes and nose are swollen and I have a continual brow ache and not much sleep. Uncle George recommended chlorodyne. Louis gave me a dose, as he thought, night before last, but it turned out to be something else, tasting like an embrocation of some sort; unless, possibly, the stuff had gone bad, and in so doing, changed its taste and smell.

I find the coffee to be doing very well, indeed, in the plantation behind the stable. We have put cacao seeds in a number of baskets and expect more next week from Mr. Steubling, also what they call here "cherry trees." I sent him some tree tomatoes and roselle plants. Lloyd and Louis took them, Louis riding the circus pinto. While the latter was being saddled, Joe gave me a horrid shock by saying, "This horse has got glanders." But it was only lampas, which accounts for his poor condition. He went well, and seems perfectly safe, and steady as a rock. On the way down, Lloyd's horse, Macfarlane, shied against him, almost knocking poor Pinto down, but the good horse took no notice whatever of the ill behaviour of the island brute.

[OCTOBER] 29TH

The rest of yesterday, after the above entry, I spent overseeing in the coffee plantation. The men burned logs left by the popies.[32]

---

[31] Dr. George Balfour, Louis's maternal uncle.
[32] An island term applied to Catholic natives.

A haughty young man called Talolo did very well, but another known as Johnny skulked behind large trees. I once came upon him unexpectedly as he was sitting on the ground. He instantly bent forward and scratched up the earth with both hands like a dog, with a great air of capacity and energy. It was almost impossible to keep them from making their fires against the feet of large trees, which in time would die from the effects of the burning and fall upon the coffee trees. My cinnamon is growing lovely, and many copal gums are coming up.

Today, just as we were about starting to do more burning, comes a policeman to arrest Pussy Wilson for stealing lime. Unfortunately he dropped bits of lime as he walked along the road, and a native detective tracked him to the house. The detective asked Lafaele for a little lime to put on his head. Lafaele, not wishing to be rude with a downright refusal, said we had none, whereas there is a large quantity on hand.

Louis took the opportunity of questioning the policeman about an affair of Lafaele's. Lafaele's story was that a year ago he had been robbed of more than seventy dollars. The thief was caught and it was agreed that Lafaele should get twelve dollars of his money, the policeman being responsible for its payment. He got but three dollars and no more. The policeman said that he had caught the man, who had no money left. He appealed to the policeman for mercy, saying that he had no father and no mother, and insisted that the policeman should adopt him. This was done, but the policeman after a time conceived the happy idea of making the thief work out the sum, and he was sent up to Vailima to Henry. Three dollars were duly earned and handed over to Lafaele, when the culprit refused to work any longer. Once again the policeman prevailed upon him to return to his enforced labours, but half a day more than served him this time and he not only deserted Vailima but the family of his adoptive father. I wonder what a London policeman would say if when he caught a thief the sly gentleman should propose his adoption as a way out of the difficulty.

Talolo amuses us very much. Belle said to him, "What shall we do when the war comes and the warriors demand our pigs?" He asked to have the question repeated. "When Malietoa says, 'Give me your pig,' what shall we do? Give it to him, I suppose? And then Mataafa will come and say the same thing."

"Oh, no," said Talolo, "Mataafa no do that; Mataafa say '*Please* give me pig.' "

Belle told him about the American Indians and how they scalped their victims, which filled Talolo with horror.

"But you Samoans cut off your wounded enemies' heads," said Belle.

"Oh," replied Talolo, "that is a very different thing. Man wounded, he feel bad. Cut off his head, he no feel bad any more. And you cut off plenty heads, take them to the Queen (king), her say, 'I am very much surprised.' "

He always uses *surprised* for *obliged*.

Our wagon is coming to pieces, but we find that Pussy Wilson understands using the pack saddles very well. One day we gave him the big white horse and the largest pack saddle with bags and sent him out to scour the country for breadfruit and taro. He was gone all day, returning in the evening dead beat, with three or four taro roots and nothing else. I presume he stopped at every native house to show off the horse and boast of his high position in Vailima. Mrs. Gurr and Miss Gurr are going to take Belle to a fancy dress ball. I have been making a crown for Mrs. Gurr, who goes as Zenobia. I think she will look very handsome.

NOV. 1ST

Yoseppi sent away. Lloyd says he feels like a person who has lost a pet dog. Yoseppi had been given his day off on Friday, so that he and Talolo should not be away at the same time. When Saturday came he wanted to go again. Lloyd said, "Go if you like, but if you do, you can't come back." He chose to go, and we now learn that there had been ill feeling between him and Talolo, so it is as well. Yoseppi had no sooner announced his determination of leaving, before another boy was hanging about, hoping to get his place. It was decided that Talolo should choose his own boy and train him to cooking. I could hardly bear the presence of the candidate for the place. Even when not looking at him I could feel his burning, eager, imploring eyes boring through my consciousness. Talolo did not take him, but brought next day a very good-looking, capable young man who seems very well adapted to the work, though his expression of extreme hauteur is rather disconcerting. We hear from Mrs. Clarke, filtered through Mrs. Stevenson, that Mr. Claxton has stated as a fact that we turned away our dear Henry, having found him out in something very wrong. Mr. C knew all about Henry, as he was here just at that time, and we were all in the first shock of the misfortune of losing him. We think there must be some mistake.

[NOVEMBER] 2ND

Mr. Haggard came to see us and spent the evening. Talolo's mother came to pay a visit by invitation, a very respectable woman indeed, quite worthy of Talolo's adoring affection. A relative came with her, almost blind with cataract. They were shown over the house and could be continually heard crying out in Samoan, "How extremely beautiful!" Even when plunged into the darkness of the cellar the same cry arose. I gave the mother a small red cross, brought from the Holy Land by a sailor who gave it to me in Marseilles. In the centre is a little magnifying glass over a photograph of Jerusalem. To the other woman I gave a little silver ornament to wear round her neck, and some ribbon to them both. It was pleasing to note Faauma showing the house with an affectation of blasé indifference. Her manner said, "No doubt all this magnificence is very surprising to you, but it is part of my daily life."

It rained heavily yesterday and is still grey and wet. On Saturday an old carpenter named Henderson came up, on the lookout for a job. I like him and he is very poor, so I was glad to have some work for him to do. I have ordered some storm shutters for my big window, and he is to do several other odd jobs. Among other things, I wanted a small door cut into the kitchen from Mrs. Stevenson's room, about three feet high and two broad. I said to him, "I want you to cut through the boards just as they are, as I cannot match the paint." "Quite impossible," was the reply. "I must have kauri wood, and panel the door." A happy thought struck me. "But I want a secret door," I said. His eyes kindled, and mystery instantly enveloped him in a dense cloud. "I can do it—yes, I can do it," said he, in a low, furtive voice, and there was no more question of kauri wood or panelling.

There is an immense deal of gossip on the beach concerning the doings at Vailima. We are supposed to be hand in glove with Mataafa and the priests. It has come to the point that we have no Protestants except ourselves on the place. But that is all self-interest; the popies are honest, industrious, capable men—[33]honest up here, I mean, and about their work. Pussy Wilson seems to have made a slip, but here he is one of our best men. Polu is the name of Talolo's boy. The mail steamer has just come in and Talolo has volunteered to go for the mail. Last Saturday Lloyd marshalled up all the men before they left for their Sunday home, and administered to each a blue pill. One unfortunate fellow was caught out hiding his in his cheek, and made to swallow it amidst shouts of laughter. I feared they would never come back, but all returned on the Sunday morning, declaring they were much improved in health. I was reminded of this just now by Lloyd coming in to say that he was sending a lot of men up to the swamp to clear the taro and bananas, and he meant to dose each one with quinine before he went. A black boy just came from Miss Gurr with a note: we could not but notice the difference between his aspect and that of the plantation boys: the Gurr boy so gay and smiling and good-looking, the latter sad, inanimate, melancholy wretches that hardly answer when you speak to them.

[NOVEMBER] 6TH

Fusi came back, I think on the fourth, honourably discharged, without a stain upon his character. Poor Talolo has been sent for to go home to his sick child, down with the influenza. We hear that influenza is raging in Apia. Today our washing man came up to say his wife was ill and the clothes must lie over until next week. Just as he was leaving I learned, to my dismay, that he was just getting the disease. A couple of days ago—

[NOVEMBER] 15TH

I get almost no time to write. I have been planting cacao seeds, about three hundred in baskets, and most of them up, or breaking ground. Also cabbage, Chinese cabbage, roselle, and an Indian plant

[33] The next nine words are suppressed in the manuscript.

for food. Today Mr. Dumet and Mr. Haggard dined with us. Mr.
Dumet pointed out to me a weed which he said was excellent eating,
cooked like asparagus. I shall try it very soon. We heard much
interesting news from these gentlemen. They told us that the C J
and the president, Baron von Pilsach, though at first recoiling from
each other, had made a sort of compact to stand by each other for
the sake of getting more power, and expected to become almost
absolute in the islands; that when things began to look uncertain
and there was a smell of failure in the air, the C J took a trip to
Fiji and the colonies, leaving the president to bear the brunt. Now
he comes back and, expressing great surprise at the state of affairs,
turns his back on the poor president. Mr. Ide, the U.S. land commissioner,[34] has resigned his position and gone home and, according
to the story brought us, intends proposing Mr. Haggard as Chief
Justice. There is no doubt but there must be a change in the government. Mr. H talked very wisely on the situation. All, or the worst,
I fear for him as C J, is on account of his being such a determinedly
patriotic Englishman. He wants an English protectorate, as do we
all. But the subject would have to be approached with great tact and
caution. The English have refused to take a protectorate before,
and may again. The next best thing would be an American protectorate. The English would have Indian coolie labour—but the English
are so bitter on the subject of America that I think they would prefer
the destruction of the island to anything American. It is odd that
the ordinary feeling of any person for his mother land is looked upon
by the most intelligent Englishman as ludicrous, but oh "wad the
power the giftie gie us." Mr. Carruthers is the only British subject
I ever saw that is an exception to the rule. He says the noisy boast-
ing of his countrymen, so vulgar and provincial, fills him with shame,
and covers him with humiliation. [35]It is the only subject on which
Louis, ordinarily so brilliant a talker, babbles like poor Poll.

A short time ago, in a bit of very "pretty fooling," Louis presented
his birthday to Mr. Ide's daughter,[36] requesting her to take the name

[34] Henry C. Ide, later Chief Justice.
[35] The following sentence is suppressed in the manuscript.
[36] Anne.

of Louisa; so, a couple of days ago we celebrated her festival on Louis's anniversary. [37]The moment that grace was said and before dinner had commenced Louis *declared* a toast in the voice of one doubtful of being obeyed. We supposed that we were to drink to Miss Ide, but no, it was "her blessed majesty the Queen." Then in an aggressive manner he turned to Lloyd, saying, "You can drink to the President *afterwards* if you like." I am writing this down hoping that Louis may see it and realize how foolish and childish and in bad taste the whole thing is. Henley, I see, is about to publish a book containing everything he can find "in praise of England." I need not say that Lloyd smiled and did not offer any but a social toast.*

Lloyd went over today and saw Captain Hufnagel. We had written a note to ask him and his wife to dine with us about ten days ago, sending the letter by way of the German firm. About eight months or a year past, Lloyd sent a letter to a veterinary surgeon belonging to one of the plantations, concerning the payment for treatment of a wounded horse, by means of the firm. The vet had only come up on Sundays, which were his own days. The letter came to him broken open, with a sharp reprimand. As we had no word from Captain Hufnagel, we feared the same fate for our invitation. He had received it the day before, nine days after it was sent. Whether closed or open, Lloyd did not ask. He tells us that he has, to his dismay, orders to stop planting cacao, so we may have all the seeds we require from Vailele.[38] He was most pleasant, and listened with but little interest to Lloyd's explanation of our stand in regard to politics. Lloyd thought he should be quite frank with Captain H, that there should be no mistakes. All the other Germans have taken an objection to the dynamite affair as a direct hostility against the German Empire. It is strange that the English can see the mote in the German eye but not the beam in their own. The whole attitude of the Germans is so excessively English.

"You have trampled on the German Emperor," cry the Germans.

---

[37] The following passage, the conclusion of which is marked by an asterisk, is suppressed in the manuscript.

[38] The German plantation.

"I suspect you want to trample on the Union Jack," cries the Englishman.

Oh, oh, what tempests in teapots. I am so very glad that Captain H is a man above such nonsense. It would be a real calamity if we should lose him too. Lloyd told him how several of our native men seemed to take an interest in cacao and talked of wanting to plant it. He was greatly pleased at the idea. When our men worked in the coffee trees we gave them coffee to drink, which many of them had never tasted before. They worked ten times better afterwards, for now they understood that something pleasant would come in time from the results of their work. Before, they continually made the mistake of pulling up a small tree now and then, but now they keep a sharp eye for the precious shrub and touch it most tenderly. Before they put out the cacao they are all to have a mug of chocolate. Captain H said that the boys we have are each one equal to two blacks. "Everybody knows," he said, "that the priests help you." I am sure there is a great deal of talk about our employing only Catholic, Mataafa boys, and all sorts of speculations concerning the great quantity of stores we are fetching up from the steamers on our big pack horses.

I told Mr. Claxton that I had given up the Protestant boys and taken on the popies in our own interests. I am very much annoyed by the Claxtons' having come up here just as Mrs. C was recovering from this influenza. Though Louis and I refused to come downstairs, and they knew why, they stopped for tea. I am tired of the Claxtons. Louis is writing, from his old notes, the story of the last Samoan war. He preferred writing a book, for boys, of Scotch history, but, as he has great quantities of material for the Samoan book and as it may be a help to an understanding of the situation [39]and may save Mataafa, I begged him to do it first, though he will get much less money for it than for the other.

[NOVEMBER] 22ND

The influenza has been raging through the islands. A few of the white residents have died, and very many of the natives. A rumour

[39] The next four words are suppressed in the manuscript.

has reached us that [40]our dear Henry is dead in Savaii. I cannot bear to believe it, and will not without positive proof. We have not a single case yet in Vailima. Lafaele is in mortal terror of the disease and begs fervently that he shall be sent on no errands to Apia. It is arranged that he is to make a melaga to Tonga after Christmas. We are all blazing with cacao fever. I have succeeded in inoculating the entire family. By a lucky chance for us, the German plantations have received orders to plant no seeds this season, so we shall have all we want. Already we have planted over six hundred, many now set out in the bush. Poor Mrs. Stevenson has had a book, called, I think, *Tropical Industries*, forced upon her by Lloyd, who keeps a sharp eye upon her to see that she reads it. He fears her enthusiasm is not at proper temperature. She seems to work away at it most gallantly. Today is Sunday, but we must all, the family and the house boys, plant the seeds we have left over from yesterday. I showed Louis, Lloyd and Joe how to roll the seeds in wood ashes and place them in the baskets yesterday. All the families who wash in Apia or the neighbourhood are ill, so we are trying to teach a couple of the work boys to wash and iron. Neither Belle nor I know exactly how laundry work should be done, so the teaching is rather difficult. Though Belle was once during the operation moved to tears, the things look better than they have done since we came to the South Seas, and we are encouraged to proceed on our wild career.

The butcher came up to Vailima day before yesterday to offer a cow for sale. Mrs. Stevenson has bought it for fourteen pounds. It has not yet arrived.

We have all been very much upset lately by the misfortunes of Mr. Gurr, who married Fanua, the maid of Apia, some time ago. Miss Gurr, or Ethel, as she prefers us to call her, has been living with the young couple for the last two or three months. They are a very gentle, charming little family, and our nearest neighbours, so we have seen a great deal of them. [41]Fanua is Henry's cousin. Mr. Gurr has been acting as manager of a bank; he also owned shares;

[40] The next two words are suppressed in the manuscript.
[41] The next four words are suppressed in the manuscript.

the business, however, belonged mostly to a Mr. Aspinall and a Mr. Hayhurst. These two gentlemen suddenly appeared in Apia, to the surprise of everyone. Mr. Gurr, who was to have dined with us on Louis's birthday, when Louis was forty-one, sent word that, owing to the arrival of these gentlemen, who proposed to dine with him, he could not come to Vailima till some time in the evening, when the three came together. Mr. Hayhurst talked the most to Louis, who rather liked him. I didn't. I thought him coarse and common. Mr. Aspinall was a black-a-vised vulgarian, with long white carnivorous looking teeth. It turned out afterwards that they had suspected Gurr of dishonest practices and had thus fallen upon him suddenly, that he should have no time for preparation. From all the facts we could gather they had some grounds to go upon, but their conduct was both singular and brutal.

Louis and his mother had a little money in the bank, which Louis was advised by Mr. Moors and Gurr himself to draw out. Of course Mr. G might, and probably was, moved to give his advice as he did because he thought it would be disagreeable to Aspinall and Hayhurst. Louis decided to draw it out, and sent a cheque for the purpose. Though the bank was open and doing business they flatly refused to give the money, but sent, almost ordering Louis to come down to Apia, as they wished to see him. Had I had my way they should have been forced to suspend payment altogether and close their bank or honour the cheque. Louis went to Apia, despite the influenza that might kill him, at the beck of these two brutes, only to be told that they did not mean to give him his money He told them to think it over and he would present his cheque again in the morning. They must have taken advice overnight, as the cheque was paid without a word when the time came, though they had told the English consul they would not pay it.

"Everything belongs to us," they said, "and we can do as we please with it." We can only suppose it to be part of the persecution of Gurr.

"*I don't know who you are*," was one of Aspinall's diamond-edged sarcasms levelled against Louis.

I should not give such people a second thought but for my sorrow for the Gurrs, especially for the two women, Fanua, a grand specimen of the high-bred Samoan, and little, fair, innocent Ethel.

Gurr explained nothing to Ethel, he could not. She knew there was something terrible in the air but asked no questions except of Belle; not exactly questions, but she made surmises.

"I know my brother is in great trouble," said she, "and I can't help thinking these two men who dined with us had something to do with it. They behaved very strangely."

Very strange, indeed, was their behaviour. They sat at the table and broke bread with the man they meant to ruin, flaunting the foods offered them by the small, terrified Ethel.

"Won't you try these tomatoes?" she asked, adding, as the man was about to help himself from the dish, "They were grown in Samoa."

"I don't want them then," was the reply. "I don't want anything that is Samoan."

They sat before their hostess, the magnificent Fanua, and said every evil thing they could think of concerning Samoan women. Their conduct was inconceivable. Mr. Gurr is a very small, slender man, who has just suffered a very painful operation for necrosis of the bone. These gallant gentlemen were perfectly safe from any physical harm whilst eating the salt and insulting the wife and sister of their victim. The cleverer of the two made underbred jokes and the other roared with laughter, while both varied the entertainment by poking Gurr viciously in the ribs with "Eh, you rascal!" followed by shouts of laughter.

The furniture in the little Gurr cottage belonged to the firm. It was instantly ordered back to Apia. The messages sent were so insolent that poor Gurr asked that his sister might come up to us until there would be no danger of her meeting these men, or, I should say, ruffians. She is here now, prattling away, and playing on her fiddle, yet with an occasional pathetic alarm in her eyes. We have offered them rooms here if they care for them. Mr. Gurr does not know yet what he had better do. It is pleasant to think we can put them all up quite comfortably, and except for the reason underneath it would be delightful to have them here. I do not feel that we quite know all concerning this affair. At any rate, even if he has stolen a bone, I am with the under dog in a fight. Besides, it would require a great deal of proof to make me believe that Gurr had ever been more than unwise.

[NOVEMBER] 30TH

Miss Gurr is gone, with a terrible tale of ruin and disgrace to carry home to her widowed mother. At the last moment, Mr. Gurr sent to say that he had not money enough to pay his sister's ticket, so Louis sent him down seven pounds. We feel very miserable about them. I am, however, pleased to hear that Mr. Carruthers has behaved very generously in the matter.

As I was working in the garden one day, I heard Belle calling out to me, "Look," she said, "here comes an *aitu*." It was Henry himself, but looking very miserable and altogether changed. He had a bad wound on the back of his head, either a spear or club blow. It looked as though there had been an attempt to assassinate him. I spoke about his marriage, but he hastily and nervously changed the subject of conversation. He came again the next day and asked for the loan of fifty dollars, and to be taken on again as overseer. He is to come tomorrow, when Louis will give him the money under the condition that he is told what use it is to be put to. He seemed greatly distressed about the condition of his "poor old family." They were poverty stricken, he said, and knew not how to work. "They don't know anything, my poor old family," were his words.

A little while before he went to Savaii he said to Louis, "I am weary of white men on the beach." Savaii, he says, is going to remain loyal to Malietoa. Louis has sent a letter to the Chief Justice to tell him that he is writing a history of Samoa and that it will run through the present "crisis." I remember when a child how frightened I was to read in a newspaper, "Great alarm! The crisis is approaching!" I imagined the crisis to be nothing less than a monstrous wild beast.

Louis, Lloyd and I have been to Apia. We met the C J just in front of Webber's house, from the windows of which we became aware we were eagerly watched by women. We talked a long time most amicably and then rode on to call upon Laulii, who had removed, so we missed her. Mr. Haggard has been turned out of his house (owned by a German) because Mr. Dowdney shot a cock that Mr. Haggard had got permission to shoot. He goes down to the Rugi building. Mr. Dowdney is the man who made the remark, "Samoa is a delightful place; you can get into a new conspiracy every day!" Louis rode the horse given me by Mr. Sewall (I call him Harold after Mr. S), and found him very pleasant to ride, though he is still thin after his accident.

Lafaele has made a cow house for the new cow, called Pauline, because she reminds us of a Paul Potter picture. We have now, in baskets and planted out, some 1200 cacaos. All yesterday Joe and I were superintending the making of a bridge over the river, the old one having rotted away. We had two trees cut down for the purpose. One of them was of the most lovely pinkish wood, with salmon-pink bark, and emitted a perfume something like sassafras and something like winter-green.

In the early part of the week I had a great fright. I was just going off to sleep at about half-past nine, when my father's portrait suddenly fell to the floor, smashing any amount of crockery that had been stored on the shelf below it. The picture was not injured, except for a bit of the frame breaking off.

Miss and Mrs. Moors lunched with us today. In the morning I planted cabbages and showed Joe what work I wanted done in the garden. Faauma came to complain that she had had no *kiki*. As Talolo looked very cross, I asked for an explanation. She had quarrelled with her husband at lunch time, and to spite him refused to eat, and now was hungry. I told her she might have more *kiki* this time, but in the future she must not quarrel with Lafaele before meals. Mrs. S [42]wants the Catholic boys to be told that they must come in to our prayers or leave. I refused to allow any interference with them. She* is [43]also very much upset with the litter connected with cacao planting, at which I do not so much wonder. The verandah in front of her door was tracked with mud, and loose boards and baskets are piled up wherever we can find room.

[42] The following passage, the conclusion of which is marked by an asterisk, is suppressed in the manuscript.
[43] The following word is suppressed in the manuscript.

12TH DEC.

So busy planting cacao that I have had no time to look at my diary. Also, twice I have been to Apia, the last time staying all night at Mr. Haggard's place. He has moved, being turned out for the shooting of the cock, and is now installed in Rugi's house. At least Abdul and the furniture are there, Mr. H himself having gone to the colonies. Abdul was a most gracious host and had everything prepared for our comfort. We even found sleeping garments laid out for Louis. Rugi's is a charming place, built in Spanish fashion, with immense rooms designed in the best taste. We felt a little heartsick when we remembered that we had once thought of buying it. Still, the fact remains that a great many people have died of fever there, and there is a marsh behind it.

The evening we spent at Mr. Moors', the only two other guests outside of our family being Mr. H. Carruthers and an officer from the American man-of-war. Mr. M's mother, a very stout, very masterful old lady; Miss Moors, a very stout, very masterful young lady. Miss Moors has a mania for changing people's names. The Moors' child they have charge of has had its name changed from Miranda to Ramona; she proposes to change little Rosy's name to Ruth, and the baby Sophia (named from the island where she was born) to Ruby. All great nonsense.

We have a new version of Henry's difficulties. Talolo says that he went to Savaii to take his place as chief, but the "family" said he was too young and appointed someone else, which throws Henry out until the present man's death. There was a "personal encounter" between the two claimants, during which Henry received the injury to his head.

Polu asked for a day's leave and never came back. He now wishes to return but Talolo indignantly refuses to allow him. The meat boy was then tried with compound duties, helping both in the kitchen and pantry. There has been a rupture with Mary. I [44]saw that she was ready to be impertinent to me and asked Mrs. S what I should do in that case, as I had no authority to dismiss her. [45]"Come straight

[44] The next eleven words are suppressed in the manuscript.
[45] The following passage, the conclusion of which is marked by an asterisk, is suppressed in the manuscript.

and tell me," was the reply. I thought it an impossible position to be placed in, but did as I was told—and wished I hadn't. I oughtn't to have but,* having started on the warpath, I thought I might as well push through and get Mary ousted from my premises, where she has been a sore thorn. She is now Mrs. Stevenson's own maid, and Faauma had the glory of taking her place. Faauma does very well indeed, though how long it will last is uncertain. The circus horse has a hurt leg. Mary rode it to town, and coming home late at night, nobody looked at it till next day. It seems to have been tethered by a rope which must have got wound round its legs and thrown it. It looks bad.

I rode the "consular horse," as Lafaele calls it, for the first time. It is a darling, with the most perfect gait possible. The first day I went to Apia, Belle accompanied me. As we were about to make the first turn on the road, both our horses stopped as though paralyzed, with their ears laid back. Nothing more terrible was in our way than a party of men, with one woman, come from across the island. It was surprising to see Belle whip up her horse, like a real horsewoman. But the acme of surprise was reached in Apia. We had stopped at Miss Taylor's shop to buy shoes, a box of which were laid on the balcony railings just above Belle's horse's head. By some accident this box fell and the horse leaped backwards. Miss Taylor caught the end of the bridle and dragged at it, the horse backing towards the embankment by the sea, until the bridle broke. I expected Belle to fall in a faint under the horse's hoofs, but no, she never changed countenance, but remained serenely on the saddle and tried to persuade Miss Taylor to let go the bridle. I am going to buy the only saddle in Samoa and present the horse, saddled and bridled, to her for a Christmas gift.

I have had hurricane shutters put up at my broad window and have ordered others for the big glass doors and Louis's windows. Mr. Maben was here yesterday to go round the bordering of Vailima with Lloyd and Joe. Joe was disappointed to find four hundred acres so small. Lloyd thought it a very large place; he was fearfully tired. Mr. Maben was greatly interested in our planting. If our experiment of planting in the bush succeeds he says we will change the whole of Samoa.

[DECEMBER] 14

A beautiful sunny day. More cacao to plant from Stuebling. I was very tired yesterday, so am not allowed to work today. Talolo has a new boy, having refused to receive "that bad Polu" back again. The "new broom," as Talolo calls him, begins well. It is now arranged that Faauma is to do all the pantry work alone, her boy to be sent away. She came to Belle and clung round her neck and begged so sweetly and prettily that this arrangement should be made that there was no gainsaying her. She has just been to make my bed, her eyes blazing with excitement and triumph. Belle comes in, despairing, to say that the pantry boy is so pathetic about leaving that she cannot bear it. He says he doesn't want money, he only wants to stay. "Has my work not been well done?" he asks. Certainly it has. "Then let me stay. I will work well without wages." It is very miserable.

Talolo brings more of Henry's story. He says that the reason given for throwing Henry out of his chieftainship was that he cannot speak the chief's language and therefore could not represent them in the fono. That was what they meant by saying he was too young. Still, a chief may always have his orator, or "talking man." I imagine they were very willing to find an excuse to oust Henry, who doubtless was very rigorous about forcing his "poor old family" to work.

Lloyd announces his determination to take up residence in a far-off native village so soon as the weather is good again, that he may perfect himself in the native tongue. He could not, at present, go to the only village I should like him to stop at, as it is a strong Mataafa place and his going would be looked upon as solely a political move. Louis had a long talk with Mr. Cusack-Smith concerning politics and our present rulers. He is hot for a change. Here is a bit of personal gossip from him concerning the C J. The Cusack-Smiths went on a melaga, closely followed by the C J. The C-S party stopped at a village for the night and gave as a present the magnificent offering of a keg of salt beef. Mary Hamilton (a native woman) was with them. She came to Mr. C-S and said that the people were delighted with their present, as now they had something handsome to offer the C J when he came, never doubting but that he would immediately make a feast for the village with the beef. Before the C-Ss left, the C J arrived and the keg of beef was presented. What was the astonishment of the C-Ss to behold the keg being rolled down to the C J's boat, intact.

"I have had a fine present," said the C J, "a keg of beef. It will feed my boatmen all through my melaga."

The feelings of the village may be imagined. It is a great pity that the C J is a man of so thrifty a soul. From a man in his position the natives expect something kingly and they get just nothing but barren thanks.

When we were in Apia the other day Louis came face to face with the baron and baroness. If a glance could kill, he said, he must have fallen before the baroness's eyes. I am very sorry for her, but for the sake of Samoa they must be made to go. Louis had another, more pleasing, meeting. He became aware of a fine manly figure on horseback, more elaborately dressed for the occasion than had yet appeared in Samoa, yellow gaiters spick and span, everything complete as possible. As the gentleman came nearer Louis discovered, to his surprise, first that it was a native and then that it was his blessed majesty himself, no other than Malietoa Laupepa, who has heretofore found a white cotton lava lava and a shirt or coat sufficient for his dignity. I think it a good plan that something should be done to show that he is above the chiefs, and dress, here, means so much.

We have had a lot of fine pineapples coming in and plenty of mangoes and oranges. My tree onions are making large bulbs but do not yet show any disposition to seed. The tomato slips are in bloom. Everything else, including the sunflowers and water melons, is growing vigorously. So are the weeds, unfortunately. Some time ago I made jelly from berries growing on trees in the bush. It was exceedingly good. The tree I cleaned is now full again and the berries are just ripening. I have made a little scent, for a trial, of mussaoi, citron, vanilla, and a fragrant gum. It is very sweet, almost heavy at first, and holds its perfume well.

Poor Mr. Gurr is ill again with his face, necrosis of the jaw. I fear it looks serious. His cheek is to be cut open again and a tooth and

piece of the jaw to be chiselled out. We are all very unhappy about
the Gurrs. We heard last week that a war party had been sent to
Mataafa's camp after men who are wanted for trial in Apia. It was
Gurr who told this to Louis.

"What do you think the result will be?" asked Louis.

"Look out on the verandah and you will see what I think," said
Gurr.

Louis looked and saw Fanua putting a rifle in order. Still, we have
had no news of trouble yet, though that seems a sure way to start
hostilities. I can hear Joe making a bridge. He and I — —

[DECEMBER] 15TH

The Catholic bishop from Tonga and a half-caste priest came to
call. The bishop a pleasant, intelligent old man. I was out overseeing
the clearing out of my coffee plantation. Thinking no one was at the
house to receive them (Louis had gone to ride, but returned just as
they came), I rushed back, barefooted, and my hair flying. Speaking
of hair reminds me that Belle surreptitiously cut my hair short round
my neck when I was trying to understand the working of a sewing
machine. Fortunately hair that curls doesn't look so badly as when
it is lank and straight. The half-caste priest told us that Mataafa
meant to call a fono if three-quarters of the Samoans came to his
banner; then he will make war. If only one-half, the issue will be
doubtful; and if less, no war.

[DECEMBER] 16TH

Mrs. Stevenson on the mare and I on Harold, the consular horse,
went to Apia to make calls and do some Christmas shopping. Bought
a saddle and other things at the German firm, where we met Captain
Hufnagel. Joe went to see the dentist at the same time, so rode down
with us. I was amused at the way Joe baited the captain about cacao.
He has promised to go to the plantation on Sunday, and I also, if
possible. My horse behaved very badly, once bolting with me on the
way down. When we came back Faauma had run away. She had been
quarrelling with Lafaele for a long time, so took that method, the
usual Samoan one, of punishing him. Lafaele saddled his horse and
went off in great agitation to hunt for her.

[DECEMBER] 17TH

At six o'clock Lafaele and Faauma appeared as usual, Faauma a little shame-faced. Belle took no notice of her little caressing ways and Faauma has been going about all day plucking at her sleeve and trying to smile into her eyes, without effect. We sent down yesterday for the disconsolate pantry boy to come back. He was to have come this morning at ten but has not turned up. I cannot but suspect that a message has been sent down to him to say that Faauma has returned and he is not wanted. He is wanted, for the fascinating Faauma is to be deposed. I shall send Talolo for him in the morning.

Henry came up to my room today with a parcel of fans. He looked so shame-faced that I suspected I was about to receive another parting present. The last was a miserable misshapen stallion that I cannot get rid of. I asked what was on his heart. He said he was ashamed to tell me, but after a little persuasion said that he must go back again to Savaii, having just received a most important letter. I had promised him a pair of pigs to take to his poor old family the first time a boat went over to his island. I said he had better take the pigs, also a sick one he thought he could cure. He was ashamed, again, about the pigs, though I found afterwards that he had brought men with him to carry them away. It was finally settled that I should have a share of the increase. After this was settled he stood in front of me, shuffling on first one foot and then the other. Suddenly he broke out, "I don't know what to do. My head is no good. I have no intelligence."

"Take my advice, Henry," said I, "and go in to Mr. Stevenson and tell him all that troubles you."

He went in, but what he did tell was forced out of him by degrees. His next neighbour was using a road through Henry's land. This road Henry closed by planting it in bananas. The neighbour and his men came and cut down the bananas. Then Henry put up a gate, when the neighbour and his followers came in a rush, armed with sticks and axes.

"I suppose there was fighting, then?" asked Louis.

Henry looked at him fixedly and repeated slowly and stolidly, "They came with sticks and axes."

Louis proposed that he attempt a compromise: let him give the road, and they give him some of their land. He is going to try that, and if all fails, leave them in peace till some law is possible. The letter was from his people to say that the neighbour had made another attack and destroyed another gate. There may be more than he has told; at any rate all the stories we have heard fall to the ground. Had it been a better time of the year, Louis would have gone over to Savaii with him.

This morning, to my surprise, I heard the notes of a flute. I ran to the verandah and looked out. The men were getting the weeds out of the peanuts, garlanded like children at a May party. Joe was overseeing, and at the same time warbling away on his flute. He would nod approval here, and disapproval there, without removing his pipe from his lips.

[DECEMBER] 18TH

I was interrupted last night in rather a startling manner. First there was a sudden report like the noise of a great gun; this was quickly followed by a rifle shot; both sounded very near. We all rushed out, thinking a battle might be beginning. Lafaele came running from his bed to ask that the arms might be served out. We waited in a good deal of excitement, but nothing more took place. It was finally concluded that men were shooting wild pigs, which would explain the crack of the rifle but not the first loud noise.

We have been having earthquakes lately. When Joe and I were overseeing in the coffee I became aware of a curious alarming sound which I had almost persuaded myself was something in my own ears. It was a hollow, buzzing rumble, very like what is called "a roaring in the ears." Then a little tremor passed through the earth, followed by a sharper shock, the noise still continuing until all was again quiet. At the first jar the men dropped their knives and huddled together, casting anxious glances at the earth and sky.

"Fire," said Pussy Wilson, pointing to the ground.

Belle says she felt a lesser shock half an hour afterwards, and Lloyd was awakened in the night by a rather heavy shock.

[DECEMBER] 19TH

Joe went down to the dentist, coming home by moonlight. I planted a few cabbages. My cabbages *must* come to something or my reputation as a gardener is gone. As none of us like cabbages I had not intended to plant them, but every white man who comes to the place asks first how my cabbages are doing. When I had none, and said so, no more interest was shown.

"They *have* grown them at one of the German plantations," was the usual remark.

I tried whitening the bridle of the consular horse with limes. While doing this I discovered that the bridle had been fastened together by two carpet tacks, the points of which passed through and must have been pricking the horse's face. It was no wonder he behaved badly. In the evening Austin announced that he would read us several chapters of a story he had written; as yet it has no title.[46] It was properly divided into chapters and paragraphs and the conversations were in inverted commas. He looked up before beginning and said, "I think I must change one of my names, for Thompson and Simpson rhyme too much." We were thunderstruck at this remark from a boy of ten. The story, so far as it went, was remarkably good. When we went in to play cards as usual Austin got his materials and wrote another chapter, his eyes shining like lamps. When he said his prayers he told his mother he wished to add something more. "Dear Lord, I thank you for a pleasant day. Dear Lord, I am glad I had no trouble with my lessons. And oh, Lord, I thank you that I have wrote—*written*—a book! Amen!!"

[DECEMBER] 20TH

Austin came upstairs today to say that he wanted some fool caps to write his story on. He made enquiries today about publishers but accepted his mother's advice to keep his tale till he was grown up and then publish it after the fashion of Mr. Ruskin. I forgot to mention yesterday that three of our chairs, made by the carpenter from our own wood, a sort of mahogany, came up. Joe, on his way to the dentist, rode on ahead to see the chairs properly packed for Pussy Wilson and Simi to carry. Simi has been working for us for some time now. He is a very handsome man, with the look of a priest, tall and with a slight stoop, and quick to understand, while Pussy is a desperate-looking ruffian. Joe waited for more than a reasonable time

[46] Austin Strong grew up to be a successful playwright.

and then started back to look for them. They were both bathing. Simi was the first to get into his lava lava and came hurrying up to Joe, saying, "That Fusi no good; he no work. That Fusi he allee time want stop; he no good, that Fusi."

The chairs, when they came, were all that could be desired: a beautiful shape, slightly different from the pattern chair (a tavern chair of pearwood, some two hundred years old) and extremely comfortable to sit in. In the ornamentation the marks of the maker's penknife show quite plainly, but they are none the worse for that.

We made up our minds today to send away the new kitchen boy. We none of us liked him and we thought his influence over Talolo was not good. Louis thought it best to explain to Talolo why the other boy was sent away. Nothing fell from the lips of the reticent Talolo but "very much surprised." When the two boys parted it seemed to be in anger. There were loud angry voices and then suddenly Talolo was playing on a flageolet Joe gave him, in an agitated way.

Lafaele has not been doing well lately. I suspected him of more skulking than I saw, so I called him in and asked what he meant by smoking and taking naps at Hunter's Rest[47] when he went to water the horses, and set him a task for today—to tear down the roof and sides of the horse shed and put up a new frame of living *fuafua* trees. He began to say that he was kept busy every moment of his time with the horses and cows.

"Look here, Lafaele," said I, "you think me allee same fool, eh? You know ship's glass? I look out ship's glass." The truth being that I could not see anything of Hunter's Rest but the tops of the cocoanuts. Lafaele hung his head, convicted.

"I won't do it any more," said he. "You look see, now, I work all right."

So I gave him Simi to help him, and an excellent day's work they have done. Fusi does not yet think it the dignified thing to work under a woman. He was slipping a big bush knife along the ground

---

[47] A small nearby ranch which Louis had leased. It provided the Stevensons with oranges, cocoanuts and bananas while their own trees were maturing; also grazing land for their cows and horses.

today, instead of pulling the weeds up by their roots. When I went down and took the knife from him his countenance was truly ferocious and he seemed not in the least mollified that I had carried down with me a very fine mango brought up by the fathers a few days ago. I was eating one and happened to see Fusi's eyes fixed longingly upon the fruit.

The pantry boy has a very bad leg, a scrofula, it looks like. He has had the same thing before, he says, and Mr. Claxton cured him, so I sent him down to be treated. We have heard nothing today from Mr. Gurr and do not know whether the operation took place or not. I trust it is over, and well over. A couple of the hurricane shutters were brought up today. There was some trickery about the fetching of them by the bush town people. Lloyd said to Faliali, "I know now why you bush people have a bad name," a most insulting remark. Lloyd is still quite ill from the effects of his walk around the boundaries. Belle made a little oil-skin for Austin, as he had expressed a desire for one for Christmas, and I oiled it today. We have bought some Samoan honey, which tastes more of burnt molasses than anything else. I am to have two hives of bees when I can send for them. The work on the roads is taking off all the men, so that it is difficult to get things up from town.

[DECEMBER] 23RD

Have been for a day or so at Mr. Haggard's new rooms in the old Rugi house; a charming place, but the air close and deathly. Lloyd and Louis both confessed to having harboured a sickening doubt as to whether we should not have bought that place instead of Vailima. Now they are satisfied, for it is certainly not a healthy situation. It was because so many people had died there that made me object to the purchase. The house is entered through a great arch closed by immense iron doors, and all the windows are barred with iron. We might have had ballrooms and a theatre, to say nothing of a separate house for Belle and cottages for servants and a studio of noble proportions, stable, etc. Just below our windows is the cottage for the billiard table. There Mr. Dowdney lived; but now a seal is on the door, for poor Dowdney is supposed to be dead. Sixty days before the seals were put on, he started away, I believe for Rose Island,[48] in a tiny schooner that was so crank that all the chains and heavy things had to be carried below in a squall. The captain was drunk when they started and carried drink with him. The last man that sailed her refused to do so again; he said she was too unsafe. Of course there is the remote chance that the passengers may be cast ashore somewhere and are unable to send a message. The terrible thing is that there are three half-caste children lost. Their sister, frightened lest they might get influenza, sent them off without the knowledge of their father.

[DECEMBER] 24TH

Last night Louis went to see Mr. Cusack-Smith. While there, Asai and another chief came in to say good-bye. They were about starting for [blank] with something like a hundred and fifty armed men to take possession of the women, children and old men of the Mataafa faction. There is much feeling on the subject. There can be no object in this movement but to provoke Mataafa to reprisals, when the man-of-war would instantly shell Malie. Talolo came down on an errand. He tells me that Mataafa knows that the women and children are to be seized.

[DECEMBER] 25TH

Christmas day. Washerwomen came with presents—tapa and fan. Henry with baskets and tapa. Fanua's women with tapa, a woolly mat, and a very valuable family mat. It is fine and soft like silk, almost brown with age, and has a goodly number of holes in it, the latter proving its antiquity and worth. Henry wished advice. He had come from Savaii for that purpose. He had seen, himself, a letter from the king, calling upon all his subjects to be ready for war and also giving the order to seize the families of the enemy.

"What am I to do?" asked Henry.

I believe he thought in his heart that he would be told to fight for Mataafa, as he told me afterwards the Vailima family are everywhere called Mataafa-ites. Louis, with my concurrence, said he must go out with his people, and the more particularly as they are loyal, he must fight for the reigning king.

[48] Near Samoa.

"That was what I thought myself," said Henry, apparently much relieved. But he wanted to consult us further. He said that the order mentioned the fact that the men must find their own ammunition and arms.

"And I haven't got anything at all," said Henry with a troubled laugh.

It was a pistol he was after. Louis thoughtlessly said, "Oh, I will buy you one," but he soon remembered that by the English law he could not.

Henry's affair with the neighbour has been amicably settled according to Louis's advice. He asked permission to come to us for advice if there were any new and confusing developments. Naturally, he would not like to be sent to attack babes and old men.

Simi came in with a message. "Well, Simi," said I, "you come fight picaninnies?" I am pleased to think that expression will be repeated to every Samoan he sees. Talolo tells me that the soldiers stopped at Tanugamanono all night, and at about six in the morning he saw them marching past at the turn of our road. Today, Lloyd and I leaned over the balcony to look at a couple of pretty women. One of them took that moment to change her lava lava. A pull and she was naked as she was born. Some instinct made her look up, and I must say she was somewhat startled. I was rather startled myself.

When Joe first arrived in Samoa he was invited to a picnic by a native lady. Arrived at the spot, he found himself the only man present amidst a bevy of native beauties, all of them very handsomely and correctly dressed for the occasion. A sudden shower came up, and what was Malosi's [49] surprise to behold all these elegant ladies pulling their garments over their heads and handing them one by one to an old dame, who hastily crushed the discarded robes into a large calabash. Satisfied that their finery was safe, the ladies then proceeded to clothe themselves after the fashion of Mother Eve, that is, with leaves.

In the morning we received a note from Joe and one from Belle to say that our people were wild with delight over their presents. When

[49] Native name for Joe Strong.

Lloyd and I were coming down to Apia we forded the river at the plantation (Hufnagel's) and made a different route. As we were crossing a broad open common, Lloyd cried out to me, "Look at the bird!" Just in front of us, on a low white stump, sat a large white owl. As we came quite close to it, it slowly turned round its head and gazed steadily at us for some moments with big, solemn, questioning eyes. It was very like an aitu. Perhaps it was one. I told this tale to Louis, which reminded him to tell me of a creature he had met in his study. It was one of those enormous salmon-coloured moths whose hearts, or something in their inside, beats against your hand when you hold them, so loudly that you can hear them. Louis cannot bear the sight of them because they are marked like a skeleton. I suppose they are a variety of the death's head moth. The wretched thing was determined to burn itself at the lamp.

I am long past trying to save the ordinary moth from its usual fate, but a moth as big as a hummingbird we can none of us bear to see going to such a terrible fate. When the little moths are scorched, it is easy enough to kill them, but it would be a brave man who could put his foot on a salmon death's head. This moth of Louis's evaded him continually and at last dropped to the floor, apparently under the table. Louis got down on his knees to look for him and to his surprise discovered that the table seemed to be on fire. He could see a beautiful glowing point, which on further examination turned out to be the insect's *eye!*

At about five o'clock we went to dine with Mr. Moors. As usual, the entertainment was delightful. None of us know what it is about the Moors' parties that makes them so enjoyable, but enjoyable they always are. There was only one person at dinner outside of our two families, a man from Savaii, but other people came in the evening, among others, Mr. Willis and his enchanting wife Laulii, and Fanua, both very well dressed in *papalagi*[50] clothes. Louis and Joe were asked to play upon their pipes. By some mistake Louis had a wrong pipe, but all the same they played away; at least sometimes one did, sometimes the other, and occasionally by some chance they played together. For such a feeble performance I never heard anything

[50] Foreign; also foreigners.

worse. Then Belle, being pressed for a recitation, repeated a few verses of Louis's. Miss Moors recited, really very well, Louis's "Christmas at Sea," and Austin poured out, with much dramatic fire and a full loud voice, "Lochinvar." There was very pretty dancing by little Miranda Moors and singing and Samoan dancing by Mrs. Gurr and Mrs. Willis. Mrs. W has a very good voice and sang with much spirit. They gave a sitting dance and one with clubs. In the sitting dance came a rather rowdy whoop which was given by Mrs. Willis with full spirit and yet with no vulgarity at all. Fanua shrieked the whoop. Two serving women came in to beat time on the floor in dancing. Both Fanua and Laulii have been maids of the village. Fanua says that she used to have nine singing girls to accompany her, one of them being our Faauma.

In the evening, at about ten, the guests departed, I with my shoes and stockings off, for it had come on to rain. We talked till late, Lloyd telling me a thing I did not know. At the time of the trial of the "criminal classes," as Lloyd called him, the *Alicia*, no doubt fraudulently wrecked, was sold at auction. The criminal classes wished to bid for her, and was allowed by Luiessii to leave the place of trial for the purpose, and returned the proud possessor of the wreck.

[DECEMBER] 26TH

The horses came down early, and the mare, as I supposed, was sent down to Moors for Belle, who had stayed there all night. We took the back road through the swamp, as the ford is more than I like to try just at the mouth of the river. There seemed something very odd about my horse, at which I had hardly looked when I mounted. It was the mare that had been given to Belle yesterday! Harold, the consular horse, had been sent to her. She would mount, as I had done, without looking at the horse, and, with Austin behind her, would start for home, the first time she had ever ventured to ride alone. Some of Harold's little ways (there is no harm in him) would frighten her to death and she might fall off, and at any rate was sure to have a miserable frightened ride. There was no telling what she might do when she discovered that she was riding a strange horse. Nor did I know how Harold would take the addition of Austin. To go back meant to lose about as much time as to go forward, so on we dashed, galloping as though for dear life, through mud and water and bush. Fortunately Louis arrived in time to stop Belle. I went on to Vailima drenched to the skin by a heavy shower. I was much alarmed about Louis. The last I saw of him he was holding his side with his hand and I saw that he had just had symptoms of a hemorrhage. It did him no harm, however.

We were most happy to be at pleasant Vailima again. Talolo, our gentle Talolo, confessed that he drank too much at Mr. Moors' on Christmas night (we lent him to Mr. Moors to help wait at table) and frightened his family when he went home to sleep.

"I lose my lava lava twice," he said, and his necktie for good. His mother was afraid of him and ran to a neighbour's, where she stayed all night. In fact, the whole family fled. We are told that a Samoan drunk is a very dangerous person.

Belle asked Talolo where he got the liquor.

"Mr. Moors' cook," he said, "he give me wine and beer, and then old Mrs. Moors shouted two bottles of champagne."

I wondered what that rigidly, frigidly, blue-ribbon old lady would say if she knew she had been accused of "shouting champagne." No doubt it was the humourous aspect of the thing that made the cook lay his theft upon the old lady, with whom he is at daggers drawn.

[DECEMBER] 28TH

Henry came in yesterday to say good-bye, and after much beating about the bush said that he wanted to take Simi with him to Savaii. It was a blow, as Simi is one of our best men. Joe has quarrelled with Fusi, who has not turned up again. In the evening I said to Simi, "Well, so you are off to Savaii."

"No!" roared Simi, "no go Savaii. Stop Vailima!"

"Mr. Strong will be glad to hear that," said I. "He was in despair at losing his best cacao man."

This morning Joe left Simi in charge of some planting, and he said he could not have done it better or more quickly himself. No doubt Simi wished to show that the compliment was not ill-bestowed.

Talolo has the Fiji man for a new broom. Tomas is his name. The first day he was here helping with the planting, he took occasion to assure me that he was no common Samoan, nor a disgusting Tongan.

"Me no Samoan man; me no Tongan man; me Fiji man. Me no German man, *no!* Me—" and here he proudly struck his breast, "me Britain!"

He is a fine handsome young fellow with eyes too much opened, like an insane person's. I trust his intellects are all right.

Last night, being Sunday, we had a service in the dining room. To our surprise, Simi, who is a popee, came in with Lafaele, Faauma and Lauilo.

With the letters by the S. F. mail packet has come a leader in the *Times* on Louis's letter concerning the president and his dynamite scheme. It looks as though the president was really finished. The *Times* article was very clever and very amusing.

Today Louis and Lloyd rode down to town, coming back in time for dinner. Lloyd came ahead of Louis, fetching Fanua with him. I had sent her Christmas box by her boy, who brought a note for Belle—an embroidered white gown, a very pretty one, indeed; I gave her the best I had. She says Mr. Gurr is now able to eat with a spoon. Heretofore he has had to suck through a straw. I was interrupted by the feeling that a horse was loose. I am never mistaken in that. It was that miserable stallion of Henry's. I have been told that if a horse eats one leaf of the [word illegible] in front of the house, he will instantly fall dead. I think that brute has eaten several bushes of it, and is ready for more. I went over in the rain to call Lafaele. All were asleep. I called him softly but woke Faauma instead. "Lafaele," she said in his ear. "Ah!" he replied in a sleepily startled voice, and then added, "Yes, Madame, what is it?" with the most perfect good nature, knowing that he would only be wakened at my request. He says no more about going to Tonga. I think Faauma has stopped that. Simi refuses, indignantly, to go to Savaii.

[DECEMBER] 31ST

Belle went down to the fancy ball that should have come off on the Prince of Wales' birthday but has been put off several times on account of the influenza. Louis went also, but came home again with the information that a hurricane was expected. All the hurricane shutters were put up and a great protection they proved, though the house was dark and airless.

1892

1ST JANUARY

Beginning to blow very heavily. In the afternoon a large tree falls
with a great crash, also a number of smaller ones. There is a curious
exhilaration in the air. The natives stand about in clusters, smiling,
and when anything comes down, shout with glee.

L O U I S . JANUARY 1ST

On Dec. 30th I rode down with Belle to go to (if you please)
the Fancy Ball. When I got to the beach, I found the barometer was
below 29°, the wind still in the east and steady, but a huge offensive
continent of clouds and vapours forming to leeward. It might be
a hurricane; I dared not risk getting caught away from my work, and
leaving Belle, returned at once to Vailima. Next day—yesterday—it
was a tearer; we had storm shutters up; I sat in my room and wrote
by lamplight—ten pages, if you please, seven of them draft, and
some of these compiled from as many as seven different and con-
flicting authorities, so that was a brave day's work. About two a huge
tree fell within sixty paces of our house; a little after, a second went;
and we sent out boys with axes and cut down a third, which was
too near the house, and buckling like a fishing rod. . . . All night it
blew; the roof was continually sounding under missiles; in the morning the verandahs were half full of branches torn from the forest.
There was a last very wild squall about six; the rain, like a thick white
smoke, flying past the house in volleys, and as swift, it seemed, as
rifle balls; all with a strange, strident hiss, such as I have only heard
before at sea, and, indeed, thought to be a marine phenomenon. Since

then the wind has been falling with a few squalls, mostly rain. But our road is impassable for horses; we hear a schooner has been wrecked and some native houses blown down in Apia, where Belle is still and must remain a prisoner. Lucky I returned while I could! But the great good is this; much breadfruit and bananas have been destroyed; if this be general through the islands, famine will be imminent; and *whoever blows the coals, there can be no war.* Do I then prefer a famine to a war? you ask. Not always, but just now. I am sure the natives do not want a war; I am sure a war would benefit no one but the white officials, and I believe we can easily meet the famine—or at least that it can be met. That would give our officials a legitimate opportunity to cover their past errors.

JANUARY 2ND

I woke this morning to find the blow quite ended. The heaven was all a mottled grey; even the east quite colourless; the downward slope of the island veiled in wafts of vapour, blue like smoke; not a leaf stirred on the tallest tree; only, three miles away below me on the barrier reef, I could see the individual breakers curl and fall, and hear their conjunct roaring rise, as it still rises at 1 P.M., like the roar of a thoroughfare close by.

F A N N Y . [JANUARY] 2ND

Towards evening thunder is heard, and we know the gale is over.

[JANUARY] 3RD

Puffy, and squalls of rain, but that is all. It is proposed that Lloyd should take a holiday and go to San Francisco.

[JANUARY] 4TH

Clear the road in the morning and send for Belle in the afternoon. Joe planting cacao. In the evening I am told that both the Fiji man (he is now kitchen boy, but is to help with cacao when required) and Simi have been spitting blood. The Fiji man seems to have a touch of pneumonia, and Simi, who stoops slightly and has a tense voice (both bad signs, to my thinking) has, I think, broken a small blood vessel. I was very angry to find that the washerwoman had, the night before, taken both men's blankets to iron upon and never returned them, so the poor fellows, both ill, had been sleeping that really cold night without a stitch of any sort, their lava lavas being soaking wet. I could not find the Fijian, but Simi came to see what could be done for him, evidently very much alarmed. He seemed to think that he must be dying when he heard we had asked about his symptoms. Louis, after tapping over Simi's lungs until he found a dull place, clapped his cupping glass upon the spot. Simi sank to the ground, where he reclined against some bricks and the cacao baskets with an expression of terror that was partly real and partly assumed. By that time the whole family and most of the natives had gathered round us, which increased his alarm. A lighted candle was brought out that Talolo might see how to use the glass, as we meant that Simi should keep it on after he went to his own place. Simi's face was a study as he perceived the cup to be partly full of his own flesh. Everybody shouted with laughter and Simi murmured something in a fainting voice, which, interpreted, was to the effect that "This was all very fine, but how was that thing to be got off?"

"It doesn't hurt you, Simi?" asked Louis.

The glass was an arching glass cup with an India rubber bulb to draw out the air; but Simi protested, looking askance at the glass as though it were a deadly serpent, that the pain was awful. It was then taken off and tried on the other men's breasts to their great delight, that Talolo might learn how to use it. Once again it was put on Simi, who sank back so weakly that the bricks slipped from under him. The last we saw of the party they were escorting Simi to bed, shouting and laughing and dancing as they went.

[JANUARY] 5TH

Packing all day for Lloyd. Louis went to town and came back without his horse, which disappeared from in front of Mr. Haggard's house. Mr. H has returned. Talolo has taken the horse (that Henry gave me) as a present from me to his family, with the understanding that if it comes back here it will be instantly shot. His family much pleased, and we much relieved.

[JANUARY] 6TH

Packing, and Joe planting cacao. Louis goes to Apia, and Lloyd also to stay all night, that he may be in time for the mail boat in the morning. Louis comes back on Mary Hamilton's[1] horse, having now lost mine. I send the boys out by moonlight to look for Harold (my horse is named Harold) and they come back with him in triumph. "It's a good horse, that consular horse," says Talolo.

[JANUARY] 7TH

Very tired in the morning, so Belle goes down alone to see Lloyd off. Joe very proud, having planted his thousandth tree today. The steamer, belated by the gale, does not come in until the middle of the afternoon. Joe and I jump on our horses, and as fast as the road will permit, hasten down to Apia. We hear the second whistle just before we arrive, and hunt frantically for a boat, but anything that floats is circling around the ship. Suddenly we spy the American consul just coming in at one of the landings.

"Mr. Blacklock, lend me your boat," I cry, and in another moment we are leaping over the water, the American flag over us. Passing the German man-of-war, we see that they are at target practice, firing right across the harbour, a most dangerous proceeding. We have no time to make a round-about course, and just as we pass, a shot sings behind us. The ship was still holding on and we swung alongside her in good style. The same thought suddenly struck both Joe and me. We were delaying the ship for a supposed consular message. The stairs were instantly dropped and at the same moment we saw Lloyd running forward to greet us.

"What shall we do?" asked Joe with an embarrassed smile.

"Get away as fast as we can," I returned, and we got away.

Belle and Fanua and Laulii and Miss Moors were at the landing. They had all been on board, also Talolo, who had begged that he might be taken. The captain made much of Talolo and gave him a glass of champagne with lumps of ice in the glass. It was a great day for Talolo, who had never seen ice before. When he went, a knot of people followed him to listen to his naïve remarks on the wonders he saw.

Last night Belle heard very sweet and mournful singing in the natives' room. As she passed the door she looked in. All were under

---

[1] Native woman, widow of Captain Hamilton.

their mosquito nets. Talolo recited the words verse by verse, and then all sang them.

"What is this?" asked Belle.

"We are singing," said Talolo, "Farewell to Loia."[2]

"What do you sing?" asked Belle again.

It was explained the song was told to go to France and look for Loia; but Loia was not there.

"Then go to Tonga and search for him there"; but Loia was not in Tonga.

"Then go all over the world and hunt until you find Loia, and give him pleasant dreams."

[JANUARY] 8TH

Have been out looking at my coffee trees with Mrs. Stevenson. We counted 80 going very well, and 226 in the nursery more than ready to go out. I am to have some of Joe's men tomorrow afternoon.

[JANUARY] 9TH

Today Mary Hamilton and a high chief named Mamea[3] came to lunch. We talked to Mamea (a very intelligent man) about many things, amongst others of our dear old friend, King Tembinoka, of whose death we have just heard. Tembinoka, it seems, had an abscess in his leg and one of his doctors lanced it with an unclean fish bone, which caused blood poisoning and the death of the king in great agony. While he was dying he arranged that Paul was to succeed him, Simon to be regent. "Tom White" is now Simon's prime minister. The king directed Paul to lay his body in the ground in the center of his new house, where the little king is to live. I can hear him say, "More better; make him fraid." He thought Paul would be safer so. We think of sending for Tembinoka's former governor (Rubarm?).[4] When we were last visiting King T, R came to me and implored me to take him away. He asked whether in case he should stow away on the ship I would let him stay with me in Samoa. I refused, saying that I was the king's friend and could not, therefore, have anything to do with the affair. R was too important a man for the king to

[2] Native name for Lloyd Osbourne.
[3] "A fine, powerfully built, handsome man, who speaks English perfectly."— Mrs. M. I. Stevenson.
[4] Raheboam.

lose. I do not care at all for Simon, and having R would be of no use to the haughty little King Paul. Mamea spoke of his pleasure in seeing us all in the native gown. He thought we set a good example to the native women.

[JANUARY] 11TH

Planting coffee the better part of the day. It looks very well, though some of Paul's plantings are dead. Simi, who went to Apia with Joe to have the horses shod, nearly broke down on the way with fatigue. He has been spitting more blood. I feel very anxious about him. We have never had a better man on the place, and I like him, besides. I had Lafaele and two stunted Savaii men to help in the coffee planting. While we were at work, Lafaele was telling me the war talk amongst the natives. When the Fiji man came to me on an errand I saw that he had his nose blackened, and stripes of black under his eyes. The war, according to Lafaele, is now really going to begin, and he declares the first battle is going to take place very close to us. "Now Madame—*please* Madame—you look out. Samoan man fight, he allee same devil—now *please*, you look out." By much questioning I gathered from Lafaele that we are marked for vengeance as Mataafas by the Malietoas and that at the first excuse the Malietoas mean to come here and demand all Mataafa men, to shoot them on the spot. Lafaele begged me, if fighting began, to send Talolo to the Catholic mission through the bush, as he was the first they would be after. I think there he is right. If there is trouble near at hand, Talolo, all of whose family are now with M, would, or might be, in danger.

While we were talking, thunder was rolling dully round the horizon, sounding very like the noise of battle. A louder volley startled Lafaele, who looked at the sky with alarmed interest. There was not a cloud to be seen, nor did I detect a single flash of lightning.

"It is strange," I said.

"No, Madame," said Lafaele, "that all right; that no thunder. War come sure now; that no thunder, that devils fight up in sky. Mean war come quick."

One of our boys was an eyewitness of a portent of war. In the village of Fagalua some people were sitting in council at the home of a chiefess, when an eel ran round the house. Some tried to catch it, when others cried out, "Do not touch it, it has no head!" All drew back in horror and watched it, and as it returned to the water, behold it had its head properly on its neck.

Belle went today to a bathing party on the invitation of Mary Hamilton. There were present a number of young native women who were surprised and delighted to find that Belle could swim like themselves. Laulii asked her whether she was a half-caste, and if not, why she was so dark. Then all said they wished me to know how grateful they were to me. Before we came here all the women married to white men were expected to dress in European fashion, otherwise they were not considered respectable. To their delight and surprise, I and all the rest of us women appeared in native dresses. But the climax seemed to be my going to a Christmas party in a very handsome black silk *holaku* with embroidered yoke and sleeves. The husbands have removed the taboo, and several of the native ladies are to have fine silk gowns made in their own pretty graceful fashion. Corsets must be agony to the poor creatures, and most of them are only the more clumsy and awkward for these European barbarities.

Mary Hamilton says she once went out in the street in Sydney in native dress, where she was followed by a crowd of boys shouting, "Hey! there goes a woman in her night-gown!" The *holaku* is only the old-fashioned sacque, which happened, fortunately, to be the mode in England when the missionaries first came to the South Seas. It was loose, cool and graceful, and so well suited the natives that it became the regulation garment of the South Pacific. I am very glad I have inadvertently done so much good.

During this period of her life Fanny often suffered from gallstones and was uncertain of the nature of her difficulty. In later years, after she had had the stones removed by a London surgeon, she wrote to Dora Williams about her former trouble. Mrs. Williams had said that rumors of her eccentricity abounded in certain circles and Fanny felt impelled to defend herself. She explained that she had had a swelling of her abdomen which she had wanted to hide from her family, and for this reason had worn the *holaku* and not in order to make a stir by being eccentric. She also said that the reason she went barefooted at certain times in Samoa was to save shoes during the rainy seasons.

Belle received a note from the Cusack-Smiths, asking for the loan of one of her play books, as they are going to get up more amateur theatricals. Every excuse for not taking a part that Belle could have thought of was put forward as a reason for not asking her to join them. It would have been more graceful to ask her and allow her to make her own excuses. It is evident from their conduct at the time of the last play as well as this that they don't want her; which is odd, as she plays much better than anyone here, and would make the affair a certain success. Perhaps Mrs. C-Smith is afraid that Belle might want the best part, which she always takes herself.

[JANUARY] 12TH

Planted coffee all morning and caught a cold. It is gusty and raining and the barometer is falling. Well, I am as ready as I can be if anything is coming. I have all the upstairs storm shutters painted, but the downstairs ones I could not lift, and I should need a ladder to reach the upper part. I must make shift to do them soon or they may warp. Joe has gone to lie down, leaving the men to fill baskets for cacao seed we expect the day after tomorrow. Captain Hufnagel says he has plenty of breadfruit trees if the firm will allow us to have them. A few days ago I sent Talolo and Lauilo to get large breadfruits from the bush. They came back with five beauties. When they were all safely planted, Lauilo told me that they had taken them from a Samoan garden when there was no one but an old woman to guard the premises.

"Old woman make big fuss," said Lauilo. "She plenty cross, but we don't mind."

Mary Hamilton has promised to see the people of the house and arrange what we shall do in the way of reparation. This evening Louis is going to begin to give lessons to such of the men as wish to learn. Lafaele and Lauilo are the two most anxious. Several simple drawing books with fair paper for copying on have come, and are now in Talolo's hands. He has quite a taste for drawing and is enchanted with his presents. It is almost too dark to write.

FEBRUARY 19

Many things have happened since I last made an entry in my diary. Lloyd, who seemed tired out, has been sent off to San Francisco. He had only been a little while gone when, to my great grief, his horse Macfarlane and my dear little Harold both died, Marfarlane first, and then Harold. Captain Tierney and his wife Lizzie came from Apiang[5] on the last *Archer* and have been several times to see us. Everybody in love with Tierney. Before he said good-bye on his last visit he asked to have the whole family sit together on the verandah, so that he might carry away with him a complete picture in his mind.

One day Joe and I found three horses in the large paddock, there against orders. They belonged to Simi, to Joe's half-caste man, and Lauilo. Joe and Louis tied up the horses and took them to the pound, where the men had to pay a dollar and a half apiece to get them out. Lauilo wept about his horse and said that Lloyd had given him permission to keep it in Vailima. As there was some doubt on the subject, though, his horse, a lovely little mare, was sent with the rest, but Lauilo had money given him privately to redeem it. I am told, to my embarrassment, that he proposes to make me a present of the mare, which I had before tried to buy from him.

We have now a black fellow named Arrick, hired from the Germans, whom we hope to teach to wash.[6] He has a rather good, shining black face, and sparkling eyes and white teeth. Joe calls him the "emblem of purity," which has been shortened to "the emblem."

This afternoon Louis was reading something aloud when his attention was directed to a brown boy standing out on the lawn in a drenching cold rain. When asked what he wanted, he replied, "Me stop here." He was brought in on the verandah and questioned further. It seemed he was a runaway and for a time had been hiding in the bush. Dines the butcher found him and took him in, and now he had run away from Dines. While he was wandering about in the bush, he said he found another runaway boy from the firm.

"Where is he?" we asked.

"Hiding over garden by the gate," was the gist of his reply.

The other boy was brought up, an impudent-looking young black,

[5] One of the Gilbert Islands.

[6] Arrick became a favorite at Vailima. According to Fanny (in her *The Cruise of the Janet Nichol*, 1914, p. 35) Arrick some years later died of homesickness, a disease the existence of which she came to believe in.

greatly terrified. It was strange to see the brown boy's nose grow pale with emotion. We let them stay the night and our kitchen boys ran to make hot tea and prepare food for them. I also gave them some dry stuff instead of the scraps of wet rag they wore tied round their loins. I am afraid the kitchen boys will be the death of Arrick, our lawful black. He is given the place of honour at their table and downs most of their food. Talolo and Lauilo, the dear softies, stand behind him and press the things on him. They eat before us and when Arrick comes into the dining room to help wait at table his stomach is distended till it sticks out in front of him like a tumour. The two runaways are very embarrassing; we cannot betray them and we cannot keep them.

[FEBRUARY] 20TH

Joe is jubilant. Ever since the horses were taken to the pound he has been hoping to catch Lafaele's horse trespassing. Last night, to his joy, there he found Lafaele's mare and colt loose on the lawn. He caught and tethered them himself and sent Talolo down to the pound with them this morning. I forgot to mention an incident that occurred yesterday. Lauilo told me that a man had found human remains in the bush behind the pig fence. The man chanced to come up to see Lafaele, and Louis made the fellow take him to the spot. Sure enough the bones of a man were there, just above my coffee plantation, but the strange thing was that there were two skulls to one skeleton. They were plainly the bones of a warrior who had taken his enemy's head and, desperately wounded himself, had crawled into the bush to die with his prize. Louis means to put up a stone over the remains.

L O U I S . 25TH MARCH

Heaven knows what day it is, but I am ashamed, all the more as your letter from Bournemouth of all places—poor old Bournemouth! —is to hand, and contains a statement of pleasure in my letters which I wish I could have rewarded with a long one. What has gone on? A vast of affairs, of a mingled, strenuous, inconclusive, desultory char-

acter; much waste of time, much riding to and fro, and little trans-
acted or at least peracted.

Let me give you a review of the present state of our live stock. —
Six boys in the bush; six souls about the house. Talolo, the cook,
returns again to-day, after an absence which has cost me about twelve
hours of riding, and I suppose eight hours' solemn sitting in council. . . . Lauilo is steward. Both these are excellent servants; we gave
a luncheon party when we buried the Samoan bones, and I assure
you all was in good style, yet we never interfered. The food was good,
the wine and dishes went round as by mechanism. — Steward's
assistant and washman. Arrick, a New Hebridee black boy, hired
from the German firm; not so ugly as most, but not pretty neither;
not so dull as his sort are, but not quite a Crichton. When he came
first, he ate so much of our good food that he got a prominent belly.
Kitchen assistant, Tomas (Thomas in English), a Fiji man, very
tall and handsome, moving like a marionette with sudden bounds,
and rolling his eyes with sudden effort. — Washerwoman and
precentor, Helen,[7] Tomas's wife. This is our weak point; we are
ashamed of Helen; the cook-house blushes for her; they murmur
there at her presence. She seems all right; she is not a bad-looking,
strapping wench, seems chaste, is industrious, has an excellent taste
in hymns—you should have heard her read one aloud the other day,
she marked the rhythm with so much gloating, dissenter sentiment.
What is wrong, then? says you. Low in your ear—don't let the papers
get hold of it—she is of no family. None, they say; literally a common
woman. Of course, we have out-islanders, who *may* be villeins; but
we give them the benefit of the doubt, which is impossible with
Helen of Vailima; our blot, our pitted speck. The pitted speck I have
said is our precentor. It is always a woman who starts Samoan song;
the men who sing second do not enter for a bar or two. Poor, dear
Faauma, the unchaste, the extruded Eve of our Paradise, knew only
two hymns; but Helen seems to know the whole repertory, and the
morning prayers go far more lively in consequence. — Lafaele, provost
of the cattle. The cattle are Jack, my horse, quite converted, my wife
rides him now, and he is as steady as a doctor's cob; Tifaga Jack, a

[7] Fanny's Elena.

circus-horse, my mother's piebald, bought from a passing circus; Belle's mare, now in childhood or next door, confound the slut! Musu—amusingly translated the other day "don't want to," literally cross, but always in the sense of stubbornness and resistance—my wife's little dark-brown mare, with a white star on her forehead, whom I have been riding of late to steady her—she has no vices, but is unused, skittish and uneasy, and wants a lot of attention and humouring; lastly (of saddle horses) Luna—not the Latin *moon*, the Hawaiian *overseer*, but it's pronounced the same—a pretty little mare too, but scarce at all broken, a bad bucker, and has to be ridden with a stock-whip and be brought back with her rump criss-crossed like a clan tartan; the two cart horses, now only used with pack saddles; two cows, one in the straw (I trust) to-morrow, a third cow, the Jersey—whose milk and temper are alike subjects of admiration—she gives good exercise to the farming saunterer, and refreshes him on his return with cream; two calves, a bull, and a cow; God knows how many ducks and chickens, and for a wager not even God knows how many cats; twelve horses, seven horses, five kine: is not this Babylon the Great which I have builded? Call it *Subpriorsford*.

During March Louis was at work on *David Balfour*. Meanwhile, as usual, there were meetings with chiefs, a few feasts, and much political gossip. In early April there was an interesting domestic drama at Vailima, involving Talolo and Faauma, Lafaele's wife, as the result of which Faauma left her husband, and Talolo was sent away. A new cook, David, was tried out, but was found inadequate. After a few days Lafaele and Talolo made it up and the latter returned to the household, much to the relief of the Stevensons, who had missed a very good cook. Faauma refused to return to her Lafaele.

April 7 was Lloyd's birthday, and the event was celebrated in native style. The native boys twisted wreaths and garlands round his head, neck and waist, and wreaths were heaped on the lunch table in decoration. The center piece of the table was a roast pig with a scarlet hibiscus blossom on its forehead and two green garlands encircling its plump body. There was an unusual heat spell which tired everyone about a week later. On the 16th Circus Jack was found dead. Later that day Malietoa himself, accompanied by Laulii as interpreter, and attended by three soldiers dressed in white coats and trousers and armed with rifles and bayonets, visited Vailima. Malietoa also wore white, with long yellow leather leggings reaching above the knee. The "king" stayed to lunch and drank kava with Louis, the latter a sign of good will. In the afternoon Louis went down to Apia to meet the steamer in case Rudyard Kipling should be on it, but the Kiplings did not come and the relations between Louis and Kipling remained purely epistolary ones.

F A N N Y . APRIL 30

I am puzzled how to catch up with my diary. So many things have taken place since last I wrote. We had a funeral over the bones found in the bush. Mr. Sewall and his father, and Mr. Haggard, came the following Sunday to our funeral. The bones were neatly packed in a box, a grave dug, and after lunch we all went up in procession to the bush. Louis made a speech, followed by the younger Mr. Sewall, who was not so felicitous as usual. For one thing, he "hoped we might often meet together on similar occasions." Afterwards we took them to see the plantation. A little way into the bush, Joe had cleared a space by the banks of a stream, and there we found a table with a cloth spread, and on it tumblers, beer and young cocoanuts and peeled oranges. Around the table were benches, with fresh leaves to sit upon. A number of our men who were too superstitious to go the funeral, and a contingent of black boys from one of the plantations, on a visit to Arrick, were waiting in wreaths to serve us. Mr. Haggard made a speech before we parted, a little more to the point than the consul's.

We have had trouble with our boys, and Lauilo is sent away for good—or bad. Talolo has been taken back, Lafaele turned away and also received again into the family. Tomas's wife, Elena, is taken on to do the washing. Simi has been having hemorrhages and at present is doing Lauilo's work. He is very haughty, anxious to please, and so far incapable. The white heifer has a calf, and the poor circus horse is dead. I had the other horses tethered out to let the grass grow, with the exception of Circus Jack, whom I left in the small paddock alone. Mrs. Stevenson was jealous for him, as she thought the tethered horses were getting the best of the grass, and insisted that he should join them. I said all I could to prevent it, as he was an old horse, and did not understand a rope; but it was of no use.

"Only Cassandraism," said his mistress.

"Very well, it's your horse. Do what you like," I said, "but you are going to kill him."

Two days after, his mangled remains were found at the bottom of the waterfall cliff. He had got himself tied up in the most extraordinary way with the rope, and in his struggles rolled over the cliff. I believe that is all the domestic news.

The political aspect is very troublous. Mr. Sewall fell under the sway of the baron and fled on the next steamer. Mr. Claxton found himself so unpopular that he left (ostensibly for his wife's health— she looked better than I had ever seen her) on the last steamer. His colleague, Mr. Whitmee,[8] was left to represent his sentiments. Unfortunately for Claxton, Mr. W came up to see Louis and is now a convert to the other side. One day, to our surprise, we were told by Laulii that Malietoa wished to pay us a visit. He came, with the queen, and took lunch with us, and day before yesterday we returned the visit. We felt in a dreadfully false position, as we were under promise to visit Mataafa the following Monday.

While we were in town a policeman came up to Louis and said that a boy had come to tell him that Mr. Stevenson was going to Malie.

"Well, what did you say?" asked Louis.

"I said," returned the officer of the peace, "that I did not know anything about Mr. Stevenson's movements."

"That was a very good answer," returned Louis.

The policeman is supposed to be still trying to find out what information he received.

We found Malietoa living in quite a common Samoan house— not even a "chief's house," either in shape or materials. The poor king was much ashamed of it. We could look out from under the eaves of the hut at the fine new house of the president, a rather galling sight, I should fancy, to the cat's-paw king. We had not been there long when a man coming from the president's house presented

[8] Rev. Whitmee of the London Missionary Society.

a small offering in a basket to the queen. I imagined from his manner that he had been sent to see who were the king's guests.

Malietoa lived in the village of Mulinuu, his seat of power. Malie, on the other hand, was the seat of power of Mataafa, the "pretender." These villages and their environs are brilliantly described by Louis in *A Footnote to History:*

Mulinuu is a narrow finger of land planted in cocoa-palms, which runs forth into the lagoon perhaps three-quarters of a mile. To the east is the bay of Apia. To the west, there is, first of all, a mangrove swamp, the mangroves excellently green, the mud ink-black, and its face crawled upon by countless insects and black and scarlet crabs. Beyond the swamp is a wide and shallow bay of the lagoon, bounded to the west by Faleula Point. Faleula is the next village to Malie; so that from the top of some tall palm in Malie it should be possible to descry against the eastern heaven the palms of Mulinuu. The trade wind sweeps over the low peninsula and cleanses it from the contagion of the swamp. Samoans have a quaint phrase in their language; when out of health, they seek exposed places on the shore "to eat the wind," they say; and there can be few better places for such a diet than the point of Mulinuu.

Two European houses stand conspicuous on the harbour side; in Europe they would seem poor enough, but they are fine houses for Samoa. One is new; it was built the other day under the apologetic title of a Government House, to be the residence of Baron Senfft. The other is historical; it was built by Brandeis on a mortgage, and is now occupied by the Chief Justice on conditions never understood, the rumour going uncontradicted that he sits rent free. I do not say it is true, I say it goes uncontradicted; and there is one peculiarity of our officials in a nutshell—their remarkable indifference to their own character. From the one house to the other extends a scattering village for the Faipule or native parliament men. In the days of Tamasese this was a brave place, both his own house and those of the Faipule good, and the whole excellently ordered and approached by a sanded way. It is now like a neglected bush town, and speaks of apathy in all concerned. But the chief scandal of Mulinuu is elsewhere. The house of the president stands just to seaward of the isthmus, where the watch is set nightly, and armed men guard the uneasy slumbers of the government. On the landward side there stands a monument to the poor German lads who fell at Fangalii, just beyond which the passer-by may chance to observe a little house standing backward from the road. It is such a house as a commoner might use in a bush village; none could dream that it gave shelter even to a family chief; yet this is the palace of Malietoa-Natoaitele-Tamasoalii Laupepa, king of Samoa. As you sit in his company under this humble shelter, you shall see, between the posts, the new house of the president. His Majesty himself beholds it daily, and the tenor of his thoughts may be divined. The fine house of a Samoan chief is his appropriate attribute; yet, after seventeen months, the government (well housed themselves) have not yet found—have not yet sought —a roof-tree for their sovereign. . . .

The way to Malie lies round the shores of Faleula bay and through a succession of pleasant groves and villages. The road is now cut up by pig fences. Eight times you must leap a barrier of cocoa posts; the take-off and the landing both in a patch of mire planted with big stones, and the stones sometimes reddened with the blood of horses that have gone before. To make these obstacles more annoying, you have sometimes to wait while a black boar clambers sedately over the so-called pig fence. Nothing can more thoroughly depict the worst side of the Samoan character than these useless barriers which deface their only road. It was one of the first orders issued by the government of Mulinuu after the coming of the Chief Justice, to have the passage cleared. It is the disgrace of Mataafa that the thing is not yet done.

The village of Malie is a scene of prosperity and peace. In a very good account of a visit there, published in the *Australasian*, the writer describes it to be fortified; she must have been deceived by the appearance of some pig walls on the shore. There is no fortification, no parade of war. I understand that from one to five hundred fighting men are always within reach; but I have never seen more than five together under arms, and these were the king's guard of honour. A sabbath quiet broods over the well-weeded green, the picketed horses, the troops of pigs, the round or oval native dwellings. Of these there are a surprising number, very fine of their sort: yet more are in the building; and in the midst a tall house of assembly, by far the greatest Samoan structure now in these islands, stands about half finished and already makes a figure in the landscape. No bustle is to be observed, but the work accomplished testifies to a still activity.

The centre-piece of all is the high chief himself, Malietoa-Tuiatua-Tuiaana Mataafa, king—or not king—or king-claimant—of Samoa. All goes to him, all comes from him. Native deputations bring him gifts and are feasted in return. White travellers, to their indescribable irritation, are (on his approach) waved from his path by his armed guards. He summons his dancers by the note of a bugle. He sits nightly at home before a semicircle of talking-men from many quarters of the islands, delivering and hearing those ornate and elegant orations in which the Samoan heart delights. About himself and all his surroundings there breathes a striking sense of order, tranquillity, and native plenty. He is of a tall and powerful person, sixty years of age, white-haired and with a white moustache; his eyes bright and quiet; his jaw perceptibly underhung, which gives him something of the expression of a benevolent mastiff; his manners dignified and thought insinuating, with an air of a Catholic prelate. He was never married, and a natural daughter attends upon his guests. Long since he made a vow of chastity—"to live as our Lord lived on this earth"—and Polynesians report with bated breath that he has kept it. On all such points, true to his Catholic training, he is inclined to be even rigid. Lauati, the pivot of Savaii, has recently repudiated his wife and taken a fairer; and when I was last in Malie, Mataafa (with a strange superiority to his own interests) had but just despatched a reprimand. In his immediate circle, in spite of the smoothness of his ways, he is said to be more respected than beloved; and his influence is the child rather of authority than popularity. No Samoan grandee now living need have attempted that which he has accomplished during the last twelve months with unimpaired prestige, not only to withhold his followers from war, but to send them to be judged in the camps of their enemies on Mulinuu. And it is a matter of debate whether such a triumph of authority were ever possible before. Speaking for myself, I have visited and dwelt in almost every seat of the Polynesian race, and I have met but one man who gave me a stronger impression of character and parts. . . .

I have now sought to render without extenuation the impressions received: of dignity, plenty, and peace at Malie, of bankruptcy and distraction at Mulinuu.

F A N N Y . [APRIL 30—Continued.]

I forgot to say that when the king was up here, Louis apologized for not having visited him, and explained that it was on account of a law made by the president, after the last visit Louis made to his majesty, to the effect that no one should see the king without asking leave from the consuls and receiving permission three days in advance. Of course Louis would not think of asking the consuls' permission to crawl into Malietoa's open hut. It was too ridiculous and undignified. The king said that no such permission was necessary and he asked us all to visit him when and as often as we wished and to pay no attention to any such law. Louis wishes very much to get Malietoa and Mataafa to work together; in no other way can there be peace in Samoa. He tried to see Malietoa alone this morning but did not succeed. He will try again tonight. He means to explain his views first to Malietoa and then to Mataafa. The last political scandals are contained in a letter written by Louis to the *Times*, which I shall pin to this page, as it explains the situation better than I can do.[9]

MAY 12TH

Louis tried in vain to get an interview with Laupepa. Not wishing to speak in the presence of spies, the arrangement was that Louis was to meet the king at Laulii's. Two appointments were made and neither kept. On the 2nd of May Louis, Belle and I, with Talolo, went over to Malie in a boat manned by Malie boys. We rather apprehended that we might be stopped, but though the whole town knew of our destination the policemen passed us with smiles and no

[9] Not pinned in diary. This no doubt refers to Louis's letter to the *Times* of London dated April 9 and April 12, 1892. See Appendix B for the letter.

obstacles were put in our way. In case of staying all night we took a waterproof bag and a big Tokelau bucket with a change of clothes. I took a dark red silk *holaku* trimmed with Persian embroidery, and Belle a dark green silk one to appear in before royalty. A little before we arrived I asked Louis to hold up a shawl for me to dress behind. When my head emerged from my gown I found him with a corner of the shawl in his fingers on his own side of the boat. He said he didn't countenance prudery.

At Malie we found the best of Joe's cacao boys and learned that they, with all the Apia men, were on strike. I was sorry that Joe had let them leave, for they were, in my opinion, quite in the right. Long before we got to the village we could see the middle part of an immense native house rising up like a church spire. Mataafa's own house was the largest and finest I had ever seen, and there were others as large. Louis tried in vain to get an interpreter and was fain to put up with Talolo, who nearly expired with fright and misery, for he could not speak the high-chief language and felt every word he uttered to be an insult to Mataafa. We have been in the habit of referring to Mataafa as "Charley-over-the-water," and toast him as "the king," waving our wine glasses over the water bottle. Talolo had some notion of what this meant and thought it a good plan to do the same. Belle saw him, to her great amusement, take a glass of water he was about to drink, wave it in the air. "Charley-in-the-water," was his mistaken and rather ominous toast.

His translation of Charley's words came to little more than "Mataafa very much surprised." Louis knew enough Samoan to have a little guess of what was going on. A number of faipules arranged themselves in a row at one end of the house, several of them sitting on the floor mats. The kava bowl was in the centre of the group, with the king's talking man beside it. Kava was first given to the king and Louis simultaneously (an extraordinary honour), then to several of the faipules, and then, by the king's orders, to the two "backs of the house" (Belle and me, whom he evidently supposed to be both wives). He was much puzzled as to which was the superior in station. He first gave me the seat of honour after Louis, and then, making a change, placed Belle where I had been. Instead of being served singly, two bowls were offered us at the same moment, so there could be no jealousy. We were thankful to get the kava, having started from Vailima at five in the morning, and consequently very tired. It was, I saw, chewed kava, but I forgot that fact before it came to my turn to drink. Before the bowl was offered to Mataafa, the bearer spilled a libation, and fresh water from a cocoanut shell was sprinkled by hand, then to the right and left. The faipules also sprinkled water to the right and left, but only one poured out a libation, and he did not touch the water.

The talking man and others made polite orations, one of them likening Louis to Jesus Christ, which embarrassed Talolo almost into idiocy. Mataafa suddenly sent for his watch, a fine gold one with a gold chain, and found it to be eleven. He asked what time we had left home and seemed distressed that we should have been so long fasting. An oblong wooden table was brought in and covered with several layers of beautiful tapa, and four chairs placed round it. We were to sit in the chairs which were draped with tapa and stuffs of *papalagi* manufacture, and have a little refreshment before dinner. The king (a Catholic) crossed himself and said grace, when a folded leaf was placed before each of us, containing a mess of arrowroot, cooked with cocoanut milk in hot stones, and we were each provided with a fresh young nut to drink. Mataafa apologized for the coming meal, saying it was all *faa Samoa*, without wine, only pig and fowls and taro. We replied that such a meal was greatly to our taste. The arrowroot was most grateful, but difficult to manage on account of its stickiness, and a little gritty with sand. His majesty advised us not to eat too much for fear of spoiling our appetites for dinner, and recommended a siesta after we had finished. While we ate, his daughter (a natural daughter, he having never married and being now under a vow of chastity) hung an immense curtain of beautiful tapa thick across one end of the room. There we found mats and pillows laid out for us and in a few seconds were all sound asleep.

In an hour and a half or so we wakened simultaneously and found that dinner was awaiting us. I forgot to say that after the speeches were made the talking man offered Louis a bit of kava, an unusual compliment, and that our present, an hundred-pound keg of beef, was presented to Mataafa. Afterwards the talking man went outside and shouted short sentences in a stentorian voice. He was informing the village and the heads of families of the nature and amount of the present received. We ate, as before, from the table, sitting on chairs, and had plates and tumblers, spoons and knives and forks. Talolo, by this time quite ill from the awful responsibility of his position, sat on the floor behind us as our retainer. Talolo is very unhappy because Tomas's wife, Elena, whom we have in to wash, is not of aristocratic birth. He carefully explained that though she belonged to his family, her position was a very humble one. It seems that Talolo's mother is a chief woman, how high I do not know, and that Talolo is himself a budding chief. I asked with much anxiety whether when Talolo "took his name" he might continue working for us. "Not at all," was the answer. "He must not use his hands. But Talolo doesn't want to take his name. He means to be the same as a white man." That was depressing, for Henry always said the same, and now I am told that he has taken his name and is chief over three villages, containing altogether some five hundred adults. Henry's people at first objected to him in every way but now they are delighted with him. I do think some credit is due to Henry's training with us for his success, for he has followed our advice in every particular, though often far removed from what the ordinary Samoan could understand.

But to return to "Charley-over-the-water." After the meal was over, Louis and he, followed by Talolo as interpreter, walked about the village and conversed as well as they could. The path is narrow, and at one place Swann, the chemist from Apia, came dashing by on his horse, almost running down the king and Louis. A guard (two accompanied the king with Winchesters) jumped forward and stopped the rude fellow, who seemed greatly frightened. We heard afterwards that he told at Apia how he was riding quietly along the road, when Louis checked his horse, explaining to him most politely and apologetically that he had better give way to native customs.

After they returned from the walk we all sat on a mat under the eaves and smoked cigarettes. A distant sound of men singing was heard and soon a procession of young men in wreaths, walking two by two, came up to us and deposited each a root of taro, to which they added a couple of young fowls, and the king an immense root of fresh kava. Speeches were made, after which mats were spread out for the dancers, who had been called by the sound of a bugle. There were two long rows of them, with two comic men, and a hunchback, apparently the king's jester. They first sang a song of welcome to us and then sang, danced and acted altogether several pieces, all well done, and some very droll indeed, the hunchback excellent particularly in an imitation of the circus that was here a while ago. Louis could not speak seriously through Talolo, as he had more to say than "much surprised," but agreed to go back to Malie again with a better interpreter. We returned by moonlight in the boat, ardent admirers of Mataafa.

About a week later Louis went again, riding across country to Malie with Charley Taylor as interpreter. They started Saturday evening in a drenching rain and came back Sunday morning, pretty early. Louis had a little better interview with M, advising him to keep the peace and make friends with Laupepa. It seemed that M held the same views. He really wishes to have Laupepa join him at Malie and hold the government there conjointly, and seems to have no intention of making war. In the early morning, about four, at the time the morning bird begins to sing, Louis was awakened by the sound of some sort of pipe playing softly a curious air. Asking afterwards what this meant, Mataafa told Louis that he always had this performance at the time of the singing of the early birds, as it conduced to pleasant dreams. His father, he added, would never allow a bird or animal to be injured and, in consequence was called "the king of the birds."

MAY 16TH

Charley Taylor came yesterday to give a lesson in Samoan to Louis, Belle and Lloyd. There has been a strike among the native workmen, and our boys having left, I have lent Lafaele to Joe. Paatalise, one of the original work boys, has come back. Being afraid to meet the strikers, he stops up here. The cacao is all in and we are going to give the men a feast. Arrick, instead of asking the permission he was sure to get, ran away for his Sunday out. He left Saturday night and, returning just at dusk the next evening, fell in with Lafaele. As the two were walking on the road just out of Tanugamanono they met Louis, riding on my horse Musu. Louis greeted them with a "talofa scri fua" and passed on. What was their terror and surprise to find Louis at home, where he had been all day. Great anxiety and alarm are felt all over the place. It is supposed that Louis sent his other self to see what Arrick and Lafaele were about.

Shortly after the plantation boys left on strike, Joe met Mr. Blacklock's black boy, who was leaving his master on account of a diet too strictly limited to rice. The man wished to come to work at Vailima, so Joe engaged him on the spot and in the afternoon late our new labourer came along the front path, carrying his mat and blanket. "Look at Arrick!" I did look at Arrick in amazement. He was leaning forward, his head protruding like a snake, watching the new arrival, with an expression of animosity that I should not like to see directed towards myself. There were murder and sudden death in the wild fixed eye of as savage a face as I ever saw. Until the new boy was out of sight Arrick remained like a black statue, moving only his lips, which emitted a sort of jabbering hiss such as I have heard a tom cat threaten an enemy with, and which even to cats seems most alarming. "That black fellow is not safe here," said I. And so he seemed to think, for that very night he mysteriously disappeared with his blanket and mat.

MAY 17TH

This afternoon who should appear but the Chief Justice, wishing to see Louis, who had just finished his Samoan history,[10] an ugly story for the C J. I went down and found our visitor talking to Mrs. S as blandly as usual. I said that Louis was not well enough to see anyone, at which Mrs. S became fearfully embarrassed, turning quite pale. So far as the C J was concerned my statement was quite true, as Louis declared to meet the man would cause him a serious illness. I offered the C J wine, beer, chocolate, and finally when he refused even water and a cigarette, I was goaded into saying, "Then you will

[10] A *Footnote to History*.

not break bread with us?" to which he smiled silently and sweetly. But I think that was the case. He informed us that the German man-of-war, the *Sperber*, was in port. I couldn't help wondering whether this might not be a hint to Louis that deportation was possible. It would be rather comic to deport Louis for trying to keep peace in the islands. But I can't think they would be so bold.

Later came Mr. Haggard and Mr. Dumet, the former with a letter sent to him from the foreign office, written to Lord Salisbury. It was a copy of a letter of false accusations against the land commission, sent to Lord Salisbury by Laupepa, patently written by Mr. Claxton, who, on the first hint of danger, found that his wife's health made it necessary for him to leave the islands in the most violent haste. I was amused to see how well Mrs. Claxton looked just before her departure, better than I had ever seen her.

It appears that the government is afraid to attempt the collection of the native taxes. It is long past the time when they should have been called in and now the time is again put off. Also the taxation of the whites is postponed. The whites propose to pay no taxes under the present state of affairs, in which view the consuls uphold them. Mr. Haggard and others say that what money the president has is almost expended, and as the only taxes likely to come in at all are from Mataafa's people the government must very shortly become bankrupt. As neither states nor individuals will lend money to so rotten and hopeless a concern it will be curious to see what will happen, for the position is unprecedented.

MAY 18TH

Mr. Haggard rode up in the evening, but Louis was gone to Laulii's. He said that the C J had received some sort of despatches that had raised his spirits to a point of buoyancy long unknown to that spinner of flimsy webs. It had nothing to do with the land commission; that they knew. At the end of the copy of the letter (a printed copy) from Claxton to Lord Salisbury was a paragraph of instructions to the the C J concerning the men-of-war expected by him. The paragraph was not blotted over, as is usually done when such mistakes occur, but simply scored with a pen and ink cross. I believe it was left purposely for Mr. Haggard to see. At any rate he did see it. On the face of it the C J seemed to have all the power he wished over the warships, but there was a hidden sting in the tail that he has not yet, apparently, discovered. Everything had to be done according to article blank and blank. Now Mr. Haggard has had the pleasure of perusing these articles, and he says that the C J will find himself able to do nothing more than send a police force by a man-of-war to any place where it is needed. We suppose that the C J, who was warned by a letter from Louis when the latter meant to attack him, thought to return the courtesy by letting Louis know the danger he ran of deportation. Louis is going to write a letter to Laupepa on the situation, advising him to make friends with Mataafa, for until the two real heads join hands there must be continual uncertainty as to the continuance of peace. That we are now at peace is owing entirely to the forbearance of Mataafa. It is feared that the C J intends some desperate move to force on war, which is his last chance to save himself or his pocket, which stands him for a soul. It was amusing, when he was here, to see a sudden flash of real interest light up his eyes when I accidentally referred to the fact that we imported all our provisions from the colonies, thereby getting them much cheaper than if we bought them here. It would be much cheaper for him, as he has refused, ever since he came, to pay the customs duties on what he fetches into the country. That was a shameless piece of meanness.

MAY 19TH

The twelfth anniversary of our marriage.[11] It seems impossible. Also impossible that two years ago (or a little more) we came up to live in the bush. Everything looks settled and as though we had been here for many years. We are going to build several Samoan houses for our people. Talolo's little brother is here, learning to take Lauilo's place. Simi has been doing the work, but with the best intentions in the world, he is rapidly destroying. Late yesterday afternoon a policeman (Scanlon, a half-caste) came up to arrest Lloyd and Joe for furious riding. Lloyd pleaded guilty, saying he thought it was all right when he was out of Apia proper, but Joe meanly said it was because they had passed the chief of police, Marguarkt, without

[11] Fanny and Louis were married May 19, 1880 in San Francisco.

bowing. Also he arrested Elena for the theft of a sewing machine. I asked Scanlon what this latter charge meant. He said it was only an attempt to annoy by a white man called Captain Nichol, to whom Elena had once been married. The couple were afterwards divorced before Folau,[12] and Nichol was told that Elena was to have for herself all that belonged to her. The only thing I know of her taking away was this hand sewing machine. Now Nichol arrests her for having stolen it. She and Tomasi, her present husband, are now in town for her hearing before Mr. Cooper. Scanlon declared she was perfectly within her rights and could come to no harm. Lafaele has been wanting to marry a pretty little girl not more than thirteen or fourteen years of age. The parents are trying to force on the match and I am told that the poor child is crying her eyes out. We have told L that if he marries the little girl she shall not come to Vailima, which I think will make an end of that. He is to be allowed to bring back Faauma if she promises to behave properly. The parents of the little girl are meanwhile wringing everything they can out of that poor old sheep, Lafaele. During the interval when my diary lapsed, we had a short sad letter from Nelly telling of the sudden, though not unexpected, death of Adolfo[13] from quick consumption. She seems herself not well, with a cough and pain in her side. I am very anxious about her. We think of sending Austin to her that he may attend school with little Louis.

MAY 22ND

The *Upolu* came in earlier than usual, on the Thursday, I think it was. Friday morning word was sent to Lafaele that his son that he had been so long expecting was awaiting him in Apia. Of course I gave him permission to have the day off. Late in the afternoon he returned in company with an old man, and a young girl about twelve or thirteen. The party laid kava at Louis's feet and seemed to expect an oration.

"But where is your boy?" I asked Lafaele.

"That my boy," was his answer, and sure enough his boy was a girl.

---

[12] A native magistrate of Apia.
[13] Adolfo Sanchez, Nellie's husband.

On Saturday Captain F of the *Upolu* came up and took lunch with us. We had nothing but vegetables, curried and cooked in all ways, but no meat. Sunday came a German vegetarian when there were no vegetables at all, and nothing but meat. I miss Lauilo very much. Our lunch was a mere scramble with four and sometimes five men rushing about the dining room, but nothing done properly. Simi, who has Lauilo's place, assisted by Mitaele (Talolo's young brother), is breaking everything we possess. He smiles with a kind tolerance when he smashes something precious, and is more like an English colonel than words can express. He will tie the best napkins round his neck, and to my horror I once saw him use one for a handkerchief.

This morning Lafaele came to me with choked sobs and said he was "too much 'fraid." I thought another horse was dead and was greatly relieved to find that the alarming occurrence was the return of Faauma. I was rather anxious to have her back, as that will break off the other connection, but I hadn't bargained for the rigid morality of Tomasi. He said plainly that he could not allow Elena to associate with whores. F was most anxious to get to work and particularly wished to help Elena, who is behind in her laundry work. I'm sure I don't know what to do, nor do I understand their morality at all. There is such a thing, no doubt, and I suppose the Fijians are more particular than the Samoans.

The little girl, who had been crying to go home, and was frightened to death of Arrick, who spoke of her most tenderly as "that little girlie" and did all he could to make her feel at ease (as had been done for him when he first came)—the little girl seems delighted with her stepmother and is as happy as possible with Faauma. Certainly F is a pretty, graceful, charming creature, but I wish she were not what Laulii calls a whore. She makes all sorts of promises, which I trust she may keep. This morning, to our surprise, she joined in the Lord's Prayer. We are getting ready to build houses for L and T. Now that the ladies cannot associate together, I must not have the houses too close, which is a bother, as it was all arranged. The "weary Christians" are come for a dancing lesson.

[MAY] 29TH

We have had the most horrid unseasonable weather for almost a week—torrents of rain and almost continuous thunder. I got a chill in the beginning and have been quite ill, but am better now. Mr. Moors has returned from Nassau,[14] which he bought without seeing it, entirely on my recommendation. I felt a little anxious about it, lest he should lose money on the speculation and be disappointed. I had told him that I believed it to be a grand island. He is delighted with the place, has found ground and is talking about building a house there. All the party but myself went to the big fono at Malie. Charley Taylor took charge of the affair and mismanaged everything. Our poor boys went down the day before to see the animals on the steamer. Dinner was ordered for them from Moors' store, but Charley Taylor (Sally Taylor as they call him) did not give them enough to eat. The steamer did not come in till after dark, and there was general disappointment. They now say that if Sally comes to Vailima they will "hit him." When the last litter of pigs was born Lafaele and Elena begged for a little one apiece, which I gave them. Elena chose a spotted boar which she named Sally Taylor, and Lafaele took what he calls a "mare pig," that is, a little sow. Both pigs have been tamed, and trot about after Elena and Faauma like pug dogs. They go to bed at night with their mistresses, like babies, and must be fed with milk at least once through the night. Both pigs came to prayers this morning. The framework of Lafaele's house is up.

[JUNE] 1ST

Louis went to Apia to ask the two sailor boys that rowed in the boat to Malie to come up to Vailima to lunch. Just as we were sitting down to dinner up comes a young man named Carr, quite drunk, who is a little mad when sober. He was clad in old pajamas, carrying his shoes in his hands, and soaked with mud and water, a wild and disagreeable looking object. He had a glass of brandy (this much to my disgust—he got it from Mrs. S) and a bath, after which he dressed in a suit of Lloyd's and sat with us at table. His conversation was anything but agreeable. He boasted that he had struck Keppel (who is certainly most irritating, but a miserable weakling in comparison with Carr, a burly young man with a sham

[14] Nassau Island, between Samoa and the Manihiki group.

Greek profile) and also that on meeting Mr. Carruthers he had struck him also. Then he went on to boast of his aristocratic blood and relations, declaring that he had a right—the third in succession—to the titles "Duke of Clarence and Avondale." I remarked that the heir, three times removed, to the dukedom had a blot on his escutcheon, that of cowardice. He had struck two men of greatly inferior strength to his own, and without warning, to say nothing of Mr. Carruthers being a man much older than himself. We were quite sickened with him and got him early to bed.

He had just gone when Louis came home with news. One of our friends heard it openly stated that Louis was to be deported. It cannot be because of his going to Mataafa to persuade the latter to keep the peace, because half the town have been on one or the other errand to Malie. The real reason, I am convinced, is that Louis tried to see Laupepa in order to tell that miserable monarch what he was going to say to Mataafa. Our first visit to Mataafa was not made until after Mr. Beckman had been there twice. We were told that we might get a place in Mr. B's boat if we wished to go at the same time; but as this permission did not come from Mr. B himself but from a native unacquainted with him we felt backward about going forward.

Having no interpreter, Louis was not able to say to Mataafa what he wished to say, namely, that so long as there were two great chiefs calling themselves king in Samoa, so long there would be two parties and continual strife and danger of war. What he advised was that Mataafa should offer to take a subordinate position under Laupepa and the two work together for the good and prosperity of Samoa. That was what he had to say to Laupepa also. Of course that is not what the C J wants. He cares nothing for the peace and welfare of Samoa. He only wants to fill his ignoble pockets with English or American silver. Louis made, as I have before mentioned, a second visit to Malie, with Charley Taylor as inefficient interpreter, and disburdened his mind. The third visit was simply to see the performances at a great fono, an excellent piece of business for the novelist, and let the old lady have an outing that she was set upon. For this—ostensibly for this—they talk of deporting Louis. I don't

see how they could do it, even though a case be brought by their little
baron before the C J. Louis was told in Apia by Paul Leonard, who
had been all day at Malie during the fono, that as Louis arrived late,
the whole function was repeated for his benefit.

[JUNE] 2ND

Carr quite sober and a little ashamed. He says he did not strike
Mr. Carruthers but only struck at him. We gave him to understand
that he could not stay here, and lent him a horse to go away on,
and some of Lloyd's clothes. Before he went I had some very plain
talk with him. He promised to go to both Mr. Cusack-Smith (to
whom he had been writing insulting letters) and to Mr. Carruthers
and apologize.

"But," said he, "if I go to Carruthers and humiliate myself before
him, he will only make some nasty remark."

"Very possible," I said, "and that will be the punishment—and
not half what you deserve—for behaving like a coward."

Louis gave him a letter, when he went, to Mr. Cusack-Smith,
offering to bear part of the expenses necessary to send Carr home.

In the afternoon came a letter from Mataafa wanting more cacao
and asking advice about the best things for Samoans to plant. "The
government," said he, "must soon face that question." If that greedy
Swede would only let these people be at peace they could go to
planting, which in the end would bring in more money than they
have had heretofore. Mr. Moors is writing a pamphlet on ramus
planting in Samoan, to send among the natives. Mataafa asked about
the paper mulberry, but we know nothing about that. He wants
something that will bring in immediate returns while waiting for
coffee and cacao to come into bearing. I am wondering if there is
enough market for kava, which grows quickly and well and is certainly very dear, even here. I planted out a lot of slips today of
a remarkably fine sort.

Lafaele's house is nearly done, but he is not pleased with it, finding it too low in the eaves. I propose to use this house for the work
boys and make another for L. Elena is teaching his "little boy"
laundry work. It seems a nice child. As they work, the two pigs are
tied to the table legs.

[JUNE] 4TH

Mr. Haggard comes to dinner, and Mr. Dumet, who stays but a short time. They bring curious news. Mr. Maben has been appointed by the king (advised by the president) to the position of secretary of state, and Mr. Willis architect to his majesty. They tell us that the miserable young man, Carr, is trying to blackmail all the people in Apia.

[JUNE] 5TH

Sunday. Austin goes to church with Mrs. Stevenson. "What did you pray so long for after the communion?" asked he. "I said the Lord's Prayer over four times before you were done."

In the afternoon Mr. Maben comes up to see Louis. He is much puzzled by his appointment, and very suspicious. He says the president seems alarmed, and withdraws from being adviser to the king except when—as provided by the Berlin treaty—his advice is asked. He seems to be copiously partaking of that bitter dish, humble pie. Maben thinks that he was given the appointment because he belongs to Louis's "gang." He came to say that his policy was all for peace, and the same as Louis's, and wished Louis to communicate with Mataafa to that effect. He is to have *carte blanche*, he says, and the moment he suspects any trickery will withdraw.

I don't understand the affair. Last week they were openly talking of deporting Louis because he had been to Malie. Now it is proposed that he communicate with M to exactly the same effect as he did on his own volition, and this from the government. Maben says that when his appointment was announced to him by the C J, that gentleman with great hilarity drank to the new secretary of state, who confessed that he was appalled at this pleasantry. There is no money to pay secretaries or anybody else, and not much chance of any taxes coming in. I am suspicious of something. I know not what, and want Louis to be very careful what he is about, or he may find himself a cat's-paw of that wily, unscrupulous Low-wegian. Maben asked Louis to write to Mataafa, but I hope he will not write, but go over to Malie and simply repeat what was said to him by Maben, and give no advice at present, nor offer any suggestions. Just say, "This is what was told me, and I was requested to repeat it to you."

There may be treachery against Mataafa hidden somewhere in the proposal. There has been so much duplicity and dishonesty and treachery surrounding those two men, the C J and the president, that I believe nothing they do does not hide some nefarious scheme. There is no doubt but I was right when I suspected the missionary, Whitmee, of having been sent here, consciously or unconsciously, by the C J. One peculiar thing is that Maben has always been the mortal enemy of Claxton. Why choose him for the post of secretary of state? Perhaps the secretary is to be a scapegoat. Maben says he is to do what he likes, and he is quite agreeable to having the seat of government at Malie, and Mataafa given the post of prime minister, which would really mean all the power. Surely the government cannot swallow such a humiliation as that. And I can't forget that when Mr. Moors was sent over on a somewhat similar errand supposing that there was to be a reconciliation between the two chiefs, he found out by accident that the C J was trying to send a man-of-war (at the same time) to bombard Malie.

I want to see Louis's feet on an open pathway, with the broad light of day upon it. I find that he was not (Louis, I am speaking of) going to consult Mr. Moors, as usual, before sending his letter to Malie. That was not natural, and not like Louis. I am sure the notion was put into his head by Maben. I have insisted that there shall be no secrecy and that Moors shall be told everything. There is the shadow of an excuse, because Moors objects to a reconciliation; but I want him to know what is going on. He has made no secret to us of what he was about.

We have just been reading an excellent pamphlet written by Moors to the Samoans on the subject of crops. It is amusing to see our own original views, that caused Moors so much amusement, now put forward, and excellently well put forward—as his own sentiments. He thinks they are his now, and no doubt has forgotten all our arguments with him on the subject. I think his paper may do much good. I hope it may.

Louis and Belle have gone to the races. It is raining, as usual, though it was brilliant sunshine when they left. Simi has been away for some days. Arrick says he has run away. The life of enforced sobriety has been too much for his endurance, I fear. The framework of Tomasi's house is going up: a fine, large house, and beautiful timbers. A cow has been in my garden and worked havoc there. I have a new place cleared near the kitchen for my garden and mean to change it. I hope I may have something to plant in it. I sent to New York for seeds and things and many of them have come up well. One sweet potato arrived in a sound state and I have taken from it about thirty sprouts. A lot of "southern cross" cabbage is up, and some eggplants; also about twenty hundred custard apples. I have engaged Henderson, the carpenter, to remove the tops of two great trees that are not safe. I am to give him three pounds and furnish the rope.

L O U I S . SATURDAY, JUNE 18TH

I must tell you of our feast. It was long promised to the boys, and came off yesterday in one of their new houses. My good Simile arrived from Savaii that morning asking for political advice; then we had Lauilo; Elena's father, a talking-man of Lauilo's family; Talolo's cousin; and a boy of Simile's family, who attended on his dignity; then Metu, the meat-man—you have never heard of him, but he is a great person in our household—brought a lady and a boy—and there was another infant—eight guests in all. And we sat down thirty strong. You should have seen our procession, going (about two o'clock), in all our best clothes, to the hall of feasting! All in our Sunday's best. The new house had been hurriedly finished; the rafters decorated with flowers; the floor spread, native style, with green leaves; we had given a big porker, twenty-five pounds of fresh beef, a tin of biscuit, cocoanuts, etc. Our places were all arranged with much care; the native ladies of the house facing our party; the sides filled up by the men; the guests, please observe: the two chief people, male and female, were placed with our family, the rest between S and the native ladies. After the feast was over, we had kava, and the calling of the kava was a very elaborate affair; and I thought had like to have made Simile very angry; he is really a considerable chief; but he and Lauilo were not called till after all our family,

and the guests, I suppose the principle being that he was still regarded as one of the household. I forgot to say that our black boy
did not turn up when the feast was ready. Off went the two cooks,
found him, decorated him with huge red hibiscus flowers—he was in
a very dirty undershirt—brought him back between them like a
reluctant maid, and thrust him into a place between Faauma and
Elena, where he was petted and ministered to. When his turn
came in the kava drinking—and you may be sure, in their con-
temptuous, affectionate kindness for him, as for a good dog, it came
rather earlier than it ought—he was cried under a new name. *Aleki*
is what they make of his own name Arrick; but instead of "the cup
of Aleki!" it was called "the cup of V*ailima*," and it was explained
that he had "taken his chief-name!" a jest at which the plantation
still laughs. Kava done, I made a little speech, Henry translating. If
I had been well, I should have alluded to my guest of all this month,
the Tongan, Tomas, and to Simile, partly for the jest of making him
translate compliments to himself. The talking-man replied with many
handsome compliments to me, in the usual flood of Samoan fluent
neatness; and we left them to an afternoon of singing and dancing.
Must stop now, as my right hand is very bad again. I am trying to
write with my left.

F A N N Y . [JUNE] 20TH

Talolo's brother, a beautiful young boy, has elephantiasis. He has
had it for a long time, about a year, he says; but was afraid to tell.
But worse than that has happened. All day Saturday Paatalise seemed
in a curious state. He would follow us about, speaking in his own
tongue, and smiling into our faces with a pathetic pleading expression like a pet dog that is hurt. Mrs. S complained to me that he
came and sat on a chair beside her and talked in a foreign tongue.
I knew he was homesick and was very sorry for him. He comes from
Wallis Island—how, I do not know; perhaps sold by his chief, or as
a stowaway on board some schooner. He was first one of Joe's plantation boys, and we, liking him very much, took him into the house
to wait at table and help Mitaele. About nine or thereabouts, on
Saturday evening, Lloyd and I were reading in my room when M

came in with something unintelligible about Paatalise. I thought we had better go and look at the boy, as he might be ill. Lloyd understood M to say that P wished to go into the bush to see his family.

"Are his family in the bush?" asked Lloyd.

"No," was the reply, which was puzzling.

We found the boy lying in his bed in a sort of stupor. Lloyd thought he had had a nightmare and was only heavy with sleep. I pulled up his eyelids and found that his eyes were drawn down and fixed, whereupon I went for Louis. While we looked at him he began making strange noises like a mouse, sometimes spitting like a cat, and struggled a little to get out of bed. I thought it better to call Joe, as I began to suspect a fit of insanity. Joe got here none too soon, as the boy soon became almost unmanageable. He said that the spirits of his dead ancestors, and also the spirits of his living family (now in Wallis) were in the bush, calling him. He leaped forward like a man diving into the sea. After this struggle I sent for Arrick. Soon there was another paroxysm, and we found we must tie him down or he would get away from us and die in the bush. Being so little used to stairs he would, no doubt, have plunged down them head first or have made a dash over the verandah railings.

We first tried with sheets wound round his body and tied under the iron bedstead with ropes. His feet we fastened with a rope to the foot of the bed. The narrow sheets, folded, were crossed over his breast and each shoulder, tied to the bed head at the upper end, then crossed again under the bed and fastened the opposite ends of the foot. After having used a pretty large coil of rope, about six sheets and a roller towel, we thought we had him secure; and, as Lafaele and Savea turned up, put them with the black boy in their charge and retired ourselves for a little rest. Lloyd had a gold ring on his little finger broken in the struggle. In about half an hour there was a call from Lafaele, and there was Paatalise, free of all his fastenings, on the point of escaping. We could think no more of humanity, and with the utmost difficulty managed to tie each wrist to an upper corner of the bed and each ankle to a lower corner, the ropes directly against his flesh. In one of his struggles Louis and Lloyd were both sitting on his leg, one directly over the knees. Suddenly the leg went up with a jerk and Louis was thrown like a ball. At the most the boy cannot be more than fifteen, and though a powerful lad, is not yet full grown. Again I left the room to recover my breath, for in this last struggle I had had to help.

Shortly after Joe came to me and said, "Paatalise is quite sensible. Come and look at him."

I asked how this had come about and was told that Lafaele had sent Savea into the bush for some leaves which, after being chewed, they had put into Paatalise's eyes, ears and nostrils. The first effect was a state of alarming coma, from which he woke perfectly sane. Joe had already loosened his hands from the bonds, and I found him sitting up with an anxious deprecating smile. Though his hands were free he made no effort to loosen his feet (which were bruised with the rope and swollen from the stoppage to circulation) until he had my permission. There was no more delirium, and everybody but Joe and I went to sleep at about half past two in the morning.

I thought Lafaele seemed a bit alarmed about the action of his remedy. Several times he took me aside to tell me that the boy would probably die at four in the morning. However, he did not die, but insisted on helping with his usual work. We allowed him to do this, thinking it better that his mind should be employed.

I had a talk with Lafaele about his remedy. He was, at first, shy of telling me anything about it, saying that its use was explained to him by his father just before the old man's death, and he had been pledged to secrecy. In fact, the leaf used is a deadly poison. The people of Tonga in olden times poisoned their enemies with it. Had anyone a spite against a family, he walked through the person's house with some chewed leaves in his mouth. If he passed food or tobacco he blew from his lips a little spray of saliva over them. I suppose he must have taken a certain risk in holding the stuff so long in his mouth. I believe it was Savea who chewed the leaves at Lafaele's request, when they were used for Paatalise. Another thing Lafaele told me: that when a person had been wounded, especially in the foot or hand, and developed lockjaw, the chewed leaves were forced up his nostrils. Very soon the jaw would relax, then all the muscles, after which the cure was certain. Joe said that when Lafaele administered the remedy to Paatalise, he smothered him, until Joe began to be alarmed. I asked if I could see a twig of the tree.

"I will send to Tonga for a piece," replied L.

I talked on other subjects for a few moments, and then returned to the charge.

"Does that tree grow very close to the house?" I asked. "It didn't take long to get the leaves."

"Oh yes," replied the simple Lafaele, "just over there. There are only two trees that I know of here in Samoa—ours, and another at Matafele."

He promised to show me the tree, and I shall send some leaves to Uncle George.

Last Thursday we gave a feast to our men. Lafaele killed a large pig, as big as I am. We bought twenty-five pounds of fresh beef, half a dollar's worth of kava, and taro and biscuits, etc. The feast was spread in one of the new houses. Speeches were made, and the kava called out in proper fashion. Everybody went away laden with spoils, and altogether it was a great success.

The same night Belle and Lloyd went to a ball given to the officers of the man-of-war (the *Curaçoa*). I asked what people were talking about in Apia, expecting to hear the last political scandal, but Bella Decker's legs seem to be the topic of conversation to the exclusion of everything else. Bella Decker is said by her mother to be fourteen, a pretty little fair girl. It seems she went to a fancy dress party as a fairy, and the question that convulses Apia is "Did Bella Decker show more of her legs than was convenable in a girl of her age?" She is said to be anywhere between fourteen and forty, and to possess a pair of legs quite worth showing. Mrs. Decker appealed to Mr. Haggard and to other dignitaries to pass an opinion, and altogether there has been a perfect tempest in a teapot.

L O U I S . TUESDAY, JUNE 21ST

To understand the full horror of the mad scene, and how well my boys behaved, remember that they *believed P's ravings*, they *knew* that his dead family, thirty strong, crowded the front verandah and called on him to come to the other world. They *knew* that his dead brother had met him that afternoon in the bush and struck him on both temples. And remember! we are fighting the dead, and they had to go out again in the black night, which is the dead man's empire. Yet last evening, when I thought P was going to repeat the performance, I sent down for Lafaele, who had leave of absence, and he and his wife came up about eight o'clock with a lighted brand. These are the things for which I have to forgive my old cattle-man his manifold shortcomings; they are heroic—so are the shortcomings, to be sure.

FANNY. JUNE 21ST

Abdul and Lauilo have come to visit us, Abdul with some birds he has shot. We have been having a little trouble with Elena. She neglects her work and is generally *musu*. Arrick, on the contrary, improves every day, and is growing quite good-looking. Yesterday we wanted some medicine for Paatalise. I sent Arrick, as the most responsible person on the place, to get it. He started on a keen run and was back inside of an hour. Three miles each way, the latter uphill, and a terrible broken stony road.

Lafaele's "little boy" leaves today at four with the old Tongan man on the *Upolu*. When we said good-bye to the old man (to whom we had made a present of a month's wages, certainly well-earned) he covered his eyes with a dramatic gesture as he turned round the corner of the verandah, as though overcome by emotion—I suppose he was.

When Belle said, "You Samoan people don't feel badly very long about anything, it seems to me," Talolo returned, "Yes, we do," quite hurt at the insinuation. "When a man's wife runs away he feel *very* bad for *two or three* days!"

Paatalise seems much better. His fever, which was terrible last night, seems gone, and he says he has no more pain in his head. I forgot to mention a pathetic act of his. The morning after his attack of mania, he came downstairs where the family were at breakfast, and kissed everybody in the pretty native fashion.

On Sunday the doctor of the man-of-war and another officer came to dinner, bringing one of the middies, a little fellow who looked about fourteen. Bernice was his name, and I never saw a boy enjoy himself more. Late in the afternoon he drank the water of two cocoanuts and ate all the meat of one, also several mummy apples, oranges innumerable, barbadines, pineapple, and I know not what. Instead of superior officers, the two men seemed more like very kind tutors. They left early because, as the doctor said, "A couple of midshipmen have got colds and I must give them some port wine negus before they go to bed." In every way it seems an unusually good sort of ship's company; the very best we have seen. We saw the published list of the officers' names. Samoan, English, where you will, the "chief" names mean the best men.

Henry was here the day of the feast and sat with the family. He says there was a rumor in Savaii that eight German men-of-war were in the harbour and that Malie and Manono had been shelled. Louis is to send him a letter by every chance. The "dreary Christian," whose bulldogs killed one of Laulii's cats, had the indecency to go again with them, when they promptly killed her remaining cat. If he brings them here they shall be shot.

L O U I S . SATURDAY, 2ND JULY

I was busy copying David Balfour with my left hand—a most laborious task—Fanny was down at the native house superintending the floor, Lloyd down in Apia, and Belle in her own house cleaning, when I heard the latter calling on my name. I ran out on the verandah; and there on the lawn behold my crazy boy with an axe in his hand and dressed out in green ferns, dancing. I ran downstairs and found all my house boys on the back verandah, watching him through the dining-room. I asked what it meant?—"Dance belong his place," they said.—"I think this no time to dance," said I. "Has he done his work?"—"No," they told me, "away bush all morning." But there they all stayed on the back verandah. I went on alone through the dining-room, and bade him stop. He did so, shouldered the axe, and began to walk away; but I called him back, walked up to him, and took the axe out of his unresisting hands. The boy is in all things so good, that I can scarce say I was afraid; only I felt it had to be stopped ere he could work himself up by dancing to some craziness. Our house boys protested they were not afraid; all I know is they were all watching him round the back door and did not follow me till I had the axe. As for the out boys, who were working with Fanny in the native house, they thought it a very bad business, and made no secret of their fears.

TUESDAY, 12TH JULY

I am doing no work and my mind is in abeyance. Fanny and Belle are sewing-machining in the next room; I have been pulling down their hair, and Fanny has been kicking me, and now I am driven out. Austin I have been chasing about the verandah; now he has gone to his lessons, and I make believe to write to you in despair. But there is nothing in my mind; I swim in mere vacancy, my head is like a rotten nut; I shall soon have to begin to work again or I shall carry away some part of the machinery. I have got your insufficient letter, for which I scorn to thank you. I have had no review by Gosse,[15] none by Birrell[16]; another time if I have a letter in the *Times*, you might send me the text as well; also please send me a cricket bat and a cake, and when I come home for the holidays, I should like to have a pony. I am, sir, your obedient servant, Jacob Tonson. P.S. I am quite well; I hope you are quite well. The world is too much with us, and my mother bids me bind my hair and lace my bodice blue.

About the third week of August the Stevensons were living a very social life. The Countess of Jersey was visiting Bazett Haggard, and Louis arranged to take her to see Mataafa, to satisfy her curiosity. Inasmuch as Mataafa was a "rebel" king her visit had to be made unofficially and as far as possible *incognita*. Louis had a great deal of fun, calling Lady Jersey his cousin Amelia Balfour. The party stayed at Mataafa's overnight, and breakfast was itself a protracted business. The following days contained much social activity and moving about, lasting into September.

[15] Edmund Gosse (1849-1928), English poet and critic, later knighted.
[16] Augustine Birrell (1850-1933), English author and politician.

MONDAY, 12TH SEPTEMBER

On Wednesday the Spinsters of Apia gave a ball to a select crowd.
Fanny, Belle, Lloyd and I rode down, met Haggard by the way and
joined company with him. Dinner with Haggard, and thence to the
ball. The Chief Justice appeared; it was immediately remarked, and
whispered from one to another, that he and I had the only red
sashes in the room—and they were both of the hue of blood, sir,
blood. He shook hands with myself and all the members of my
family. Then the cream came, and I found myself in the same set of
a quadrille, I don't know where the devil they fished it from; but it
is rackety and prancing and embraceatory beyond words; perhaps
it is best defined in Haggard's expression of a gambado. When I
and my great enemy found ourselves involved in this gambol, and
crossing hands, and kicking up, and being embraced almost in common by large and quite respectable females, we—or I—tried to
preserve some rags of dignity, but not for long. The deuce of it is
that, personally, I love this man; his eye speaks to me, I am pleased
in his society. We exchanged a glance, and then a grin; the man
took me in his confidence; and through the remainder of that prance,
we pranced for each other. Hard to imagine any position more ridiculous; a week before he had been trying to rake up evidence against
me by brow-beating and threatening a half-white interpreter; that
very morning I had been writing most villainous attacks upon him
for the *Times*; and we meet and smile, and—damn it!—like each
other. I do my best to damn the man and drive him from these
islands; but the weakness endures—I love him. This is a thing I
would despise in anybody else; but he is so jolly insidious and
ingratiating! No, sir, I can't dislike him; but if I don't make hay of
him, it shall not be for want of trying.

Yesterday, we had two Germans and a young American boy to
lunch; and in the afternoon, Vailima was in a state of siege; ten
white people on the front verandah, at least as many brown in the
cook house, and countless blacks to see the black boy Arrick.

Which reminds me, Arrick was sent Friday was a week to the
German Firm with a note, and was not home on time. Lloyd and
I were going bedward, it was late with a bright moon—ah, poor dog,

you know no such moons as these!—when home came Arrick with his head in a white bandage and his eyes shining. He had had a fight with other blacks, Malaita boys; many against one, and one with a knife: "I KNICKED 'EM DOWN, three four!" he cried; and had himself to be taken to the doctor's and bandaged. Next day, he could not work, glory of battle swelled too high in his threadpaper breast; he had made a one-stringed harp for Austin, borrowed it, came to Fanny's room, and sang war-songs and danced a war dance in honour of his victory. And it appears, by subsequent advices, that it was a serious victory enough; four of his assailants went to hospital, and one is thought in danger. All Vailima rejoiced at this news.

THURSDAY, 15TH SEPTEMBER

On Tuesday, we had our young adventurer[17] ready, and Fanny, Belle, he and I set out about three of a dark, deadly hot, and deeply unwholesome afternoon. Belle had the lad behind her; I had a pint of champagne in either pocket, a parcel in my hands, and as Jack had a girth sore and I rode without a girth, I might be said to occupy a very unstrategic position. On the way down, a little dreary, beastly drizzle beginning to come out of the darkness, Fanny put up an umbrella, her horse bounded, reared, cannoned into me, cannoned into Belle and the lad, and bolted for home. It really might and ought to have been an A1 catastrophe; but nothing happened beyond Fanny's nerves being a good deal shattered; of course, she could not tell what had happened to us until she got her horse mastered.

Next day, Haggard went off to the Commission and left us in charge of his house; all our people came down in wreaths of flowers; we had a boat for them; Haggard had a flag in the Commission boat for us; and when at last the steamer turned up, the young adventurer was carried on board in great style, with a new watch and chain, about three pound ten of tips, and five big baskets of fruit as free-will offerings to the captain. Captain Morse had us all to lunch; champagne flowed; so did compliments; and I did the affable celebrity life-sized. It made a great send-off for the young adventurer. As the boat drew off, he was standing at the head of the gangway, supported by three handsome ladies—one of them a real full-blown

[17] Austin Strong, who was sent to school in Monterey.

beauty, Madame Green, the singer—and looking very engaging himself, between smiles and tears. Not that he cried in public.

My, but we were a tired crowd! However it is always a blessing to get home, and this time it was a sort of wonder to ourselves that we got back alive. Casualties: Fanny's back jarred, horse incident; Belle, bad headache, tears and champagne; self, idiocy, champagne, fatigue; Lloyd, ditto, ditto. As for the adventurer, I believe he will have a delightful voyage for his little start in life. But there is always something in a mite's first launch.

SEPTEMBER 30TH

David Balfour done, and its author along with it, or nearly so. Strange to think of even our doctor here repeating his nonsense about debilitating climate. Why, the work I have been doing the last twelve months, in one continuous spate, mostly with annoying interruptions and without any collapse to mention, would be incredible in Norway. . . . Vital—that's what I am at, first: wholly vital, with a buoyancy of life. Then lyrical, if it may be, and picturesque, always with an epic value of scenes, so that the figures remain in the mind's eye forever.

OCTOBER 8TH

Suppose you sent us some of the catalogues of the parties what vends statues? I don't want colossal Herculeses, but about quarter size and less. If the catalogues were illustrated it would probably be found a help to weak memories. These may be found to alleviate spare moments, when we sometimes amuse ourselves by thinking how fine we shall make the palace if we do not go pop. Perhaps in the same way it might amuse you to send us any pattern of wall paper that might strike you as cheap, pretty and suitable for a room in a hot and extremely bright climate. It should be borne in mind that our climate can be extremely dark too. Our sitting-room is to be in varnished wood. The room I have particularly in mind is a sort of bed and sitting-room, pretty large, lit on three sides, and the colour in favour of its proprietor at present is a topazy yellow. But then with what colour to relieve it? For a little work-room of my own at the back, I should rather like to see some patterns of unglossy —well, I'll be hanged if I can describe this red—it's not Turkish and it's not Roman and it's not Indian, but it seems to partake of the two last and yet it can't be either of them because it ought to be able to go with vermilion. Ah, what a tangled web we weave— anyway, with what brains you have left choose me and send me some—many—patterns of this exact shade.

A few days ago it was Haggard's birthday and we had him and his cousin to dinner. . . . And there was of course a special verse for each one of the party. . . . Fanny's verse was less intelligible, but it was accompanied in the dance with a pantomime of terror well-fitted to call up her haunting, indefatigable and diminutive presence in a blue gown.

NOV. 2ND

On Saturday we expected Captain Morse of the *Alameda* to come up to lunch, and on Friday with genuine South Sea hospitality had a pig killed. On the Saturday morning no pig. Some of the boys seemed to give a doubtful account of themselves; our next neighbour below in the wood is a bad fellow and very intimate with some of our boys, for whom his confounded house is like a fly-paper for flies. To add to all this, there was on the Saturday a great public presentation of food to the King and the Parliament men, an occasion on which it is almost dignified for a Samoan to steal anything, and entirely dignified for him to steal a pig.

All this made it very possible that even if none of our boys had stolen the pig, some of them might know the thief. Besides the theft, as it was a theft of meat prepared for a guest, had something of the nature of an insult and "my face" in native phrase "was ashamed." Accordingly, we determined to hold a bed of justice. It was done last night after dinner. I sat at the head of the table, Graham on my right hand, Henry Simile at my left, Lloyd behind him. The house company sat on the floor around the walls—twelve all told. I am described as looking like Braxfield[18] as I could manage with my appearance; Graham, who is of a severe countenance, looked like Rhadamanthus; Lloyd was hideous to the view; and Simile has all the fine solemnity of a Samoan chief. The proceedings opened by

---

[18] Robert MacQueen, Lord Braxfield, the "Hanging Judge" (1722-1799), who inspired the creation of the chief character in RLS's *Weir of Hermiston.*

my delivering a Samoan prayer, which may be translated thus—
"Our God, look down upon us and shine into our hearts. Help us
to be far from falsehood so that each one of us may stand before
Thy Face in his integrity."—Then, beginning with Simile, every one
came up to the table, laid his hand on the Bible, and repeated clause
by clause after me the following oath—I fear it may sound even
comic in English, but it is a very pretty piece of Samoan, and struck
direct at the most lively superstitions of the race. "This is the Holy
Bible here that I am touching. Behold me, O God! If I know who
it was that took away the pig, or the place to which it was taken,
or have heard anything relating to it, and shall not declare the same
—be made an end of by God this life of mine!" They all took it with
so much seriousness and firmness that (as Graham said) if they
were not innocent they would make invaluable witnesses. I was so
far impressed by their bearing that I went no further, and the
funny and yet strangely solemn scene came to an end.

FANNY . DEC. 23RD

My diary has been long neglected. About the time I stopped writing we found Joe Strong out in various misdeeds: robbing the cellar
and store-room at night with false keys. In revenge, when he found
that he was discovered, he went round to all our friends in Apia and
spread slanders about Belle. We turned him away and applied for a
divorce for Belle, which was got with no difficulty, as he had been
living with a native woman of Apia as his wife ever since he came
here—an old affair begun when he was here before. Also, he had
been engaged in an intrigue with Faauma. He came up here late
one night to beg forgiveness and ask to be taken back. I was so
shocked at seeing him that I had an attack of angina, which seems
to remain with me. Louis was made sole guardian of the child, who
has been sent to Nelly to school.

The Jerseys have been and gone, trailing clouds of glory over the
island. The dear Haggard has since moved in the clouds. They were
a selfish "champagne Charley" set, with the exception of the daughter, Lady Margaret Villers, a tall, leggy, awkward young girl of the

best English sort; gracious and gentle, and simple with the pretty simplicity of youth. Lady Jersey tall and leggy and awkward, with bold black eyes and sensual mouth; very selfish and greedy of admiration, a touch of vulgarity, courageous as a man, and reckless as a woman.

1 8 9 3

Fanny's diary has a hiatus the first months of 1893, her first entry being July 3; but Louis's diary-letters were very full during this period.

L O U I S . JANUARY 24, 1893

This ought to have gone last mail and was forgotten. My best excuse is that I was engaged in starting an influenza, to which class of exploit our household has been since then entirely dedicated. We had eight cases, one of them very bad, and one—mine—complicated with my old friend Bluidy Jack.[1] Luckily neither Fanny, Lloyd or Belle took the confounded thing, and they were able to run the household and nurse the sick to admiration.

Some of our boys behaved like real trumps. Perhaps the prettiest performance was that of our excellent Henry Simile, or, as we sometimes call him, Davy Balfour. Henry, I maun premeese, is a chief; the humblest Samoan recoils from emptying slops as you would from cheating at cards; now the last nights of our bad time when we had seven down together, it was enough to have made anybody laugh or cry to see Henry going the rounds with a slop-bucket and going inside the mosquito net of each of the sick, Protestant and Catholic alike, to pray with them. . . .

After the other seven were almost wholly recovered, Henry lay down to influenza on his own account. He is but just better and it looks as though Fanny were about to bring up the rear. As for me, I am all right, though I *was* reduced to dictating *Anne*[2] in the deaf and dumb alphabet, which I think you will admit is a *comble*. . . .

[1] Hemorrhages from the lungs.
[2] *St. Ives.*

Do not bother at all about the wall-papers. We have had the whole of our new house varnished, and it looks beautiful. I wish you could see the hall; poor room, it had to begin life as an infirmary during our recent visitation; but it is really a handsome comely place, and when we get the furniture, and the pictures, and what is so very much more decorative, the picture frames, will look sublime.

In the middle of February, Louis was at sea on the *Mariposa* with Fanny and Belle. They had gone on a month's lark, and Fanny, in good fettle, was reported by him to have eaten a whole fowl for breakfast, "to say nothing of a tower of hot cakes." Louis himself was feeling very jolly, despite the fact that he had been rather sick and had had two small hemorrhages.

FEBRUARY 21, 1893

Fanny is on deck. I have just supplied her with the Canadian Pacific Agent, and so left her in good hands. You should hear me at table with the Ulster purser and a little punning microscopist called Davis. Belle does some kind of abstruse Boswellising; after the first meal, having gauged the kind of jests that would pay here, I observed, "Boswell is Barred during this cruise."

But on the return voyage matters were not so jolly. Belle had "dentistry troubles," Fanny was quite ill, although apparently mending, and Louis had cooked up a fine pleurisy.

Poor Fanny had very little fun of her visit, having been most of the time on a diet of maltine and slops—and this while the rest of us were rioting on oysters and mushrooms. . . . Take it for all in all, it was huge fun: even Fanny had some lively sport at the beginning; Belle and I all through. We got Fanny a dress on the sly, gaudy black velvet and Duchesse lace. And alas; she was only able to wear it once. But we'll hope to see more of it at Samoa; it really is lovely. Both dames are royally outfitted in silk stockings, etc. We return, as from a raid, with our spoils and our wounded. I am now very dandy: I announced two years ago that I should change. Slovenly youth, all right—not slovenly age. So really now I am pretty spruce;

always a white shirt, white necktie, fresh shave, silk socks, oh, a great sight!

APRIL 5TH

Well, there's no disguise possible; Fanny is not well, and we are miserably anxious. . . .

FRIDAY, 7TH

I am thankful to say the new medicine relieved her at once. A crape has been removed from the day for all of us. To make things better, the morning is ah! such a morning as you have never seen; heaven upon earth for sweetness, freshness, depth upon depth of un-imaginable colour, and a huge silence broken at this moment only by the far-away murmur of the Pacific and the rich piping of a single bird. You can't conceive what a relief this is; it seems a new world. She has such extraordinary recuperative power that I do hope for the best. I am as tired as man can be. This is a great trial to a family, and I thank God it seems as if ours was going to bear it well. And oh! if it only lets up, it will be but a pleasant memory. We are all seedy, bar Lloyd, Fanny, as per above; self nearly extinct; Belle utterly overworked and bad toothache; Cook, down with a bad foot; Butler, prostrate with a bad leg. Eh, what a faim'ly!

SUNDAY

Grey heaven, raining torrents of rain; occasional thunder and lightning. Everything to dispirit; but my invalids are really on the mend. The rain roars like the sea; in the sound of it there is a strange and ominous suggestion of an approaching tramp; something nameless and measureless seems to draw near, and strikes me cold, and yet is welcome. I lie quiet in bed to-day, and think of the universe with a good deal of equanimity.

APRIL 16TH

Several pages of this letter destroyed as beneath scorn; the wailings of a crushed worm; matter in which neither you nor I can take stock. Fanny is distinctly better, I believe all right now; I too am mending, though I have suffered from crushed wormery, which is not good for the body, and damnation to the soul.

17TH

My dear fellow, politics is a vile and a bungling business. I used to think meanly of the plumber; but how he shines beside the politician!

THURSDAY, APRIL 20

A general, steady advance; Fanny really quite chipper and jolly—self on the rapid mend, and with my eye on *forests* that are to fall—and my finger on the axe, which wants stoning.

25TH APRIL

To-day we had a ride down to Tanugamanono, and then by the new wood paths. One led us to a beautiful clearing, with four native houses; taro, yams, and the like, excellently planted, and old Folau—"the Samoan Jew"—sitting and whistling there in his new-found and well-deserved well-being. It was a good sight to see a Samoan thus before the world.

SUNDAY [APRIL]

A heavenly day again! the world all dead silence, save when, from far down below us in the woods, comes up the crepitation of the little wooden drum that beats to church. Scarce a leaf stirs; only now and again a great, cool gush of air that makes my papers fly, and is gone.—The King of Samoa has refused my intercession between him and Mataafa; and I do not deny this is a good riddance to me of a difficult business, in which I might very well have failed. What else is to be done for these silly folks?

All the while Louis is constantly absorbed in his writings, and writes often and copiously to Colvin about them, especially about *David Balfour* and *The Ebb Tide.*

SUNDAY, JUNE 4TH

Yesterday, 12:30, in a heavenly day of sun and trade, I mounted my horse and set off. A boy opens my gate for me. "Sleep and long life! A blessing on your journey," says he. And I reply, "Sleep, long life! A blessing on the house!" Then on, down the lime lane, a rugged, narrow, winding way, that seems almost as if it was leading you into Lyonesse, and you might see the head and shoulders of a giant looking in. At the corner of the road I meet the inspector of taxes, and hold a diplomatic interview with him; he wants me to pay taxes on the new house; I am informed I should not till next year; and we part, *re infecta*, he promising to bring me decisions, I assuring him that, if I find any favouritism, he will find me the most recalcitrant tax-payer on the island. Then I have a talk with an old servant by the wayside. A little further I pass two children coming up. "Love!" say I, "are you two chiefly proceeding inland?" and they say, "Love! yes!" and the interesting ceremony is finished.

TUESDAY, 6TH

I am exulting to do nothing. It pours with rain from the westward, very unusual kind of weather; I was standing out on the little verandah in front of my room this morning, and there went through me or over me a wave of extraordinary and apparently baseless emotion. I literally staggered. And then the explanation came, and I knew I had found a frame of mind and body that belonged to Scotland, and particularly to the neighbourhood of Callander. Very odd these identities of sensation, and the world of connotations implied; highland huts, and peat smoke, and the brown, swirling rivers, and wet clothes, and whisky, and the romance of the past, and that indescribable bite of the whole thing at a man's heart, which is—or rather lies at the bottom of—a story.

FANNY. JULY 3RD, 1893

Nothing talked of, nor thought of, but the impending war. The president is gone, and the C J to go. Mr. Maben is secretary of state. The three consuls are helping to run the now bankrupt government. Native clans, mostly reluctant, are at last coming in to support Laupepa. A few days ago Louis and Pelema[3] went over to the rebel outposts to see what was going on. Armed Samoans were guarding the ford on the Vaiusu[4] road, the next ford after the Gasegase River. They gave pleasant greeting and our men went on to Vaiala to the house of Poor White Man.[5] They came back quite wild with excitement, burning to join in the fray. It is going, I see, to be a difficult

[3] Native name for Graham Balfour, cousin and biographer of RLS.

[4] A village about half-way between Apia and Malie.

[5] A chief named Faamoina. Poor White Man, or Papalagi Mativa, the native equivalent, was his nickname.

task to keep Louis from losing his head altogether. Shortly after, Belle and I and Louis went over the same road, that Belle might take sketches. It was odd how much notice we attracted, beginning even before we entered Apia, everyone most friendly, talofas on every side.

As we neared Vaiusu, Louis gave directions that we should ride very fast, lest we be forcibly stopped. I said, "Go, then, and I will follow." But I had no intention of flying through the town. For one thing (and the principal) I had a touch of lumbago, aggravated by a sudden leap of my horse; and for another, I had a childish distaste for showing anything but a calm demeanour before a possible enemy. In consequence, we both came to humiliation. In the middle of the town is a small bridge. Just before this bridge my wretched horse stopped dead and began to bend at the knees and shiver. I couldn't tell whether she was pretending to be afraid or was about to have a fit (to which she is subject). At any rate, I could not make her move. There was nothing to do but sit and wait for what would happen, for by this time Belle and Louis had sped far out of sight. People sitting before their huts looked at me curiously at first, apparently wondering what I would be at, but when they understood the situation, a man and a boy came out and began leading or rather dragging forward the unworthy Vaivai, who certainly justified her name (malingerer or feeble one). In the meantime Louis, having missed me, had started back and was a good deal alarmed to see me, as it appeared, in the hands of possible hostile natives.

Soon after this episode, we came to a flag of truce, a white rag fastened by a triangle of sticks to a cocoanut tree; then another, and yet a third. Nearing the village of Vaiala, we heard a fife and drum, and quite suddenly found ourselves in the midst of a large party of stalwart young warriors playing cricket. There was not a gun to be seen, nor were there any sentinels at the ford where Louis had passed them before. At the house of the chief, his wife ran out to meet us. Young men took our horses, the lady kissed us both, and led us into the house, where the chief sat on a fine mat, a dozen or so serious-looking small chiefs sitting in a circle under the eaves. Kava was made. I noticed that the supply was scant and was glad that we had brought a little as a present, in the usual Samoan fashion. We also took some native tobacco.

A white man named Rea, a collector of taxes, was sitting in the circle waiting—he said, to our surprise—for the Chief Justice, who had some business with Poor White Man relating to a land claim. While we were talking and passing the usual Samoan compliments, Belle, who had instantly rushed off to make sketches, came back and entered into a whispered conversation with our hostess, who gave her the astonishing *tala*[6] that Louis and the three consuls had announced their intention of taking Mataafa's head.

On the way back we stopped for Belle to make a sketch at the ford, and again for a sketch of one of the flags of truce. At this latter place Belle must have dropped her whip. As we went on, we passed the C J, looking much thinner than when I saw him last, very rigid, and with his outward squint very marked. We stopped in the bed of a stream for Belle to make another sketch, when she discovered the loss of her whip. Louis would ride back after it, leaving us with a bearded oldish native and several younger men. As Louis galloped off, the older man made a sign, whereupon two long-legged youths flew after like young colts. I imagine they thought Louis was following the C J to do him an injury. They appeared to be part of the C J's escort. He, when we met him, was accompanied by a powerful black and a young Samoan.

While Louis was away, the elder Samoan talked to Belle in his own tongue.

"Who is that woman?" he asked insolently, pointing to me.

"You should say 'Who is that lady?'" said Belle. "Why do you look at her like that?" she added. "Don't you think she is pretty?"

"She is a pig-face," was the reply. The word pig-face is the most insulting epithet possible in the Samoan language.

Half angrily and half jeeringly, as she is used to talk to our own men when they misbehave, Belle taunted him with his cowardliness, saying, "A man who does not know how to address ladies cannot be much of a warrior." She made him repeat the words after her, "You

[6] Gossipy tale.

are a beautiful lady, and your mother is a beautiful lady," at which his friends laughed at him with much enjoyment.

Louis came back without the whip. We did not tell him of the rudeness of the man, who handed Belle a switch from a tree for her horse most politely, and bade us each *tofa* as we rode off.

That evening Belle and Louis went to a ball. Mrs. Decker, who was there, told Belle that she was for the first time thoroughly alarmed, as she believed there was going to be an attack upon the whites. A chief, whose name she gave, told her that the first thing the government soldiers meant to do was to kill Tusitala[7] and his family. A native man, who asked to buy Mr. Fring's rifle and was refused, cast a glance round the store, saying, "Well, that's all right. I'll get it by and by for nothing. There's plenty of good food in the store and I'll get that too."

At a council of chiefs in Apia, one of them rose up and said, "Why are we about to shed each other's blood while these white men sit in their houses and laugh at us? Why should they not suffer?" There was not a word of answer. The white men at Mulinuu may find that in forcing these unwilling natives to war they have unloosed a tiger that will be hard to chain again.

Of our house people, only Iopu, the cook's assistant, has left us, with his wife. They went originally to assist at the death bed of a relation who was thrown from his horse and fatally injured on the way home from a visit to Vailima, and now they are prevented from coming back by fear of getting into trouble concerning the war.

Mr. Maben, at the ball, was told by Louis of the threats that had been made against him by government men. Louis also said that he wished it understood that he meant to protect himself and his property to the best of his ability. Mr. M asked to what camp our men belonged. At that time we had noncombatants from both camps, on hearing which information Mr. M said nothing but sighed dismally. Now we have not only noncombatants but three government warriors, and four more want to come in tomorrow. They say

[7] Tusitala, meaning "writer of tales," was the Samoan name for RLS. Fanny was called Aolele, meaning "flying cloud," also Tamaitai, or "lady of the house." RLS's mother was known as Tamaitai Metua, or "old lady of the house," Belle as Teuila, or "beautifier of the ugly," and her son, Austin, was called Ositini.

they wish to stay here until the war actually begins. One of the three had his gun and ammunition with him. The gun he gave to Lloyd to lock up for safe-keeping, but the cartridges he could not part with, but carried them with him all through his work. Tonight, however, he asked for his gun, as he had to show up with it at Mulinuu. Pelema, on the contrary, believes he means to sleep with it like a child with a new toy.

Talolo has had permission from his high chief to stay with us. Sina, his wife, is expecting a baby. All her beautiful hair has been cut off to make warriors' headdresses, and she is quite a plain-looking girl without it. Henry (Simile), after much vacillation has decided also to stay with us. Then there are Sosimo, Misifolo, and my man Leuelu, of whom not one could be dragged away. A fine old man, taller than Lloyd, who just shaves six feet, from the opposite side of the island, announces his determination not to leave us till the war is over, and is to bring his child. He is, I believe, a lukewarm supporter of Laupepa. My poor old Lafaele asked if he might not come back to stay for the war, but mentioned that he hoped Simile would fight. He cannot get over his jealousy of Henry, nor lose hope of one day stepping in his shoes. Today we had five sisters from the convent to lunch with us, two French, one colonial, and two Samoan. Louis went after them, taking two horses, as we only expected two sisters. On the way they met a war party of about fifty men, armed with guns and bush knives. The *tala* now is that Mataafa has run away to Manono.

[JULY] 4TH

Lloyd has been down to the village. He found them in a great state of excitement about the war. They asked him what they were to do if Mataafa took the village, and begged him to put up an American flag over a little "chief house" that belongs to him and Fono in some sort of uncertain partnership. He told them that he had no authority to hoist the flag and reminded them that this is a different war from the last, when there was ill feeling on both sides. It is disgusting to think that if the two high chiefs, Laupepa and Mataafa, had been allowed by the government to make friends, as Louis advised and as they wished to do, there would have been no war and all would now be prosperity and peace. I do not wonder that the natives hang back and are unwilling to fight when they do not understand what it is all about.

Henry comes up from town and says the three consuls had a meeting yesterday and proposed to hold back the war until the arrival of the mail ship on Thursday, in hopes they may receive instructions from their governments. One of our former men came up yesterday to draw out his wages (almost all the men have left their wages with Lloyd). I asked him if he meant to act like a coward and take the heads of wounded men. He said he would take all the heads he could get and carry them to Mulinuu. I reasoned with him, as did Lloyd, but he stood respectfully firm. No doubt, he said, we were right, but each people had its own customs. The black boys were cannibals and ate their enemies, and the Samoans cut off the heads of wounded men, and he must hold by the customs of his country. I wonder with what countenance the government would receive a basket of heads. I am afraid that they have not thought to forbid this abomination, or haven't dared.

Lloyd saw Mrs. Blacklock last night, and she said that now it is universally believed that Mataafa is at Vaia at the priests' place. Apia seems to be greatly alarmed at the thought of the atrocities that are in store for them if Mataafa takes the town. The place is alive with tales of every sort, probably all untrue. Natives are trying to sell their belongings. I bought a large fine mat, at the urgent request of a young man, for six dollars. In times of peace it would have been worth forty or fifty dollars. A man has just sold Henry five fowls for three shillings, the usual price being one shilling apiece.

We ate our fat pig, so that can no longer be a temptation to foraging parties. We have laid in a great lot of kava and have a fair amount of food on hand. Of course it may all be taken from us but it is better to run the chance.

Mr. Moors is not here, having gone to the Chicago Fair. For some reason, only explainable by Joe Strong, he is our bitter enemy; more particularly Lloyd's and mine, we two being Joe's pet aversion. Also his friend, Mr. Carruthers. I was rather sorry about Carruthers, as he is almost the only man with the education of a gentleman here.

I believe his reputation is a good deal clouded, but of that I know nothing. They tried to tell me all about him in Fiji, but I refused to listen, as I saw what was meant—to put me on my guard against him. That kind of talk always angers me.

I have not, I believe, mentioned that Austin is in Monterey with my sister Nelly, and Mrs. Stevenson at home in Scotland by this time. If the war is on, at least that is a comfort.

We have had strange unseasonable weather for the time of the year: gloomy, lowering, with occasional wind and battering rain. Our first breadfruit tree is beginning to bear.

In these exciting times it is really dreadful to find oneself in the position of the British female. Lloyd and Pelema are young, and of course intolerant, but it is a little surprise to find Louis with the same ideas. I suppose if our house should be attacked, Belle and I must retire to a back apartment with some crochet work and not ask what is going on. A strange thing that would be for a person of my spirit. I was never a coward in my life and never lost my presence of mind in any emergency, and I have met some very serious ones.

Our men came home at about three to say that we must not (we women) go to the ball, as it would in all probability be no more nor less than an orgy. They had many exciting talas! Belle and I had made up our minds to strike for freedom, and announced the fact, whereupon our horses were sent for, that we might at least go to Apia. I was told to dress plainly, which I did, though I had meant to go for once in full dress. I wore a little yellow native gown. Louis in deep sulks at our attitude, Lloyd sweetly amiable, Pelema keeping out of sight. The ball a great success. One hundred and fifty people present, no orgies, and every American woman with an elaborate new gown, except the Vailimaites. I left early, for fear Louis would get too tired, but the rest stayed till three. Louis went home, as it was very cold on the verandah, and he wished to be early at his work.

[JULY] 5TH

Belle and I thought it would be a good plan to stay all day and make sketches (Belle's sketches) of war preparations. Sent our horses home and spent the day making a few calls and getting lots of materials for the pictures. Boats passing and coming in, armed men marching to and fro to the sound of drums and bugles, which the performers couldn't play upon. Maben was at the table at dinner. I told him we wished to go to Mulinuu but would not go if he objected. He said, "Go, by all means," but recommended the afternoon as a better time than the morning, which would be very quiet. It is a long sunny walk, so we thought we would take the chance of the morning.

[JULY] 6TH

Wearing shoes after so long going barefoot, and tramping about on the hard road, had made my feet sore, and swelled them so that I was quite lame, but I would have gone if I had had to walk on my head. It was suggestive to see the white traders of Apia, who a short time ago called the Samoans "niggers" and made them walk behind like dogs, parading the street cheek by jowl with well-oiled warriors. As we neared Mulinuu we met Fatulia,[8] who showed great anxiety and alarm when we told her where we were going. She hesitated a little while, saying she would prefer to go with us but had some important business on hand. We assured her we had no fear, and proceeded on our way. We looked back and saw she was doing the same, dear soul, and also saw Maben coming behind us at some little distance.

Several armed men passed us, some saying *talofa* and some not. A young warrior joined us and spoke to Belle, asking where we were going, why we did not go to Malie instead; and when Belle affected not to understand, asking again why we did not go to Mataafa, and then demanded the number of firearms at Vailima. At that moment Maben, who must have walked very fast, stepped up beside me, and the man fell humbly in the rear. Maben walked with us as far as the president's house and we went on alone.

Finding a good spot to get a sketch of the street, we sat down on the ground. A woman from a house nearby called to us to come in, which we did. It was a large, prosperous-looking Samoan house, with rifles hanging against the sides. Two women of middle age received us most politely, offering taro and kava. They knew us and spoke of

[8] Wife of Seumanutafa.

Belle's having taken sketches on the last melaga and talked together about Iopo and the *togafiti* concerning him. Belle asked, "What *togafiti*?" but when they saw she understood them they ceased speaking of Iopo. Two very pretty girls came in and posed to be sketched, also a beautiful young man, who maintained a determined silence all the time we were there, a sardonic smile on his face and in his eyes. He steadily scraped the rust from cartridges with a knife, watching us with sharp side glances.

It rained while we were there, and I was cold. The woman gave me a tapa to wrap round me, saying that it was a Samoan shawl. The sketches done, we went on as far as the house of the Chief Justice. As Belle was drawing it, three men, powerful, dangerous-looking fellows, came out from a house behind and looked over her shoulder. They were polite and friendly and, after the house was drawn, posed for Belle in a row, all in the same attitude, with their hands behind them. With "love" and "may you live," we parted and turned our steps homeward. After this we met no one who was not, or seemed not to be, friendly. One woman ran out and apologized that she had no food to offer us, and children followed us, calling out salutations.

I had a touch of sore throat, so stopped at Swann the chemist's and got a gargle, and then to the International,[9] where we had some ginger beer and cake, and back to the hotel we started from. Here we found Louis, still in the sulks. He stayed a little while and then went home, saying he would send down our horses. All the afternoon Mr. Haggard, who had had more to drink than was good for him, and besides was quite intoxicated with excitement and romantic feeling— He had several guns, a pistol and lots of ammunition and declared that he and all concerned with the land commission were, in case of the town being "rushed," going to hold the little match-box of a building where their office is. To complete the romantic effect, he bitterly wanted women to protect, and besought Belle and me to remain in town, ready to fly to the commissioners' office. He said we would lie under a table (on the upper floor) and hand cartridges out to him.

[9] An Apia hotel.

"No," I said, "I do not wish to be found dead, lying under a table, shot through the stomach."

"Well, then," he rejoined, "*I'll* go under the table and hand cartridges to *you*, and you can shoot."

His scheme was not attractive and I steadily refused. His last word was, "You are going to sell your life for a few banana trees."

I had several talks with Maben while I was there. I said, "Your people tell me that they are going to cut off the heads of the wounded and carry them in to Mulinuu. Who are these heads for? You, or the three consuls? And to what use are you going to put them? Will it not be embarrassing to the government to have a basket of heads laid at their feet?"

Maben tried to explain to me that having taken a head was equivalent to an English soldier receiving the Victoria Cross and that it took a good deal of courage to rush into the enemy's lines and cut off the head of a wounded man and carry it away. But I fear it is generally after a battle that the victorious party goes over the ground with knives and hatchets, gathering their dreadful trophies. A man came here to say good-bye to his brother before going to fight. He told how he had been taken through the last war by his father, he being a young boy, that he might learn how to fight.

"It was a great thing," he said to his brother, "to be beside a mighty warrior like our father; but when he took a head, oh that was dreadful! I tried to run away and held my hands over my eyes and screamed and cried, but now our father is dead (he went mad with excitement and died a raving lunatic), I must take his place and do what he did. I must take heads too, now, but oh it's a dreadful thing to do."

I also told Maben that I knew there were many threats among the government men against us, and that if any harm came to one of my family a white man's life should pay for it, not a native's.

"These Samoans have never wished to fight, but are fighting by the orders of white people. Now I want to know whose war this is. I want to know who is responsible if harm comes to one of my family. Is it *your* war?"

"No," said Maben, "it's not my war."

"Then is it the three consuls' war?"

Maben then tried to change the subject. The truth is it *is* the three consuls' war, and I fear they have started a ball a-rolling that cannot be easily stopped. The horses came, and we went home, Louis still in the sulks. Lloyd told how he had made himself responsible for poor old Fono's war outfit. It consisted of a cheap little trade hatchet, a small piece of tobacco, and four boxes of matches. It is all too dreadful and pathetic.

[JULY] 7TH

The government men have been allowed to go out and take their positions, but the consuls have told them that they must not begin to fight until after the mail steamer has come in. We are assured that fighting cannot begin before Monday next, the government having given strict orders to that effect. The steamer came in in the morning. Belle and Lloyd went down with Louis to meet her. They missed the captain, who was lunching at one of the plantations. The steamer had brought American sailors for the *Adams* to Honolulu, the *Adams* to come directly here. She was not at Honolulu at the time, so we do not know when to look for her. Mrs. Stevenson writes that the furniture was to leave in June. We may have no house to put it in when it comes. One body of men have been stationed on the Vaiusu road, and another sent round the mountain to cut off Mataafa's retreat. To our amusement, the men who went round the mountain went home at night to sleep. They said it was not comfortable, poor children. In the evening we were a little startled by seeing fireworks let off from a German man-of-war. There are two in the harbour, the *Buzzard* and the *Sperber*.

[JULY] 8TH

All the boys wanted to go to the races today. We let most of them go. They came home in good time, reporting that fighting had begun and there were almost no natives at the races. For two days we have been expecting the Gurrs, but they do not come. Fanua has been ill, and we thought a change and rest might do her good. Lloyd and Pelema have put up the lawn tennis things, although the lawn is not ready. It is a good plan to keep the boys amused. I brought up linen and embroidery for that little minx, Sina, for her baby clothes. As we sat round the table after dinner, at about seven o'clock a note came from Mr. Gurr to say that there had been desperate fighting at Vaitele,[10] eleven heads at Mulinuu, many wounded brought in to the mission house, and a number dead. Louis jumped up and said he must ride down to the mission at once.

"I will go, too," said I, whereupon Louis, who had agreed the night before to "bury the hatchet," said then he wouldn't go. Upon second thoughts, however, he said he would go; and then Lloyd said if we went he would go also. We had horses up, Jack for Louis, Soifu for Lloyd and Old Upsala for me. I found Upsala a very easy pleasant horse to ride, but a little touched in the wind. He trotted along, quite fast enough, with a long smooth stride.

We had, I had forgotten to say, heard a *tala* from Talolo when he returned from the races, to the effect that there had been some kind of a fight between Haggard and the manager of the Tivoli; that Abdul had gone to his master's rescue and had been more or less damaged, being hurt on the cheek bone. Talolo saw Abdul and asked him about the affair. Abdul replied that he did not wish to talk about his master's affairs; that he would tell me if he saw me, but no one else.

The night was starry but dark, so we carried a lantern with us. As after the village the road is good, we left our lantern there. Had we been on any other errand, I should have thought the ride delightful. We stopped first at the Tivoli and Louis went in to see if Maben were there. He was not, but poor Haggard was lying asleep on a sofa in the verandah. Old Joe the boatman, who has lost one hand by dynamite in the usual South Sea fashion, stood on the front steps beside a German sailor, swaying from side to side, quite drunk. He announced to the sailor that Lloyd was a fine gentleman, and to the Universe that a star was speeding across the sky towards Malie to rest over Mataafa's head.

"There it goes—look!" he shouted. "And to hell with Laupepa!" Lurching forward, he discovered my presence for the first time, crying out as he did so, "By Gawd! By Gawd, Miss!"

Then on to the mission house. People were running back and forth

[10] A village.

over the lawn, and lights shone through all the windows. Mr. Clarke came to meet us and said it was quite true, he had [blank] wounded men, and three dead had been brought in, that eleven heads had been brought in to the government, and were there hanging in baskets on a tree near the king's hut in Mulinuu. Amongst them was the head of a village maid, a thing unheard of in Samoa. Gurr and Fanua were there with Mrs. Clarke, who was very bad with a cold. Mrs. C, who is much of an invalid and pretty deaf, told us about the difficulties she had had at dinner that day in arranging her party. They just had to go in anyhow, by two's or by three's, as it happened. She was too hard of hearing to know that at the same time Fanua was telling us how her adopted mother, Fatulia, had looked at the heads brought in, and amongst them had recognized the last three blood relations she had in the world.

Poor Fanua was very restless and excited. Her husband said she neither ate nor slept, and could not keep still a moment.

Tomorrow morning a party goes out to bury the dead left on the field. We were told that Mataafa took no heads, that he was beaten back so quickly that he had no time. This I do not believe. The party that is to go out in the morning to bury the dead seems a proof that there are mutilated bodies still lying there. No Samoan would leave the body of one of his party lying all night where the head might be in danger of capture.

Mr. Krause told Louis that he saw a number of dead bodies, he thought about ten, though he only counted five, being carried into Apia, and one of them was headless. All the heads, we were told, were from Savaii, even the poor girl's. According to custom, Fanua is to go in the morning to look at the heads.

Louis went in where the wounded were lying at the mission. The German man-of-war doctor, considerably under the influence of drink (he had been dining with Mr. Beckman), seemed to be doing his work well enough; and Louis said it was pleasant to see the pink young German sailors helping the doctor and Mr. Clarke. Two men were dying: one shot through both lungs, a very fine, handsome old man of an unusually dark colour for a Samoan. I saw and remarked such a man from the hotel verandah. Quite a young boy was having his arm dressed for a flesh wound. Two people held his legs lest he should struggle, but he kept still and made no complaint. Miss Large happened to pass the group, when she said, "I don't believe you know that his leg is hurt." On examination he was found to be shot through both thighs.

[JULY] 9TH. SUNDAY

Food is being sent to the front by the families of the fighting men. Lloyd sent a basket to Fono. I trust he may be living to receive it. It contained enough kava for two large bowls, three tins of meat, and some ship's biscuits. I don't suppose he will use the kava himself but will present it to some high chief; but to receive it and be able to offer it to his superior puts him in a very genteel position. I suppose a couple of baskets of champagne would be its equivalent in England. We hear that the heads have been, some of them, returned to Malie, according to the custom the girl's head wrapped in silk handkerchiefs. Three more were brought in last night, and more wounded men. Yandall[11] has come up from Haggard's with a flag, but we have our old *Casco* flag flying over the house already, and an American flag ready to hoist over Lloyd's cottage, if it seems necessary, at any time. When we went down to town last night—

L O U I S .   SUNDAY, 9TH JULY

Well, the war has at last begun. For four or five days, Apia has been filled by these poor children with their faces blacked, and the red handkerchief about their brows, that makes the Malietoa uniform, and the boats have been coming in from the windward, some of them 50 strong, with a drum and bugle on board—the bugle always ill-played—and a sort of jester leaping and capering on the sparred nose of the boat, and the whole crew uttering from time to time a kind of menacing ululation. Friday they marched out to the bush; and yesterday morning we heard that some had returned to their houses for the night, as they found it "so uncomfortable." After dinner a messenger came up to me with a note, that the wounded were arriving at the Mission House. Fanny, Lloyd and I

[11] Described by Moors as a half-caste Britisher.

saddled and rode off with a lantern; it was a fine starry night, though pretty cold. We left the lantern at Tanugamanono, and then down in the starlight. I found Apia, and myself, in a strange state of flusteration; my own excitement was gloomy and (I may say) truculent; others appeared imbecile; some sullen. The best place in the whole town was the hospital. A longish frame-house it was, with a big table in the middle for operations, and ten Samoans, each with an average of four sympathisers, stretched along the walls. Clarke was there, steady as a die; Miss Large, little spectacled angel, showed herself a real trump; the nice, clean, German orderlies in their white uniforms looked and meant business. (I hear a fine story of Miss Large—a cast-iron teetotaller—going to the public-house for a bottle of brandy.)

The doctors were not there when I arrived; but presently it was observed that one of the men was going cold. He was a magnificent Samoan, very dark, with a noble aquiline countenance, like an Arab, I suppose, and was surrounded by seven people, fondling his limbs as he lay: he was shot through both lungs. And an orderly was sent to the town for the (German naval) doctors, who were dining there. . . . Back to the hospital about 11:30; found the German doctors there. Two men were going now, one that was shot in the bowels— he was dying rather hard, in a gloomy stupor of pain and laudanum, silent, with contorted face. The chief, shot through the lungs, was lying on one side, awaiting the last angel; his family held his hands and legs; they were all speechless, only one woman suddenly clasped his knee, and "keened" for the inside of five seconds, and fell silent again. . . .

FANNY. [JULY] 10TH

Mataafa is routed, and after firing Malie, burning all except his own private house, which he thought dangerous to the church nearby, fled to, it is supposed, Manono. Poor White Man's house, where we drank kava the other day, is in ashes, and Poor White Man gone, no one knows where. I cannot bear to think of the kind old man, with his two lame legs (he had fe fe in both), a homeless fugitive. Mataafa's son[12] was killed with a hatchet. He was so close to his enemy that he could not get his gun in position, received a blow in the side of his head from a hatchet, fell, and was decapitated. A relation of his on the government side brought in the headless trunk, carried on a pole, and wrapped in old mats. The man who took his head walked first with the head wrapped in a piece of fine mat and was followed by the bearers of the body. This son of Mataafa eloped with his wife, whose relations never forgave her, she being a *taupo-sa*, or sacred maid. When the husband went out to fight, the wife refused to leave him. They were both killed in the same fight and her head was one of those brought in to the government. In all, three heads of women have been brought in to Mulinuu, a thing unheard of before in Samoa. Women have been shot because they ran in the way of shots, but no fighting man ever before dreamed of taking a woman's head, which, as Henry says, means disgrace to the children's children. I hear no corroboration of the *tala* of the sending back a girl's head to Mataafa with the handkerchiefs around it.

Mr. Dines' wife's cousin (or brother) took a head that was smeared in the usual manner, with black. When he presented it at Mulinuu the black was washed off and he discovered it to be the head of his beloved brother. Mr. Dines said that when he saw him last he was sitting with the head in his hands, kissing it, and bathing it with tears. If I mistake not, these two men are near relatives of Laupepa's. Fatulia's stepson brought in the head of her brother. To receive the heads, the king sat on the steps of the office of Maben, in the house that was the president's.

Louis saw Maben yesterday and demanded that the takers of women's heads should be punished. I think, from what Maben said, that he is afraid to take any steps at all. Well, there was a woman's head for each great power, or, if one likes better, for each consul. It is now conceded that, so far as known, Mataafa took no heads and committed no atrocities. He may have had no opportunity, but I believe he would try to prevent the taking of heads, as he has talked

---

[12] Leaupepe, actually Mataafa's nephew, but called his son, in the Samoan custom.

of those matters so much with his white friends. But now, driven to the wall, everything lost, all he held most dear gone forever, I should not like to think of the chance of reprisals.

Henry came in this morning from Apia with a strange pallid countenance and said he wished to put a question. A number of men in Apia wished him to do so. The question was, "Whose war is this? Who made this war?" We answered, "The three consuls," of course. I did not think of it at the time, but I believe he had been told that it was Louis. It is too terrible to think that Louis held Mataafa back, when had he fallen on Mulinuu and Apia he would have been upheld and now safe and happy, with all his loved ones round him, at the expense, possibly, of a few worthless lives. In his anxiety to do the right and profit by his friends' counsel he has come to ruin, and probably a shameful death.

Louis commands that we keep the peace with Maben; not only that, but to be friendly with him. Until the blood of women is washed from Maben's hand I cannot touch it. I do not myself feel innocent. Thinking we did right both for Mataafa and for Samoa, and for the fear of bloodshed, we counseled peace. But the fact is that remotely, because of our advice, these women's heads were brought in to the representatives of the three great powers, and like cowards they sit silent. Poor old Laupepa, who when Dines saw him was shaking as though with ague, is only a tool and cipher. The present advisers to the king, Cusack-Smith, Beirman, and Blacklock, made and directed the war, and gave orders to the army (if army it can be called). Laupepa signed what he was told to sign.

Misifolo did not come back this morning as usual. This was not like him. We asked the other boys if they knew what was the matter. It came out that he had eloped with a young girl from Talolo's village, Talolo being the go-between. After lunch Louis went down to the mission to help nurse the sick, though I had thought they wanted none of us. Lloyd and I went later to Fanua's to ask her to take us to Fatulia's that we might try to say how sorry we felt for her in her terrible sorrow. She had gone to Savaii but just before we arrived. Sitione took a head in the fight. He was seen covered with fresh blood, having just cut off the head. That "fresh blood" sounds horribly like the decapitation of a wounded man. The night before, Louis sent Pelema to the Clarkes to see if they wanted help (rather to Pelema's disgust, I fear). He saw the wounded men and said the one shot through both lungs looked just like the description I gave of the man who called me "pig-face." It is supposed he will die, poor wretch. At the crossroads we met Louis, returning, with his horse, Jack, dead lame. He had, apparently, received a chilling reception from the mission, who had been fighting among themselves. Pelema had the same experience the night before. Mr. Hills was to go to Manono in the morning to look after Mataafa's wounded.

After lunch Pelema ordered his horse in a very mysterious way. After he was gone, Lloyd told me that his destination was Malie. He asked L to go with him but L said he could not bear to see the place now, burnt and destroyed and in the hands of its enemies. He came back in time for dinner. At Malie he met Daplyn[13] and Christian and Much, little Janney and Davis, all of whom had come by boat. He saw an immense procession of a very wild and savage sort, the people daubed with black and decked with feathers and streamers, dancing and going through the pantomime of head hunting. The men who had taken heads in the fight carried in their teeth great lumps of raw pork cut in the semblance of heads. Quite to his surprise, he met Iopo, who received him like a long-lost brother, his face blacked, but the dispenser of weapons had had the good sense to give no gun into the hands of our "wild Irishman," as we always called him. Iopo said he and his wife were most anxious to get home to Vailima and would come as soon as they were allowed.

Belle was very much amused by my poor old Lafaele, who came to see me on Sunday. He wants to come back in a week, when his month will be up with Carruthers. Lloyd told him that instead of the sixteen shillings a week he got from Carruthers he would only get his old wages, thirteen shillings here.

"Never mind money," said Lafaele. "I no care for that. I like come back because I love Madame too much."

Belle declared that his expressions hardly sounded proper. It was

[13] A. J. Daplyn, a Sydney artist. A painting by him of RLS now hangs in Stevenson House, Monterey.

the translation of *alofa*, which Lafaele has learned since he left. Mr. Dines came up late and looked at Jack. He has a wind gall on his knee and an abscess in his hoof.

[JULY] 11TH

Belle has made some excellent pictures of the war. Today she could not remember exactly what her notes meant of the president's house, so we rode down to take a look at it. As we passed the door, intent on studying the building, we both saw Maben with the tail of our eyes, writing at a table just inside, where the king received the heads. He seemed thunderstruck at the sight of us and remained in the same position, his pen in the air, when we came back. We affected to be quite unconscious of his proximity and examined the house like "intending" burglars. We met Seu[14] on the road, marching at the head of a considerable body of armed men. Seu ran to meet us, holding out both hands, greeting us most warmly, almost affectionately. I could plainly see a thrill run through his party at the sight. They stepped on one side, giving us the road, and all who caught our eyes gave us *talofa*.

On the way back, we stopped at Laulii's. She was in such a state of excitement that she could hardly speak English at all. She informed us that all Fatulia's relatives were killed, including the half of a brother. She meant a half-brother. She is in great fear of reprisals for the women's heads. The man who is known to have taken one woman's head is from her town of Laulii, where she was once maid. If there were reprisals she really would be in danger, but I am sure that is impossible. At the gate we were met by the bride and Loia. On the bank by the gate, to our surprise, sat [blank]. Talolo said the man had brought him a letter, but was altogether very reticent. The Atuas[15] go tonight in their boats to Manono after Mataafa, and the others in the morning. In the town there seemed no sign of rejoicing over their victory. All the faces looked sad and anxious, and depression and gloom seemed lying on the town. I think they are shocked at having killed so many of their friends, and humiliated by the taking of women's heads. In all fourteen heads were brought in to

[14] Seumanutafa, chief of Apia.
[15] Atua, a district of Upolu.

the government, eleven men's and three women's. Henry says Savaii will go solidly for Mataafa. They have no fear of the men-of-war and are delighted to get a real high chief to themselves. But no one can tell in the least.

Henry says the account of the opening of the fight, generally told, and believed by him, is as follows. The Laupepas stopped in front of the Mataafas, who were behind a stone wall. They lowered their guns and Tofi and Asi[16] called out to the Mataafas to put down their guns and come out and have a friendly talk, this being quite *faa Samoan.* When the Mataafas came, their chief smoked with the others, talking and laughing, when Asi gave the Mataafa a Judas kiss. This was the signal for the Laupepas, who shot the Mataafas as they ran to cover. We have heard exactly this story from a number of people, up to the point of the kissing.

"Then," they said, "the fighting suddenly began. Some say that the Mataafas shot two of the Laupepas, but nobody knows really how it began, except that it started instantly upon the kissing."

I wonder—I wonder at the forbearance of these Samoans. Were I a Samoan I would, and I believe successfully, agitate for a massacre of the whites. Clarke, the other night, told Louis that the *Germans!* were going to take up Mataafa's cause. But who could believe that? He also hinted that Louis had made this war. I am almost tempted to wish he had. Things in that case would be very different now. When we were in town we stopped at the photographer's, thinking he might have photographs of war incidents. He had none.

Belle said, "Why did you not run out with your camera when the heads were brought in?"

"I thought more of my carcass than my photographs," was the reply.

"It was a pity," pursued Belle, "that you did not get a photograph of the women's heads."

"Oh," returned he with polite hopefulness, "there may be more."
[JULY] 12TH

Our fine old man has been snatched from us. It seems he is a

16 Samoan chiefs.

"suspect." One of his family came for him before and the old man bought him off with five dollars. But this man said he must go or be outlawed by his clan. Never did warrior depart so unwillingly. The man who came was a fine handsome fellow and the first, who accepted the five dollars, was still better. They say there are only twelve of them altogether. Pelema has seen six, each a model of strength and manly beauty. We had kava made, but the stranger hurried away without partaking, though he was willing to take some food and a cup of tea. Kava may be of the nature of salt. Our poor old man said he had better go at once, that there should be no appearance of unwillingness on his part, but would return later in the day. He had a fine send-off, with foods and quantities of kava root in a basket. The man who came for him says the expedition to Manono is off, as they have information that Mataafa is in Savaii. They mean to feast today, and leave tomorrow for Savaii.

The *tala* now is that the Laupepas are disgusted with the queen (she is not the king's true wife and is an out-islander besides, and a coarse, rowdy, fat woman, not in the least like a Samoan). According to the *tala*, the war party going to Savaii do not mean to fight at all, but will propose peace to Mataafa, and after that is arranged they will return and oust the queen.

It seems to me that the power of the three consuls and Maben is nil. When hundreds of fighting men get off as far as Savaii I imagine they will pay small heed to these four whites in Apia.

Talolo has been up to speak to me. He said he had a dreadful thing to tell me: that Sina's brother, Afega, was one of the men who brought in a girl's head. He seems to have had a letter, and says his mother is in Manono and that Mataafa, after landing his war party in Manono, pressed on to Savaii alone, hoping to rouse the whole island. He expected Manono to be attacked and left his men there to fight. I think, myself, it was to engage the attention of the enemy while he was busy in Savaii. Talolo has heard this *tala* and believes it; but I told him that I must write nothing in my book for fact that was not strictly true.

Here is the *tala*. The *taupo-sa* was shot in the knee and fell in a sitting position. A man ran up to her with a small hatchet. The girl cried out, holding her hands before her in a supplicating manner, "*faa moli moli*, I am a woman." But the man, shouting that he did not care what she was, proceeded to hack off her head with his hatchet.

It is denied that Sitione took a head. I am sure, now, that Sina's legal marriage will not come off. Talolo says she is ashamed when anybody looks at her, because of the disgraceful act of her brother. The old man talked to Talolo, telling him that Sina's family were far too low and common for him to fasten himself to for life. "That old man is just like a father to me," said Talolo, "he does everything I tell him." This afternoon Talolo is going out to make it his business to find out the exact truth about the three women, their names, and who took their heads.

Henry says a man, who saw the first woman's head brought in, told him that the hair was short, but short in the woman's fashion, with a fringe cut across the forehead and curling thick around the neck, "six inches long, just like yours, madame," he added. I told him if I could bring Sina's brother to punishment, the more shameful the better, I should do it. He said that was what he wished.

The *tala* now is that Mataafa went to Savaii and was told to go away, as they wished to have nothing to do with him. Pelema, who went to town, brought back this *tala*. Also that the reason for the anger of the soldiers against Laupepa's wife was that Laupepa excused himself for not attending the fono at Malie because his wife "was not well."

It seems that the villagers of Falealili in Atua have the right, when marching in wartime, to kill anyone who crosses their path. They happened to pass in front of the Tivoli, where Haggard was leaning over the balcony. There seemed to be a little bustling of some young men who were on the road, and when the young men ran for the mission, Haggard, thinking it all fun, applauded. No fun was intended, however. The young men saved themselves, but poor old Krause was, as Pelema said, "nearly scragged." They also met the Chief Justice who, after some rough hustling, began to see what was meant and got himself out of the road.

Sina has gone to Apia. Talolo expects her back but I do not. The

Japan plums that Pelema and I planted out on the arrival of the last steamer have blossoms on them. In the evening Louis got a note from Mr. Clarke, a very nervous *faa moli moli* letter. When we first went down to the mission I was convinced that we were "intruders," and it seems we were. I never could have gone myself, but Louis was in such a frantic state of excitement that I was determined to keep him in sight. I have never personally meddled with the missionaries, though always good friends enough without any intimacy. I have never put my foot inside the church and am not likely to do so. To begin with, once would be enough to establish a precedent, and I've seen all I wish of that sort of thing in a small community. Louis was mad enough once to give a sort of sermon, by request, in their Sunday school. Such scandals flew, in consequence, as never were heard of except amongst religious folk. I did not go to hear the Sunday school sermon.

[JULY] 13TH

Louis sent a rather curt note to Mr. C in reply to his of yesterday. Lloyd—.

[JULY] 17TH

I have not been able to write in my diary for real downright anger. Louis went to town and had all Maben's talk filtered through Haggard and Blacklock [17]and came home filled with the *tala* that Mataafa is an intriguing coward, and in a letter to go with Belle speaks, without really intending it, I believe [about five words missing].* A little while ago all the talk was of Mataafa, the powerful chief, whom all respected. That was when they were afraid of him. Now, when they are afraid of their own men, and Mataafa is a childless fugitive, all the stones are thrown at him. To begin with, my sympathies are always with the "underdog in the fight." But, besides, I remember, when Mataafa was the man before whom all trembled, we offered our friendship and broke bread with him. If I gave him loyalty then, fifty thousand times more do I give it now. They say they have found compromising letters from Louis addressed to Mataafa. That is not true, as Louis wrote no compromising letters.

[17] The following passage, the conclusion of which is marked by an asterisk, is suppressed in the manuscript.

[18]But this diary of mine I now make a compromising document: compromising to one purpose, and I intend to do everything in my power to save Mataafa: doubtless very little, but it shall be my utmost. And if Louis turns his face from him by the fraction of an inch,* I shall wear black in public if they murder him, or if he is brought in to Apia a prisoner I shall go down alone and kiss his hand as my king. Louis says this is arrant mad quixotism. I suppose it is; but when I look at the white men at the head of the government and cannot make up my mind which is the greater coward, my woman's heart burns with shame and fury and I am ready for any madness.

A little while ago both Maben and Blacklock talked of the war to me, and before me, making it clearly understood that they were going to let loose the dogs of war. Now that they are alarmed lest they get bitten, the whole burden is thrown upon Malietoa Laupepa. "He was so *determined*," said Haggard yesterday, "that no one could move him." I said that was something new, to find the amiable old sheep, at whom they have all been laughing, suddenly turned into the determined wolf.

As we sat on the verandah Mr. Haggard's interpreter, Yandall, appeared with a wound in his head and a bruise on his jaw. He had, while in a boat over which the American flag was flying, and with a "safe conduct" from Laupepa in his possession, been struck from another boat and knocked senseless. Haggard was very meek on the subject. Suddenly I rose up and said vehemently that all the white men in Samoa were cowards, and left the party. I am afraid I behaved very badly. [19]At luncheon healths were being drunk, and I drank the health of "H. J. Moors, my worst enemy and the only white man clinging to Samoa who is not a coward."*

Yandall brought news of an English man-of-war having arrived. This morning an uncle of Simile's who has been in the war, a native of Savaii, came to see him. He was taller, older, better looking and

---

[18] The following passage, the conclusion of which is marked by an asterisk, is suppressed in the manuscript.
[19] The following passage, the conclusion of which is marked by an asterisk, is suppressed in the manuscript.

more "chieflike" than Simile, but otherwise just like him, with the same wrong eye. I tried in vain until this afternoon to extract his news from the reticent Henry. This is what he finally told me: that Savaii asks for a fono at which both Laupepa and Mataafa shall be present.

"If this is refused by the white men, what then?" I asked.

"That's the trouble," replied Henry.

"Well?" said I.

"Then they go with Mataafa," confessed Henry reluctantly.

A while ago I was called to receive the information that our fine old man, the unwilling warrior, was returned, and in the kitchen. He jumped up from his bread and tea, his first desire, and ran to meet me with glowing eyes. He said he had returned on account of ill health. Lloyd was unfeeling enough to tease him about his "high-chief sickness." He seems to think that he may be allowed to stop now at Vailima. He looks thin and starved, poor old soul.

Belle has just received a note from town telling us that it is said that a scheme of ours (Belle's and mine) to get food to a sick old chief in Manono has so far been successful. Another compromising statement if my diary should be overhauled. No one has to do with it but us, or really me, myself, as Belle only talked about it, while I gave the money; very little indeed, but it was all I had of my very own, that I had earned myself and had kept for a good many years. I only found it the other day, in a hiding place of my own. I thought sometime I might wish a few shillings for a private charity and hid it away for that purpose. Well, it has paid for a few biscuits and a little salt beef for a sick and suffering old man whose name, Poor White Man, was given to him because he could never refuse help to any poor white man. They do not seem to be rushing to *his* aid now, "to any alarming extent." [About ten words missing.] The note received said also that all the warships are going over to Manono, supposedly on a peaceful errand, and that the German warships are under the command of the English captain.

Louis has come home. He has not seen any of the Maben [about ten words missing]. The captain of the man-of-war turned out to be a Catholic and with no desire for indiscriminate bloodshed.

He said that he would go over to Manono and ask Mataafa to come on board his ship and have a friendly talk. He will propose that Mataafa give himself up, and the captain will ensure his safety. Louis was to write a letter to M, and if possible the captain will take Father Broyer with him. So much treachery has been used towards Samoans by the whites that some such step is necessary. In case of M's refusal the captain will be compelled to bombard.

Pelema has had the true and exact story of the attack on Yandall. He was in a cutter hired by Janney, an American, and the American flag was flying. They were returning from Manono, whence Yandall was fetching his children and his very aged grandmother under a "safe conduct" from the king. Some men in a boat came up to them, looking, as they said, for the wounded from Mataafa's camp, to take their heads. The missionaries had offered to receive Mataafa's wounded and care for them, under a safe conduct from the government. They denied having any wounded on board, and either Janney or Hall pointed to the flag. The men in the boat, at that, struck Yandall on the head with a musket, and on the cheek with an oar, and began to drag him from the boat, saying they were going to cut off his head and that he was a bad man. Just after he was struck, a woman in Janney's boat threw an English flag over Yandall's head. He was dragged into the assailant's boat and carried off, flag and all, if I understand correctly. Yandall is a British subject. Janney's boat followed after them until they landed and carried Yandall off into the bush, where the white men supposed he was being murdered. Seeing a chief walking along, the white men appealed to him to save Yandall, and gave him a present of a tin of biscuit. He finally said that Yandall would not be killed, because of being in company with the two white men, but that other attempts would be made to murder him. The white men then came back, and the unfortunate Yandall followed afterwards. Yandall complained that his old grandmother, nearly a hundred years of age, had been maltreated. From all I can make out, the ill treatment was not very serious, consisting mostly of her being roughly dragged out of the boat and hustled about on shore. Louis took a note sheet of things that he wished to remember to speak to the captain about.

Maben may propose that Mataafa's followers, some 800, on Manono, be disarmed until it can be settled what to do with them. If that happens, and it would sound most reasonable to a foreigner, they may be all massacred. If it looks at all necessary, Louis will offer to go with the ship to Manono. He has, first, to go to Cusack-Smith to ask permission to send his letter to Mataafa. It seems very undignified for Louis to do so but I suppose it is the right thing. C-Smith is such a poor, little, imitative creature, with such a comically ugly face, that it is rather shocking to ask him anything. He has the most ferocious curled-up moustaches on the meanest mug possible. His wife is a tall, slashing, rather vulgar good-looking lass. The question any woman asks herself is how could she marry such a pallid brownie? Louis came home very late. He had seen the captain again and given his letter. The captain has given his word that he will not give up the persons of Mataafa nor any of his chiefs. He has promised to keep them on his ship.

[JULY] 18TH

All the ships left early in the morning. In the afternoon, late, the two German ships came back with the news that Mataafa had surrendered and was on board the English ship with twenty-eight of his chiefs, Poor White Man among them.

[JULY] 19TH

Early this morning Louis and Lloyd went to Apia to meet the returning ship, having been told that it would be in soon after daylight. They were the first aboard, and the only friendly faces the prisoners had seen. Mataafa looked old and broken and made a wandering speech to Louis. One of the chiefs tried in vain to speak to Lloyd and at last, when he managed to get in a word, asked if they were to lose their heads. There seemed a good deal of feeling in the wardroom about the behaviour of their ship. The captain had given Mataafa three hours to come to a decision, a very short time for the slow ceremonial Samoans. He was getting very anxious, when the chiefs turned up only fifteen minutes before the time was up. The wardroom officers said the prisoners spent the night in weeping. Blacklock was to have a governor, a really trustworthy person, appointed as governor, and the Aana[20] people were to remain with him to guard the rank and file, who were disarmed. The ship had hardly turned to leave before flames broke out. The guards were burning the houses already. Mataafa fell on his knees to the captain and besought him to save his helpless people. Blacklock, I believe, went back and reported that there was no danger to life. While Louis and Lloyd were on board, the prisoners were divided, and twelve sent on board the German man-of-war. There is a *tala* that Jack Eina, Henry's cousin, who was acting as interpreter, asked about the captain's word of honour that he had given to the effect that the prisoners were not to leave the English ship, and was sent ashore to the Catholic mission. What, indeed, about the captain's word of honour? Being among English people, I had taken up their ideas, that such a thing as an Englishman's word of honour existed. The captain's excuse was that he gave his word on the strength of *Laupepa's having given his!* The man whose honour hangs round the neck of that poor sheep is in a bad way indeed. The wardroom seemed to feel their position rather sharply. And well they might; already fire and treachery on their hands.

All day my poor Talolo lay prone, with his face covered. I, not yet awakened to the fact that an Englishman's honour was of very brittle material, tried to console him by a beautiful picture of that chameleon attribute, but he only murmured something about "white all the same—Manono chiefs"—referring to the treachery against them when dynamite, bought from the American consul, Blacklock, and laid by order of the Chief Justice, so nearly blew them all in atoms. It is a very interesting thing to see how the English and American consuls hold by each other. The English consul knows that the dynamite was bought from Blacklock, and Blacklock knows of a discreditable monetary transaction in which the English consul was concerned. They *must* be friends. It is very decent behaviour that so many men in Apia know this thing of the English consul, which would ruin his career if known, and yet do not tell it, for most of them despise and hate him.

[20] Aana, a district of Upolu.

To go back to the ship. Lloyd went to shore and got tobacco, ava,[21] an ava bowl and strainer and scraper. Also a crucifix for Mataafa that had belonged to the priest, Father Didier, who was on one of the many schooners that have disappeared, and eight white lava lavas for the chiefs, who had nothing but a bit of tapa to wear. Charley Taylor sent the best shirt he could find as a present to M. Lloyd was very much overcome at the sight of M and the chiefs, with their anxious eyes and suppressed excitement, and confessed to tears. Before he went for the ava he went to another part of the ship, where Poor White Man was waiting with the chiefs to be sent aboard the German man-of-war. Lloyd said the old man was magnificent. He held his head in the air like an old lion and said his heart was strong. He had fought on the side of the right and he had no fear, whatever was his fate. Religion was not mentioned. He only spoke as a man. Mataafa, on the contrary, had a saintlike expression and only said he left all to God, in whom he put his trust. In telling the story, Lloyd broke out, "It was hard times on the old man to have nothing more than that to trust to," which was very like the parson's "Has it come to that?"

When Lloyd came back with the ava, Poor White Man was on the German ship, so he and his presents had to be carried there. Lloyd kissed the old man, to the wonder of the white men, and in a few minutes had a hint that he had better leave. The chiefs crowded around him to shake hands, reaching over each other's heads to do so. Their gratitude was out of all proportion to the service rendered; but the poor souls must have felt very friendless, with not a single person coming near them, and glad to see a kind face.

Louis saw Cusack-Smith and spoke about the head-hunting. I think there is no doubt but Laupepa wished to refuse the heads brought in to him, but did not dare to do so without Maben's support. I fear that Maben kept out of the way for that very reason. He did not dare to advise the king not to receive heads in the face of the men who brought them in. It is such a difficult thing for a woman to believe a man to be a coward. I do not forget Maben's burst at a dinner party at Haggard's, when he said no man did any-

[21] Kava.

thing whatever for the good of his country or his fellow men except as it served him for his own interest. Well, Maben's sly shifty eyes said the same thing. I had begun to like him, really because he was Louis's countryman.

When the two house boys had finished their work they went out to Talolo and for hours I heard impassioned prayer rising from the native house. They fully believe that Talolo's mother and brother have been treacherously deserted by the English captain and that they are now lying dead and decapitated. And the worst of it is that they may be right. I could not face up to Talolo to tell him about the captain's breach of faith and the burning houses he left behind him with only Blacklock's word to assure him that the unarmed prisoners were safe in the hands of their enemies.

Louis asked Blacklock what he had done about sending the governor.

"Oh, I have spoken to the king."

"And what is the name of the chief trustworthy enough for such a position?"

"Never asked," was the reply; and then he volunteered the information that he wished to hang Mataafa to a cocoanut tree, and described his visit to his fallen enemy, how he insulted the old man when he went aboard the ship.

We have seen two instances, one of English honour, the other of American chivalry; only thank God the American is only a sham article, being of English colonial birth, and bearing all the marks of Jewish extraction. Sewall was a ranting schoolboy, but neither of these things were possible to him.

"Burning houses!" said he (Blacklock). "They were not houses. They were only native huts."

I know what a "native hut" is, for I have built three, and would feel it a serious loss if one were burned. It was as though the Queen should say of the burning of Blacklock's house, "It was not a palace. It was only an auctioneer's wooden house."

It is curious to see Fanny so full of prejudice at this moment; but she was not entirely herself during the events described. From all I have heard and read, she had fewer prejudices than most people. Louis himself, as we have seen, was capable of seeming so pro-British as to appear anti-American. Louis was once questioned by a correspondent as to whether he was anti-Semitic. His reply was vigorous and disarming and, as one might expect, in the negative.

[JULY] 20TH

Early this morning Talolo and all the men set to cooking native food for the prisoners. Lloyd and Pelema left at 11 in the morning with heavy loads for four men. Taro cooked in the ground, fine large ones of the best sort, one hundred *poli samis*, young cocoanuts, and bananas. They have not yet returned. At 12 last night the mail steamer came. Mr. Harris was on board and came ashore to wake up poor Haggard to receive a bag for Louis, containing game and celery. Belle's pictures went off. May they cheer the hearts of the government officials—cowards all! Louis received a note from Mrs. Cusack-Smith yesterday to say that she had put down his name for a five-dollar subscription for the wounded.

[22]I wish I were able to write a little tale that I might save some money of my own. I know that people speak of my [about eight words missing]. I don't mind that so much, for there is such a blessing and pleasure in sharing anything in the [about six words missing]. All the money I have earned [about eight words missing] away to other people. Of the last I got twenty-five dollars out of a hundred and fifty, which I sent to my dying brother-in-law. I wonder what would become of a man, and to what he would degenerate, if his life was that of a woman's: to get the "run of her teeth" and presents of her clothes, and supposed to be always under bonds of the deepest gratitude for any further sums. I would work very hard to earn a couple of pounds a month, and I could easily earn much more, but there is my position as Louis's wife, therefore I cannot. Louis comes in and proposes to send [about two words missing] which is rather awkward: both about the German boy and the above, which looks like begging for money, which idea would shame me beyond measure.*

Lloyd home. Saw the captain, who seemed much displeased by

[22] The following passage, the conclusion of which is marked by an asterisk, is suppressed in the manuscript.

Blacklock's conduct about the burning of the houses. The other day, Blacklock informed Louis, with shuddering horror, "The captain's a Papist."

"Good God!" was Louis's reply. Query: is B Christian or Jew? Lloyd saw the chiefs on the English ship; was told that they might, of course, receive visitors. "They are not criminals, but prisoners of war." The captain had been heard assuring Mataafa over and over again, always in the same form of words, that his life was safe while on board. M seems to have finally understood, and the chiefs seemed quite cheerful and at home. A loud shout from the German ship, a long way off, was heard. Lloyd recognized it as the shouting of ava, our ava. The captain wished to send a responsible white man to Manono and said why not Lloyd, to which Lloyd replied that he was a Mataafa sympathizer. Lloyd went to the German ship to distribute food but was politely informed that no one was allowed to speak to the prisoners. Two of the officers came up to dinner; very pleasant, right sort of people, one with a stammer that somehow made one like him the better for it. Talolo, who is still very ill, flew about to get dinner for them, and produced a very creditable meal. I had told the boys they might come in after dinner and see the officers. So soon as coffee was served, I saw shirts being drawn over brown shoulders at the open door of the hall. They all filed in, Talolo at their head, a very presentable body of men. Talolo made a little speech of welcome and the two officers, who were not prepared for orations (they knew not their Samoan yet), were quite embarrassed. The one because he could think of nothing to say, the other because he had plenty to say, but could not, on account of his stammer.

[JULY] 21ST

Mataafa wants Henry for an interpreter. I thought he ought to go, though he is not a good interpreter. I am afraid of some tricky half-caste being imposed on M. The rest did not seem to agree with me, so no more is said. Lloyd went down to C-Smith to take the protest against head hunting. I don't know why that should remind me of Louis's first meeting with any of the officers of the warship. One of the men who dined here was at the Tivoli, apparently awaiting someone very anxiously. As Louis stopped a moment at the door, the man asked eagerly, "Are you Mr. Smith?"

"Why the hell *should* I be Smith?" was Louis's savage reply, at which the stranger incontinently fled.

Lloyd came back to say that notices were up in town, signed by the three consuls, ordering the soldiers to disperse and return to their own homes. The last time Louis was in town he asked Black-lock if it would not be a good idea to disarm the men as they came in. "Yes," said B, "but I am afraid we have not large enough a force," which was an odd way for one to speak of his own forces. I think Frankenstein is more and more alarmed by his monster. Aside from anything else, it was utter madness to put firearms into the hands of three thousand uncivilized men, that, unarmed, are well nigh uncontrollable. If the *Adams*, the American ship, came in, there would be an attempt to disarm, but not otherwise. No gun or am-munition carried away will ever appear again [about ten words miss-ing]. The C J has fallen out of sight. He is neither mentioned nor remembered. Lloyd said tonight, speaking of Tom Balfour, "He's a superior sort of Isla made on an inferior pattern." Louis did not seem like himself. I believe the influenza did him more damage than we thought. Sometimes, they say, people are a year or more getting over it. Misifolo has quarrelled with his bride already. He has a bad cold, also Talolo and the old man. I gave them all three a davis powder. Sosimo carelessly pulled the heart out of one of my most cherished plants. I can hardly forgive him.

SUNDAY [JULY] 23RD

Had Carrick, editor of the *Herald*, to lunch; asked Daplyn, who wandered up late in the afternoon and stayed to dinner instead. We were very much annoyed by the Saturday's paper, which appeared as Blacklock's mouthpiece. The day the mail steamer for S. F. came in, the *Herald* printed an "extra," in which it was mentioned that when the Manono houses were seen to be burning, *Blacklock* ordered the man-of-war back. We gave Carrick to understand that this would not do. He seems a pleasant enough person, though I fear Aunt Maggie would rise up against him, he being so plainly "Glasgow."

Willis came, had some beer, and talked a lot of foolishness, but told an amusing story against himself. The last time he was here he told me about a man who had received a knife wound "right through his enterials." He talks of a "ligitous man." He and Carrick left together. Then came three officers from the man-of-war, followed by Haggard. H has broken with the manager of the Tivoli and has gone back to his old place, the Rugi mansion. He had also quarrelled with Maben, I fancy about Louis, though H said on account of Mataafa. H is now very friendly toward Mataafa, as indeed most people seem to be. I think Louis started the feeling of chivalry towards a great man fallen. The officers say that the sailors vie with each other in paying them attention, and that as many as a hundred cigars have been offered them at once.

Carrick brought an ugly *tala* to the effect that all but nine of the chiefs on the English man-of-war had been taken by Maben to the jail; that instead of assuring himself of their safety Maben left them to be taken by their enemies, by whom they were insulted and beaten. I could not help telling the officers how Blacklock had boasted to Louis of having insulted Mataafa on board their ship. It was almost impossible to get them to understand that anyone could commit such an act of cowardice, much less boast of it. Carrick said that he had heard, and it was generally believed on the beach, that Louis had gone immediately on the arrival of Mataafa to visit him, but was ordered off instantly by the captain. He asked if he might mention the true story in his letter to the colonies and also in his own paper. Louis answered, "Certainly." After that no one can say that Louis did not stand by Mataafa in the time of his defeat.

[JULY] 24TH

All day visitors coming and going from the native house. The Manono prisoners have come in, and Talolo has seen his mother, looking well, he said, but with "much business at her heart." Fali, in passing his own village, was rescued by a party of men, and has disappeared. No one seems to have mentioned the circumstance. The natives are now wondering why the prisoners are not allowed to disperse with the king's men, the war being over. It is said that quite a large amount of ammunition and many arms were discovered in Manono. This store was seized by the guard, and they now refuse to give it up, having at once sent it away to a safe place, doubtless to be used when the taxes are claimed.

This afternoon the captain of the man-of-war turned up with Mrs. Cusack-Smith. Mr. C-S, who, when Louis asked what steps were to be taken about killing the wounded and bringing in heads, asked that a petition should be sent to Laupepa, sent back the one Louis wrote, as we expected he would. He said it was "too Samoan." Louis had purposely made it like that so that the translation might be easy. Also he objected, on the behalf of any possible white atheist who might be asked to sign the document, that no reference should be made to the Samoans' belief in God. In fact, he wished something rather short and curt, and "thoroughly British," enclosing a sort of example, so to speak. He said as this production of his had no literary merit (it hadn't) he would be glad if Louis would pull it together. Louis made it short, but so thoroughly curt and British and to the point that I think C-S will be embarrassed to know what to do with it. All were very much pleased with the captain. Our men had errands that took them continually across the lawn in front of the house, or rather made errands that they might stare at the captain. I think the latter was surprised to find that we had not had a single Mataafa soldier on the premises, but, on the contrary, a good many government soldiers. Belle had shown her sketches on Sunday, the ones that were not quite good enough to send to the papers, and the captain at once asked for them.

Mr. Haggard told me that it was quite true that Sitione had taken a head, for he met him on the street carrying a pole over his shoulder, the end of the stick being thrust into the neck of the head, from which the blood had been running down his back, so that he presented a horrid spectacle. Our stout, dignified magistrate, Folau, was seen dancing and capering, half-naked, his face besmeared with black, at the front of a procession, carrying a head. The man who had the head, tossed and caught it in his hand as Folau leaped like an ape, distorting his countenance with savage grimaces.

While the captain was taking tea on the verandah, whom should

I spy on the path over the lawn but Iopo. Belle and I jumped up, at which Iopo came running to us with beaming smiles and little cries of joy. Louis followed, and Iopo sank on one knee before him and kissed his hand. Iopo told us that there was a *tala* to the effect that we would not receive him, or any other man who had fought for the government, back again. He ran round and round the place, picking up the threads of his old duties, looking into this thing and that with the utmost eagerness. He did not come to stay this time, to his grief and ours. I am sure he was sincere. After the brother who was hurt died, another brother fell ill, and also Tali, his wife. Some of the mission people are taking care of Tali, who has something that sounds like quinsy. The other members of the family say they are tired out with the long illness of the brother who died, and refuse to help with the nursing of this one. Poor Iopo had been across the island, on foot, after an old woman, but she also refused her aid, so the tired man had to tramp back again. He looks greatly changed, thinner, and his forehead heavily marked with lines of care and privation. Iopo cannot stand too much of that sort of thing, as his lungs are weak. He has twice had hemorrhages since he has been here.

Just in time for dinner, Mr. Gurr and Fanua came to stay a few days, to get a change for the latter, who is threatened with consumption. Louis looks much better again. He was in no condition for the fatigues and agitations consequent on the war, and certainly my savage attack concerning our conduct to Mataafa could not have been good for him. He called me an "idiotic Enthusiast." Well, he's another, and I insist on his being consistent; at least to his own ideals. It is not in him to be either a philosopher or a cynic.

They say that Maben's scanty locks have turned quite white during this war. Well they might. If ever a man had the chance to play a fine showy part, that man was Maben. Unfortunately he had not the courage nor the wit. One thing that amused Mataafa very much was the fact that the land commission had been sitting every day as usual and going on with their work, war or no war. Mataafa threw up his head and laughed aloud at the thought. Mr. Haggard, who stayed all night, had a touch of sunstroke this morning. He was sitting on the verandah reading a book before breakfast, bareheaded in the full glare of the sun. It looked to me almost like a slight stroke of paralysis.

[JULY] 25TH

Planted beans all morning with Leuelu. Worked in the garden, as I often do, hatless, the noon sun beating straight on my head. If anyone should have a sunstroke it is certainly I, but I find not even discomfort in the sun. I had meant to plant all afternoon but was persuaded to make calls instead, a poor substitute for the heavenly pastime of planting. I also made a large quantity of kerosene emulsion, a rather disgusting business.

Belle and I called on Mrs. Blacklock, a very pleasant young native woman, then on Mrs. Frings, a pretty young woman with very fine eyes and a drunken husband, then Mrs. Janney, another native wife of a white man, the latter a little mad, then Mrs. Schlueter, a most charming native woman with a pleasant, very fat, German husband; and then home, where we met Mrs. Clarke at the gate, and a couple of the new ship's officers, who were drinking tea on the verandah. I am rather tired of Mrs. Clarke; her chatter is so empty and interminable; in fact I am out of accord with the whole mission. The officers were pleasing enough but I think were a little startled. First one of them mentioned casually that the chiefs imprisoned on board the German ship had been put to menial labour. Belle gave a cry of indignation and looked as though she were about to strike the speaker with her fan or whip. I forget which she had in her hand. Soon after, the other man said he thought it a pity that Mataafa had so persistently refused the vice-kingship.

"Who told you that he refused it?" asked Louis.

"Mr. Cusack-Smith," was the reply.

"Then he lied in his throat!" shouted Louis, springing to his feet in a hot fury.

They must think that Vailima is a sort of imitation Wuthering Heights.

Janney told us about the attack on his boat, and that the people who made it said plainly that they were searching for the wounded to kill them. When they found there were no wounded they said,

"Well, this is a bad fellow," referring to Yandall. "We'll cut off his head." Melly, his Samoan wife, insisted that the story of the cutting off the head of a living girl was strictly true.

Pelema and Mr. Gurr made a turnstile at the gate today. Tomorrow Pelema goes to see some alleged ruins, with Yandall as guide.

[JULY] 26TH

Lloyd went to Apia, took some ava and tobacco to Mataafa, and learned on board that all the chiefs were to be deported instantly. The chiefs begged to know where they were to be sent. He was able to inform them that on account of the English ship being short of coal, the *Sperber* was to take them to the Tokelaus. Lloyd hastened back to get ava and tobacco for Faamoina (Poor White Man), but just as he was getting into the boat he saw her steam off. He hastened home to tell us the news, and found us just about to start to see Mataafa. I felt very badly that I was not allowed to go before. It was thought to be "not convenable" that ladies should show any sympathy with their broken friends *until the captain had called!* What sort of a devil from hell is the British matron, and why should I, of all people in the world, take her for my pattern in conduct? It is like being a sham paralytic. I fear I shall carry away something yet. I always despised Mary Shelley, and here I am no whit better. I despise myself and that's the fair truth. The other day Lloyd and Pelema went to see the Fathers, and ava was served to them in the cathedral. Mrs. Blacklock spent the afternoon and stayed to dinner. Pelema came home very tired and has been cross ever since.

[JULY] 27TH

Lloyd told me this morning that a story had gone over to Falilatie that he and Pelema had been killed with Yandall in a boat, and the old chief, Tagaloa; and the whole village wept and mourned them. It seems the men that Lloyd chased up the road at the beginning of the war were the very same lot who ran amuck through Apia.

Sina has been quarrelling, not to say fighting, with Talolo, and has gone to his mother. She threw stones at Talolo and struck him and bit him, and he smacked her face. It is proposed by the family that she stay with the mother-in-law until the baby is born. Then she must leave, and I suppose they will keep the child. We hear that

Haggard is better. There is a *tala* that the prisoners, who are still in Mulinuu, must pay 30,000 dollars, 6,000 pounds. That they can't do. It is probably not true. Tomorrow or next day there is to be a great fono. Laupepa did not go on board the man-of-war while Mataafa was there. I presume he was not allowed, lest the two high chiefs, on meeting, should weep on each other's necks and become reconciled. If they had, it would have been a comic incident indeed, and it is quite in keeping with the Samoan character and customs that they should have done so.

Thus ends Fanny's diary, on the inside back cover of the ledger. Possibly another volume followed, but I rather think not—the long lapses toward the end of the present diary seem to indicate that the writing of it was a heavy burden in view of her many other commitments.

In August, 1893, there was illness at Vailima, with almost everybody taking quinine. Only Fanny was feeling well. Louis wrote to Colvin:

Fanny seems on the whole the most, or the only, powerful member of the family; for some days she has been the Flower of the Flock. Belle is begging for quinine. Lloyd and Graham have both been down with "belly belong him" (Black Boy speech). As for me, I have to lay aside my lawn tennis, having (as was to be expected) had a smart but eminently brief hemorrhage. I am also on the quinine flask.

SEPTEMBER 5TH[23]

I have again and again taken up the pen to write to you, and many beginnings have gone into the waste paper basket (I have one now —for the second time in my life—and feel a big man on the strength of it). And no doubt it requires some decision to break so long a silence. My health is vastly restored, and I am now living patriarchically in this place six hundred feet above the sea on the shoulder of a mountain of 1500. Behind me, the unbroken bush slopes up to the backbone of the island (3 to 4000) without a house, with no inhabitants save a few runaway black boys, wild pigs and cattle, and wild doves and flying foxes, and many particoloured birds, and

[23] To George Meredith.

many black, and many white: a very eerie, dim, strange place and hard to travel. I am the head of a household of five whites, and of twelve Samoans, to all of whom I am the chief and father: my cook comes to me and asks leave to marry—and his mother, a fine old chief woman, who has never lived here, does the same. You may be sure I granted the petition. It is a life of great interest, complicated by the Tower of Babel, that old enemy. And I have all the time on my hands for literary work. My house is a great place; we have a hall fifty feet long with a great red-wood stair ascending from it, where we dine in state—myself usually dressed in a singlet and a pair of trousers—and attended on by servants in a single garment, a kind of kilt—also flowers and leaves—and their hair often powdered with lime. The European who came upon it suddenly would think it was a dream. We have prayers on Sunday night—I am a perfect pariah in the island not to have them oftener, but the spirit is unwilling and the flesh proud, and I cannot go it more. It is strange to see the long line of the brown folk crouched along the wall with lanterns at intervals before them in the big shadowy hall, with an oak cabinet at one end of it and a group of Rodin's (which native taste regards as *prodigieusement leste*) presiding over all from the top—and to hear the long rambling Samoan hymn rolling up (God bless me, what style! But I am off business to-day, and this is not meant to be literature). . . .

For years after I came here, the critics (those genial gentlemen) used to deplore the relaxation of my fibre and the idleness to which I had succumbed. I hear less of this now; the next thing is they will tell me I am writing myself out! and that my unconscientious conduct is bringing their grey hairs with sorrow to the dust. I do not know—I mean I do know one thing. For fourteen years I have not had a day's real health; I have wakened sick and gone to bed weary; and I have done my work unflinchingly. I have written in bed, and written out of it, written in hemorrhages, written in sickness, written torn by coughing, written when my head swam for weakness; and for so long, it seems to me I have won my wager and recovered my glove. I am better now; have been, rightly speaking, since first I came to the Pacific; and still, few are the days when I am not in some physical distress. And the battle goes on—ill or well, is a trifle; so as it goes. I was made for a contest, and the Powers have so willed that my battle-field should be this dingy, inglorious one of the bed and the physic bottle. At least I have not failed, but I would have preferred a place of trumpetings, and the open air over my head.

This is a devilish egotistical yarn. Will you try to imitate me in that if the spirit ever moves you to reply? And meantime be sure that way in the midst of the Pacific there is a house on a wooded island where the name of George Meredith is very dear, and his memory (since it must be no more) is continually honoured. . . .

TUESDAY, 12TH SEPTEMBER

Yesterday was perhaps the brightest in the annals of Vailima. I got leave from Captain Bickford to have the band of the *Katoomba* come up, and they came, fourteen of 'em, with drum, fife, cymbals and bugles, blue jackets, white caps, and smiling faces. The house was all decorated with scented greenery above and below. We had not only our own nine out-door workers but a contract party that we took on in charity to pay their war-fine; the band besides, as it came up the mountain, had collected a following of children by the way, and we had a picking of Samoan ladies to receive them. Chicken, ham, cake, and fruits were served out with coffee and lemonade, and all the afternoon we had rounds of claret negus flavoured with rum and limes. They played to us, they danced, they sang, they tumbled. Our boys came in the end of the verandah and gave *them* a dance for a while. It was anxious work getting this stopped once it had begun, but I knew the band was going on a programme. Finally they gave three cheers for Mr. and Mrs. Stevens, shook hands, formed up and marched off playing—till a kicking horse in the paddock put their pipes out something of the suddenest —we thought the big drum was gone, but Simile flew to the rescue. And so they wound away down the hill with ever another call of the bugle, leaving us extinct with fatigue, but perhaps the most contented hosts that ever watched the departure of successful guests. Simply impossible to tell how well these blue-jackets behaved; a most interesting lot of men; this education of boys for the navy is making a class, wholly apart—how shall I call them?—a kind of

lower-class public school boy, well-mannered, fairly intelligent, senti-
mental as a sailor.

In October Louis went to Hawaii for a few weeks of change, taking
Talolo with him, but became ill and had to have Fanny come and fetch
him home. By November they were home again, and soon Louis, Fanny,
Belle and Lloyd were driving in a hired carriage to the prison where the
native chiefs were held, carrying kava and tobacco as gifts. Christmas
came, and the Stevensons were hosts at a large party. The next day they
attended a native feast at the jail.

I am a sort of father of the political prisoners, and have *charge
d'âmes* in that riotously absurd establishment, Apia Gaol. The twenty-
three (I think it is) chiefs act as under-gaolers. The other day they
told the Captain of an attempt to escape. One of the lesser political
prisoners the other day effected a swift capture, while the Captain
was trailing about with the warrant; the man came to see what was
wanted; came, too, flanked by the former gaoler; my prisoner offers
to shew him the dark cell, shoves him in, and locks the door. "Why
do you do that?" cries the former gaoler. "A warrant," says he.
Finally, the chiefs actually feed the soldiery who watch them!
The gaol is a wretched little building, containing a little room,
and three cells, on each side of a central passage; it is surrounded
by a fence of corrugated iron, and shews, over the top of that, only
a gable end with the inscription O *le Fale Puipui*. It is on the edge
of the mangrove swamp, and is reached by a sort of causeway of turf.
When we drew near, we saw the gates standing open and a prodigious crowd outside—I mean prodigious for Apia, perhaps a hundred
and fifty people. The two sentries at the gate stood to arms passively,
and there seemed to be a continuous circulation inside and out. The
Captain came to meet us; our boy, who had been sent ahead, was
there to take the horses; and we passed inside the court, which was
full of food, and rang continuously to the voice of the caller of
gifts; I had to blush a little later when my own present came, and
I heard my one pig and eight miserable pineapples being counted
out like guineas.

1 8 9 4

And so the year 1893 ended. At the end of January he was writing, "Yes, if I could die just now, or say in half a year, I should have had a splendid time of it on the whole. But it gets a little stale, and my work will begin to senesce; and parties to shy bricks at me; and now it begins to look as if I should survive to see myself impotent and forgotten. It's a pity suicide is not thought the ticket in the best circles." He had but ten months to live.

In February he reports to Colvin that they have given a ball at Vailima, in March that he is struggling with *St. Ives*, which he was never to finish. In April he writes to Charles Baxter, who was then planning the Edinburgh Edition of Stevenson's works, and requests literary materials which he desires for *St. Ives*. In May he communicates to Baxter his delight and gratitude over the projected collected edition, and there is discussion with Colvin about what is to be included. In June, in a letter to his cousin Bob (R. A. M. Stevenson), he explains his involvement in island politics.

But it is impossible to live here and not feel very sorely the consequences of the horrid white mismanagement. I tried standing by and looking on, and it became too much for me. They are such illogical fools; a logical fool in an office, with a lot of red tape, is inconceivable. Furthermore, he is as much as we have any reason to expect of officials—a thoroughly commonplace, unintellectual lot. But these people are wholly on wires; laying their ears down, skimming away, pausing as though shot, and presto! full spread on the other tack. I observe in the official class mostly an insane jealousy of the smallest kind, as compared to which the artist's is of a grave, modest character—the actor's, even; a desire to extend his little authority, and to relish it like a glass of wine, that is *impayable*. Sometimes, when I see one of these little kings strutting over one of his victories—wholly illegal, perhaps, and certain to be reversed to his shame if his superiors ever heard of it—I could weep. The strange thing is that they *have nothing else*. I auscultate them in vain; no real sense of duty, no real comprehension, no real attempt to comprehend, no wish for information—you cannot offend one of them more bitterly than by offering information, though it is certain you have *more*, and obvious that you have *other*, information than they have; and talking of policy, they could not play a better stroke than by listening to you, and it need by no means influence their action. *Tenez*, you know what a French post-office or railway official is? That is the diplomatic card to the life. Dickens is not in it; caricature fails.

All this keeps me from my work, and gives me the unpleasant side of the world. When your letters are disbelieved it makes you angry, and that is rot; and I wish I could keep out of it with all my soul. But I have just got into it again, and farewell peace!

In June Graham Balfour arrived, and then Lloyd and "Aunt Maggie." Louis was feeling well physically, but his writing balked. He wrote to Henry James on July 7th:

And when that is wrong, as you must be very keenly aware, you begin every day with a smarting disappointment, which is not good for the temper. I am in one of the humours when a man wonders how any one can be such an ass to embrace the profession of letters, and not get apprenticed to a barber or keep a baked-potato stall. But I have no doubt in the course of a week, or perhaps to-morrow, things will look better.

But in September he was still wrestling with *St. Ives*. In that month also he saw the beginning of the Road of Gratitude, or Road of the Loving Heart—a road developed and finished by Samoans who wished to express their gratitude to him for all his aid and sympathy in their trials. It was his private road which they worked on, and he was profoundly moved. In October his spirits were improving, and soon he began dictating *Weir of Hermiston*, and feeling all his old powers—more, feeling at the summit of his achievement. He felt well physically, and optimistic about the future. And then, on the afternoon of December 3, 1894, at the age of forty-four, he was struck down by a cerebral hemorrhage. His mother, writing from Vailima to her sister, Jane Whyte Balfour, described the tragic event the following day.

"How am I to tell you the terrible news that my beloved son was suddenly called home last evening. At six o'clock he was well, hungry for dinner, and helping Fanny to make a mayonnaise sauce; when suddenly he put both hands to his head and said, 'Oh, what a pain!' and then added, 'Do I look strange?' Fanny said no, not wishing to alarm him, and helped him into the hall, where she put him into the nearest easy-chair. She called for us to come, and I was there in a minute; but he was unconscious before I reached his side, and remained so for two hours, till at ten minutes past 8 P.M. all was over.

"Lloyd went for help at once, and got two doctors wonderfully quickly—one from the *Wallaroo* and the other, Dr. Funk, from Apia; but we had already done all that was possible, and they could suggest nothing more. Before the end came we brought a bed into the hall, and he was lifted on to it. When all was over his boys gathered about him, and the chiefs from Tanugamanono arrived with fine mats which they laid over the bed; it was very touching when they came in bowing, and saying '*Talofa,* Tusitala'; and then, after kissing him and saying '*Tofa,* Tusitala,' went out. After that our Roman Catholic boys asked if they might 'make a church,' and they chanted prayers and hymns for a long time, very sweetly. . . . We had sent for Mr. Clarke, who stayed with us till all was over; Louis wished to be buried on the top of Vaea Mountain, and before six this morning forty men arrived with axes to cut a path up and dig the grave. Some of Mataafa's chiefs came this morning; one wept bitterly, saying, 'Mataafa is gone, and Tusitala is gone, and we have none left.'. . .

"They have just gone up the mountain now. The letters must be posted tonight, and I scarcely know what I am writing. None of us has realised yet what has happened, and we shall only feel it all the more as days go by. . . . I feel desolate indeed, and don't know what I shall do. . . ."

On the ninth of December "Aunt Maggie" wrote again to Jane Balfour.

"Life seems to have stood still with us since Tuesday, and none of us can do anything but think over our loss, which only grows greater as we begin dimly to realise it. No one, at least, was ever more universally mourned than my beloved son. . . . The ascent to the top of Vaea Mountain was a very difficult matter, and many of the men found it more than they could manage. The coffin left half an hour before the invited guests, as the labour of climbing with it was so great; but there were many relays of loving Samoan hands ready to carry their dear Tusitala to his last home amongst them, and they took the utmost pains to bear him shoulder high, and as steadily and reverently as possible. Behind them came the few near and good friends that we had invited to be present; and when they reached the top of the mountain they found the coffin laid beside the grave, and covered with the flag that used to fly over us in those happy days upon the *Casco*. . . .

"As soon as it was lowered into its place, and the wreaths and crosses thrown in till it was hidden from sight, our house-boys seized the spades from the 'outside' boys[24] who had dug the grave; no hands but theirs, who had been specially 'Tusitala's family,' should fill it in, and do the last service for him that was left to them. Mr. Clarke read portions of the Church of England burial-service, and also a prayer written by Louis himself, which he had read at family worship only the night before his death; and Mr. Newell[25] gave an address in Samoan, which made all who understood it weep; and prayed also in the same language, that Louis loved so well. . . .

"I must tell you a very strange thing that occurred just before his death. For a day or two Fanny had been telling us that she knew— that she *felt*—something dreadful was going to happen to some one we cared for; as she put it, to one of our friends. On Monday she

[24] That is, those doing the outside work on the estate.
[25] Rev. J. E. Newell, of the London Missionary Society, who rose from a sick-bed to make the address.

was very low about it, and upset, and dear Lou tried hard to cheer her. He read aloud to her the chapter of his book that he had just finished, played a game or two of Patience to induce her to look on, and I fancy it was as much for her sake as his own that the mayonnaise sauce was begun upon. And, strangely enough, both of them had agreed that it could not be to either of *them* that the dreadful thing was to happen! Thus far, and no further, can our intuitions, our second sight, go. . . .

"Sosimo, Lou's special boy, is quite inconsolable; he keeps Tusitala's room in exquisite order, and when Fanny and I were there this morning, we were touched to find two glasses filled with beautiful fresh white flowers on the table beside his bed."

On December 16 she writes:

"Another Sunday without my child; his leaving us was so swift and sudden, that I seem only now to begin to realise that I shall see him on earth no more. . . . Yesterday we had another sad scene to go through, the paying-off of the outside boys; their last work had been to make a better road to the top of the mountain, and it was finished yesterday. In the afternoon we all assembled in the hall, the first time that it had been used since the funeral; and Lloyd made a speech, explaining how sorry we were that we could not keep them any longer now that Tusitala had left us, and thanking them for all their loving services. One of them replied, saying how happy they had been here, that they had always been made to feel themselves like members of the family, had been well fed and taken care of when they were sick, and that they were very sorry to go away and leave us. Then they sang a couple of songs of farewell to Tusitala that two of them had composed, and we drank kava together and shook hands with them all. Some of them kissed our hands, as they said, *Tofa, soifua*, 'Farewell, may you live.' . . .

"Of the outside boys we have only kept our old friend Lafaele, who takes care of the cows and pigs, Leuelo, Fanny's boy, who works in the garden, and a Tongan who has only one eye, and is delicate as well. Some time ago Lloyd suggested to Louis that as he was of little use, he had better be sent away; but Louis replied that he had no home to go to, and there was every chance of his becoming altogether blind, and that as long as *he* was at Vailima, the Tongan should have a home there too."

JANUARY 13, 1895:

"I don't think I told you of a remark made by the doctor of the *Wallaroo* that haunts me constantly. We were watching round dear Lou, Fanny and I were rubbing his arms with brandy, and his shirt-sleeves were pushed up, and showed their thinness; some one made a remark about his writing, and Dr. A said, 'How can anybody write books with arms like these?'

"I turned round indignantly and burst out with, 'He has written *all* his books with arms like these!'

"I don't think I was ever before so terribly impressed with the greatness of the struggle that my beloved child had made against his bad health. He has written at the rate of a volume a year for the last twenty years, in spite of weakness which most people would have looked on as an excuse for confirmed invalidism; and he has lived, too, and loved his life in spite of it all. Do you remember how years ago, when some one was comforting him by saying that the Balfours always got stronger as they grew older, he replied, 'Yes; but just as I begin to outgrow the Balfour delicacy, the Nemesis of the short-lived Stevensons will come in and finish me off!' That has been at the back of my mind all these years, and you see it has come true."

Of all the messages of condolence which came to her, perhaps the finest which Fanny received—a tribute to her as well as to Louis—was a letter from Henry James.

"My dear Fanny Stevenson," it began, "What can I say to you that will not seem cruelly irrelevant or vain? We have been sitting in darkness for nearly a fortnight, but what is our darkness to the extinction of your magnificent light? You will probably know in some degree what has happened to us—how the hideous news first came to us via Auckland, etc., and then how, in the newspapers, a doubt was raised about its authenticity—just enough to give one a flicker of hope; until your telegram to me via San Francisco—repeated also from other sources—converted my pessimistic convictions into the wretched knowledge. All this time my thoughts have hovered round you all, around you in particular, with a tenderness of which I could have wished you might have, afar-off, the divination. You are such a visible picture of desolation that I need to remind myself that courage, and patience, and fortitude are also abundantly with you. The devotion that Louis inspired—and of which all the air about you must be full—must also be much to you. Yet as I write the word, indeed, I am almost ashamed of it—as if anything could be 'much' in the presence of such an abysmal void. To have lived in the light of that splendid life, that beautiful, bountiful thing—only to see it, from one moment to the other, converted into a fable as strange and romantic as one of his own, a thing that has been and has ended, is an anguish into which no one can enter fully and of which no one can drain the cup for you. You are nearest to the pain, because you were nearest the joy and the pride. But if it is anything to you to know that no woman was ever more felt with and that your personal grief is the intensely personal grief of innumerable hearts—know it well, my dear Fanny Stevenson, for during all these days there has been friendship for you in the very air. For myself, how shall I tell you how much poorer and shabbier the whole world seems, and how one of the closest and strongest reasons for going on, for trying and doing, for planning and dreaming of the future, has dropped in an instant out of life. I was haunted indeed with a sense that I should never again see him—but it was one of the best things in life that he was there, or that one had him—at any rate one heard of him, and felt him and awaited him and counted him into everything one most loved and lived for. He lighted up one whole side of the globe, and was in himself a whole province of one's imagination. We are smaller fry and meaner people without him. I feel as if there was a certain indelicacy in saying it to you, save that I know that there is nothing narrow or selfish in your sense of loss—for himself, however, for his happy name and his great visible good fortune, it strikes one as another matter. I mean that I feel him to have been as happy in his death (struck down that way, as by the gods, in a clean, glorious hour) as he had been in his frame of mind. And, with all the sad allowance in his rich full life, he had the best of it—the thick of the fray, the loudest of the music, the freshest and finest of himself. It isn't as if there had been no full achievement and no supreme thing. It was all intense, all gallant, all exquisite from the first, and the experience, the fruition, had something dramatically complete in them. He has gone in time not to be old, early enough to be so generously young and late enough to have drunk deep of the cup. There have been—I think—for men of letters few deaths more romantically right. Forgive me, I beg you, what may sound cold blooded in such words—or as if I imagined there could be anything for you 'right' in the rupture of such an affection and the loss of such a presence. I have in my mind in that view only the rounded career and the consecrated work. When I think of your own situation I fall into a mere confusion of pity and wonder, with the sole sense of your being as brave a spirit as he was (all of whose bravery you shared) to hold on by. Of what solutions or decisions you see before you we shall hear in time; meanwhile please believe that I am most affectionately with you. . . . More than I can say, I hope your first prostration and bewilderment are over, and that you are feeling your way in feeling all sorts of encompassing arms—all sorts of outstretched hands of friendship. Don't, my dear Fanny Stevenson, be unconscious of mine, and believe me more than ever faithfully yours, Henry James."[26]

In April, 1895, Fanny, tired and ill, set sail for San Francisco. She spent the summer of that year in California, wintered in Hawaii, during which time Lloyd married, and in May of the next year, accompanied by Belle, returned to Vailima. But soon it became evident to her that with Louis gone and her children needed elsewhere, she could no longer be happy in that place. Accordingly, she sold Vailima to a Russian merchant named Kunst, whose heirs in turn sold it to the German government, whereupon it became the residence of the German governor of Samoa. During World War I New Zealand occupied Upolu, and Vailima, with many changes and enlargements made, stood under the Union Jack as the British government house.

Fanny went to England in 1898, where she underwent a major opera-

[26] From *The Life of Mrs. Robert Louis Stevenson*, by Nellie Van der Grift Sanchez, pp. 222-25. Charles Scribner's Sons, 1920.

tion, and in December traveled through France, Spain and Portugal. She purchased a home in San Francisco, made excursions into Mexico, lived for a while at lonely Rancho El Sausal, six miles from Ensenada, in Lower California, visited Europe in 1906 and 1907, and in 1908 made her last home in Santa Barbara, California, where she died February 18, 1914, like Louis of a cerebral hemorrhage. In the spring of 1915 Belle and her husband sailed for Samoa with Fanny's ashes, in accordance with her mother's request. On June 22 they were finally interred beside the remains of Louis. The small crowd on the mountaintop above Vailima included Sitione (now Amatua), Laulii, and Mitaele. Under the name Aolele the following inscription was placed in bronze on Fanny's tomb:

> Teacher, tender comrade, wife,
> A fellow-farer true through life,
> Heart whole and soul free,
> The August Father gave to me.

The monument also contains lines in memory of Louis—his own *Requiem:*

> Under the wide and starry sky,
> Dig the grave and let me lie.
> Glad did I live and gladly die,
> And I laid me down with a will.
>
> This be the verse you grave for me;
> *Here he lies where he longed to be;*
> *Home is the sailor, home from the sea,*
> *And the hunter home from the hill.*

Appendix A

VAILIMA PRAYERS, by ROBERT LOUIS STEVENSON
(Prayers written for family use at Vailima)

FOR SUCCESS

Lord, behold our family here assembled. We thank Thee for this place in which we dwell; for the love that unites us; for the peace accorded us this day; for the hope with which we expect the morrow; for the health, the work, the food, and the bright skies, that make our lives delightful; for our friends in all parts of the earth, and our friendly helpers in this foreign isle. Let peace abound in our small company. Purge out of every heart the lurking grudge. Give us grace and strength to forbear and to persevere. Offenders, give us the grace to accept and to forgive offenders. Forgetful ourselves, help us to bear cheerfully the forgetfulness of others. Give us courage and gaiety and the quiet mind. Spare to us our friends, soften to us our enemies. Bless us, if it may be, in all our innocent endeavours. If it may not, give us the strength to encounter that which is to come, that we be brave in peril, constant in tribulation, temperate in wrath, and in all changes of fortune and down to the gates of death, loyal and loving one to another. As the clay to the potter, as the windmill to the wind, as children of their sire, we beseech of Thee this help and mercy, for Christ's sake.

FOR GRACE

Grant that we here before Thee may be set free from the fear of vicissitude and the fear of death, may finish what remains before us of our course without dishonour to ourselves or hurt to others, and, when the day comes, may die in peace. Deliver us from fear and favour; from

The following Vailima Prayers are reprinted from *Miscellanea*, Volume 26, *The Works of Robert Louis Stevenson*; copyright 1923 by Charles Scribner's Sons, 1951 by Alan Osbourne; used by permission of the publishers: "For Continued Favours," "For Mind and Body," "For Fellowship," "For Home," "For Renewed Power" and "For Strength."

mean hopes and cheap pleasures. Have mercy on each in his deficiency; let him be not cast down; support the stumbling on the way, and give at last rest to the weary.

At Morning

The day returns and brings us the petty round of irritating concerns and duties. Help us to play the man, help us to perform them with laughter and kind faces, let cheerfulness abound with industry. Give us to go blithely on our business all this day, bring us to our resting beds weary and content and undishonoured, and grant us in the end the gift of sleep.

Evening

We come before Thee, O Lord, in the end of Thy day with thanksgiving. Our beloved in the far parts of the earth, those who are now beginning the labours of the day what time we end them, and those with whom the sun now stands at the point of noon, bless, help, console, and prosper them.

Our guard is relieved, the service of the day is over, and the hour come to rest. We resign into Thy hands our sleeping bodies, our cold hearths and open doors. Give us to awake with smiles, give us to labour smiling. As the sun returns in the east, so let our patience be renewed with dawn; as the sun lightens the world, so let our loving-kindness make bright this house of our habitation.

Another for Evening

Lord, receive our supplications for this house, family, and country. Protect the innocent, restrain the greedy and the treacherous, lead us out of our tribulation into a quiet land.

Look down upon ourselves and upon our absent dear ones. Help us and them; prolong our days in peace and honour. Give us health, food, bright weather, and light hearts. In what we meditate of evil, frustrate our will; in what of good, further our endeavours. Cause injuries to be forgot and benefits to be remembered.

Let us lie down without fear and awake and arise with exultation. For His sake, in whose words we now conclude.

In Time of Rain

We thank Thee, Lord, for the glory of the late day and the excellent face of Thy sun. We thank Thee for good news received. We thank Thee for the pleasures we have enjoyed and for those we have been able to confer. And now, when the clouds gather and the rain impends over the forest and our house, permit us not to be cast down; let us not lose the savour of past mercies and past pleasures: but, like the voice of a bird singing in the rain, let grateful memory survive in the hour of darkness. If there be in front of us any painful duty, strengthen us with the grace of courage; if any act of mercy, teach us tenderness and patience.

ANOTHER IN TIME OF RAIN

Lord, Thou sendest down rain upon the uncounted millions of the forest, and givest the trees to drink exceedingly. We are here upon this isle a few handfuls of men, and how many myriads upon myriads of stalwart trees! Teach us the lesson of the trees. The sea around us, which this rain recruits, teems with the race of fish: teach us, Lord, the meaning of the fishes. Let us see ourselves for what we are, one out of the countless number of the clans of Thy handiwork. When we would despair, let us remember that these also please and serve Thee.

BEFORE A TEMPORARY SEPARATION

Today we go forth separate, some of us to pleasure, some of us to worship, some upon duty. Go with us, our guide and angel; hold Thou before us in our divided paths the mark of our low calling, still to be true to what small best we can attain to. Help us in that, our maker, the dispenser of events—Thou, of the vast designs, in which we blindly labour, suffer us to be so far constant to ourselves and our beloved.

FOR FRIENDS

For our absent loved ones we implore Thy loving-kindness. Keep them in life, keep them in growing honour; and for us, grant that we remain worthy of their love. For Christ's sake, let not our beloved blush for us, nor we for them. Grant us but that, and grant us courage to endure lesser ills unshaken, and to accept death, loss, and disappointment as it were straws upon the tide of life.

FOR THE FAMILY

Aid us, if it be Thy will, in our concerns. Have mercy on this land and innocent people. Help them who this day contend in disappointment with their frailties. Bless our family, bless our forest house, bless our island helpers. Thou who hast made for us this place of ease and hope, accept and inflame our gratitude; help us to repay, in service one to another, the debt of Thine unmerited benefits and mercies, so that when the period of our stewardship draws to a conclusion, when the windows begin to be darkened, when the bond of the family is to be loosed, there shall be no bitterness of remorse in our farewells.

Help us to look back on the long way that Thou has brought us, on the long days in which we have been served not according to our deserts but our desires; on the pit and the miry clay, the blackness of despair, the horror of misconduct, from which our feet have been plucked out. For our sins forgiven or prevented, for our shame unpublished, we bless and thank Thee, O God. Help us yet again and ever. So order events, so strengthen our frailty, as that day by day we shall come before Thee with this song of gratitude, and in the end we be dismissed with honour. In their weakness and their fear, the vessels of Thy handiwork so pray to Thee, so praise Thee. Amen.

SUNDAY

We beseech Thee, Lord, to behold us with favour, folk of many families and nations gathered together in the peace of this roof, weak men and women subsisting under the covert of Thy patience. Be patient still; suffer us yet awhile longer to endure and (if it may be) help us to do better. Bless to us our extraordinary mercies; if the day come when these must be taken, brace us to play the man under affliction. Be with our friends, be with ourselves. Go with each of us to rest; if any awake, temper to them the dark hours of watching; and when the day returns, return to us, our sun and comforter, and call us up with morning faces and with morning hearts—eager to labour—eager to be happy, if happiness shall be our portion—and if the day be marked for sorrow, strong to endure it.

We thank Thee and praise Thee; and in the words of Him to whom this day is sacred, close our oblation.

FOR SELF-BLAME

Lord, enlighten us to see the beam that is in our own eye, and blind us to the mote that is in our brother's. Let us feel our offences with our hands, make them great and bright before us like the sun, make us eat them and drink them for our diet. Blind us to the offences of our beloved, cleanse them from our memories, take them out of our mouths for ever. Let all here before Thee carry and measure with the false balances of love, and be in their own eyes and in all conjunctures the most guilty. Help us at the same time with the grace of courage, that we be none of us cast down when we sit lamenting amid the ruins of our happiness or our integrity: touch us with fire from the altar, that we may be up and doing to rebuild our city; in the name and by the method of Him in whose words of prayer we now conclude.

For Self-Forgetfulness

Lord, the creatures of Thy hand, Thy disinherited children, come before Thee with their incoherent wishes and regrets: Children we are, children we shall be, till our mother the earth hath fed upon our bones. Accept us, correct us, guide us, Thy guilty innocents. Dry our vain tears, wipe out our vain resentments, help our yet vainer efforts. If there be any here, sulking as children will, deal with and enlighten him. Make it day about that person, so that he shall see himself and be ashamed. Make it heaven about him, Lord, by the only way to heaven, forgetfulness of self, and make it day about his neighbours, so that they shall help, not hinder him.

For Renewal of Joy

We are evil, O God, and help us to see it and amend. We are good, and help us to be better. Look down upon Thy servants with a patient eye, even as Thou sendest sun and rain; look down, call upon the dry bones, quicken, enliven; recreate in us the soul of service, the spirit of peace; renew in us the sense of joy.

For Continued Favours

O God who givest us day by day the support of Thy kindly countenance and hopeful spirit among the manifold temptations and adventures of this life, having brought us thus far, do not, O God, desert us, but with Thy continued favours follow us in our path. Keep us upright and humble, and O Thou who equally guidest all mankind through sun and rain, give us Thy spirit of great mercy.

For Mind and Body

Give us peace of mind in our day, O Lord, and a sufficiency of bodily comfort, that we be not tortured with changing friendships or opinions nor crucified by disease, but ever in strength, constancy and pleasantness, walk in a fair way before Thy face and in the sight of men; and if it please Thee, O Lord, take us soon in health of mind and honour of body into Thy eternal rest.

For Fellowship

God, who hast given us the love of women and the friendship of men, keep alive in our hearts the sense of old fellowship and tenderness; make offences to be forgotten and services remembered; protect those whom we love in all things and follow them with kindness, so that they may lead simple and unsuffering lives, and in the end die easily with quiet minds.

For Home

Lord, behold us come before Thee this night, once more assembled. Help us in our troubles, correct us in our faults, give us to see so far as may be needful, help us to see as far as may be right, and yet not further, in all vicissitudes of our career. For them that are absent, we offer Thee our supplications. Be good to the green and to the ripe. Prepare the child for the arena. To our absent mother, give my armfuls, the last gleanings of the harvest of her life, so that she may go down there where she must go in the beauty of a serene evening, not without its songs. Help us one and all to bear, and to forbear, for Thy name's sake, and let this home of ours endure all strokes of enemies from without and of enemies from within, until we shall be gathered, one by one, into Thy garner of the dead and resting, nevertheless not as we will but as we shall serve in the unknown design.

For Renewed Power

O God, who throughout life hast pursued us with Thy mercies and Thy judgments, and in love and anger led us daily forward, as Thou has not been weary in the past, be not weary yet awhile. Pardon our dull spirits, and whether with mercy or with judgment, call us up from slumber.

For as we kneel together, in this cruel state, weak folk, with many weaker depending upon our help, sinful folk, with the whole earth ministering temptations, we would desire to remember equally our need and Thy power. Save us, O Lord, from ourselves. The prayer that we lifelessly repeat, hear, Lord, and make it live, and answer it in mercy.

Let us not judge amiss, let us not speak with cruelty; our kindness to others, suffer it not to weary. May we grow merciful by tribulations, liberal by mercies. Thou who sendest Thy rain upon the just and the unjust, help us to pardon, help us to love, our fellow-sinners.

For Strength

O God, who has brought us to the end of another day, of use or of uselessness, pardon, as is Thy wont, the manifold sins and shortcomings of our practice, the discontent and envy of our thoughts; enable us this night to enjoy the repose of slumber and waken us again to-morrow, with better thoughts and a greater courage, to resume the task of life. Bless to us the pleasures, bless to us the pains of our existence. Suffer us not to forget the bonds of our humanity; give us strength, give us the spirit of mercy, give us the power to endure. Leave us not indifferent, O God, but pierce our hearts to resolve and enable our hands to perform, as before Thy face in the sight of the eternal. Watch upon our eyes, ears, thoughts, tongues, and hands, that we may neither think unkindly, speak unwisely, nor act unrighteously.

Guide us, Thou who didst guide our fathers; and upon this day more especially set apart for prayer, receive our penitent and grateful thought; and hear us, when we pray for others and ourselves; that they may be blessed and we be helped; and give us, beyond our deserts to receive, beyond our imaginations to expect, the grace to die daily to our evil, and to live ever the more and ever the more wholly to Thee and to our fellow-sufferers.

Appendix B

LETTER TO THE TIMES, BY ROBERT LOUIS STEVENSON

Samoa, April 9, 1892

Sir,—A sketch of our latest difficulty in Samoa will be interesting, at least to lawyers.

In the Berlin General Act there is one point on which, from the earliest moment, volunteer interpreters have been divided. The revenue arising from the customs was held by one party to belong to the Samoan Government, by another to the municipality; and the dispute was at last decided in favour of the municipality by Mr. Cedarcrantz, Chief Justice. The decision was not given in writing; but it was reported by at least one of the Consuls to his Government, it was of public notoriety, it is not denied, and it was at once implicitly acted on by the parties. Before that decision, the revenue from customs was suffered to accumulate; ever since, to the knowledge of the Chief Justice, and with the daily countenance of the President, it has been received, administered, and spent by the municipality. It is the function of the Chief Justice to interpret the Berlin Act; its sense was thus supposed to be established beyond cavil; those who were dissatisfied with the result conceived their only recourse lay in a prayer to the Powers to have the treaty altered; and such a prayer was, but the other day, proposed, supported, and finally negatived, in a public meeting.

About a year has gone by since the decision, and the state of the Samoan Government has been daily growing more precarious. Taxes have not been paid, and the Government has not ventured to enforce them. Fresh taxes have fallen due, and the Government has not ventured to call for them. Salaries were running on, and that of the Chief Justice alone amounts to a considerable figure for these islands; the coffers had fallen low, at last it was believed they were quite empty, no resource seemed left, and bystanders waited with a smiling curiosity for the wheels to stop. I should add, to explain the epithet "smiling," that the Government has proved a still-born child; and except for some

250

spasmodic movements which I have already made the subject of remark in your columns, it may be said to have done nothing but pay salaries.

In this state of matters, on March 28, the President of the Council, Baron Senfft von Pilsach, was suddenly and privately supplied by Mr. Cedarcrantz with a written judgment, reversing the verbal and public decision of a year before. By what powers of law was this result attained? And how was the point brought again before his Honour? I feel I shall here strain the credulity of your readers, but our authority is the President in person. The suit was brought by himself in his capacity (perhaps an imaginary one) of King's adviser; it was defended by himself in his capacity of President of the Council; no notice had been given, the parties were not summoned, they were advised neither of the trial nor the judgment; so far as can be learned, two persons only met and parted—the first was the plaintiff and defendant rolled in one, the other was a judge who had decided black a year ago, and had now intimated a modest willingness to decide white.

But it is possible to follow more closely these original proceedings. Baron von Pilsach sat down (he told us) in his capacity of adviser to the King, and wrote to himself, in his capacity of President of the Council, an eloquent letter of reprimand three pages long; an unknown English artist clothed it for him in good language; and nothing remained but to have it signed by King Malietoa, to whom it was attributed. "So long as he knows how to sign!"—a white official is said thus to have summed up, with a shrug, the qualifications necessary in a Samoan king. It was signed accordingly, though whether the King knew what he was signing is matter of debate; and thus regularised, it was forwarded to the Chief Justice enclosed in a letter of adhesion from the President. Such as they were, these letters appear to have been the pleadings on which the Chief Justice proceeded; such as they were, they seem to have been the documents in this unusual cause.

Suppose an unfortunate error to have been made, suppose a reversal of the Court's finding and the year's policy to have become immediately needful, wisdom would indicate an extreme frankness of demeanour. And our two officials preferred a policy of irritating dissimulation. While the revolution was being prepared behind the curtain, the President was holding night sessions of the municipal council. What was the business? No other than to prepare an ordinance regulating those very customs which he was secretly conspiring to withdraw from their control. And it was a piece of duplicity of a similar nature which first awoke the echoes of Apia by its miscarriage. The council had sent up for the approval of the Consular Board a project of several bridges, one of which, that of the Vaisingano, was of chief importance to the town. To sanction so much fresh expense, at the very moment when, to his secret knowledge, the municipality was to be left bare of funds, appeared to one of the Consuls an unworthy act; and the proposal was accordingly disallowed. The people of Apia are extremely swift to guess. No sooner was the Vaisingano bridge denied them than they leaped within a measurable distance of the truth. It was remembered that the Chief Justice had but recently (this time by a decision regularly obtained) placed the municipal funds at the President's mercy; talk ran high of collusion between the two officials; it was rumoured the safe had been already secretly drawn upon; the newspaper being at this juncture suddenly and rather mysteriously sold, it was rumoured it had been bought for the officials with municipal money, and the Apians crowded in consequence to the municipal meeting on April 1, with minds already heated.

The President came on his side armed with the secret judgment; and the hour being now come, he unveiled his work of art to the municipal councillors. On the strength of the Chief Justice's decision, to his knowledge, and with the daily countenance of the President, they had for twelve months received and expended the revenue from customs. They learned now that this was wrong; they learned not only that they were to receive no more, but that they must refund what they had already spent; and the total sum amounting to about $25,000, and there being less than $20,000 in the treasury, they learned that they were bankrupt. And with the next breath the President reassured them; time was to be given to these miserable debtors, and the King in his clemency would even advance them from their own safe—now theirs no longer—a loan of $3,000 against current expenses. If the municipal council of Apia be far from an ideal body, at least it makes roads and builds bridges, at least it does something to justify its existence and reconcile the rate-payer to the rates. This was to cease: all the funds husbanded for this end were to be transferred to the Government at Mulinuu, which has never done anything to mention but pay salaries, and of which men have long ceased to expect anything else but that it shall continue to pay salaries till it die of inanition. Let us suppose this raid on the municipal treasury to have been just and needful. It is plain, even if introduced in the most conciliatory manner, it could never have been welcome. And, as it was, the sting was in the manner—in the secrecy and the surprise, in the dissimulation, the dissonant decisions, the appearance of collusion between the officials, and the offer of a loan too small to help. Bitter words were spoken at the council-table; the public joined with shouts; it was openly proposed to overpower the President and seize the treasury key. Baron von Pilsach possesses the redeeming rudimentary virtue of courage. It required courage to come at all on such an errand to those he had deceived; and amidst violent voices and menacing hands he displayed a constancy worthy of a better cause. The council broke tumultuously up; the inhabitants crowded to a public meeting; the Consuls, acquainted with the alarming effervescency of feeling, communicated their willingness to meet the municipal councillors and arrange a compromise; and the inhabitants renewed by acclamation the mandate of their representatives. The same night these sat in council with the Consular Board, and a *modus vivendi* was agreed upon, which was rejected the next morning by the President.

The representations of the Consuls had, however, their effect; and when the council met again on April 6, Baron von Pilsach was found to have entirely modified his attitude. The bridge over the Vaisingano was conceded; the sum of $3,000 offered to the council was increased to $9,000, about one-half of the existing funds; the Samoan Government, which was to profit by the customs, now agreed to bear the expense of collection; the President, while refusing to be limited to a specific figure, promised an anxious parsimony in the Government expenditure, admitted his recent conduct had been of a nature to irritate the councillors, and frankly proposed it should be brought under the notice of the Powers. I should not be a fair reporter if I did not praise his bearing. In the midst of men whom he had grossly deceived, and who had recently insulted him in return, he behaved himself with tact and temper. And largely in consequence his *modus vivendi* was accepted under protest, and the matter in dispute referred without discussion to the Powers.

I would like to refer for one moment to my former letter. The Manono prisoners were solemnly sentenced to six months' imprisonment; and, by some unexplained and secret process, the sentence was increased to one of banishment. The fact seems to have rather amused the Governments at home. It did not at all amuse us here on the spot. But we sought consolation by remembering that the President was a layman, and the Chief Justice had left the islands but the day before. Let Mr. Cedarcrantz return, we thought, and Arthur would be come again. Well, Arthur is come. And now we begin to think he was perhaps an approving, if an absent, party to the scandal. For do we not find, in the case of the municipal treasury, the same disquieting features? A decision is publicly delivered, it is acted on for a year, and by some secret and inexplicable process we find it suddenly reversed. We are supposed to be governed by English law. Is this English law? Is it law at all? Does it permit a state of society in which a citizen can live and act with confidence? And when we are asked by natives to explain these peculiarities of white man's government and white man's justice, in what form of words are we to answer?

April 12

Fresh news reaches me; I have once again to admire the accuracy of rumour in Apia, and that which I had passed over with a reference becomes the head and front of our contention. The *Samoa Times* was nominally purchased by a gentleman who, whatever be his other recommendations, was notoriously ill off. There was paid down for it £600 in gold, a huge sum of ready money for Apia, above all in gold, and all men wondered where it came from. It is this which has been discovered: The wrapper of each rouleau was found to be signed by Mr. Martin, collector for the municipality as well as for the Samoan Government, and countersigned by Mr. Savile, his assistant. In other words, the money had left either the municipal or the Government safe.

The position of the President is thus extremely exposed. His accounts up to January 1 are in the hands of auditors. The next term of March 31 is already past, and although the natural course has been repeatedly suggested to him, he has never yet permitted the verification of the balance in his safe. The case would appear less strong against the Chief Justice. Yet a month has not elapsed since he placed the funds at the disposal of the President, on the avowed ground that the population of Apia was unfit to be entrusted with its own affairs. And the very week of the purchase he reversed his own previous decision and liberated his colleague from the last remaining vestige of control. Beyond the extent of these judgments, I doubt if this astute personage will be found to have committed himself in black and white; and the more foolhardy President may thus be left in the top of the breach alone.

Let it be explained or apportioned as it may, this additional scandal is felt to have overfilled the measure. It may be argued that the President has great tact and the Chief Justice a fund of philosophy. Give us instead a judge who shall proceed according to the forms of justice, and a treasurer who shall permit the verification of his balances. Surely there can be found among the millions of Europe two frank and honest men, one of whom shall be acquainted with English law, and the other possess the ordinary virtues of a clerk, over whose heads, in the exercise of their duties, six months may occasionally pass without painful disclosures and dangerous scandals; who shall not weary us with their surprises and intrigues; who shall not amaze us with their lack of penetration; who shall not, in the hour of their destitution, seem to have diverted £600 of public money for the purchase of an inconsiderable sheet, or at a time when eight provinces of discontented natives threaten at any moment to sweep their ineffective Government into the sea to have sought safety and strength in gagging the local press of Apia. If it be otherwise—if we cannot be relieved, if the Powers are satisfied with the conduct of Mr.

Cedarcrantz and Baron Senfft von Pilsach; if these were sent here with the understanding that they should secretly purchase, perhaps privately edit, a little sheet of two pages, issued from a crazy wooden building at the mission gate; if it were, indeed, intended that, for this important end, they should divert (as it seems they have done) public funds and affront all the forms of law—we whites can only bow the head. We are here quite helpless. If we would complain of Baron Pilsach, it can only be to Mr. Cedarcrantz; if we would complain of Mr. Cedarcrantz, and the Powers will not hear us, the circle is complete. A nightly guard surrounds and protects their place of residence, while the house of the King is cynically left without the pickets. Secure from interference, one utters the voice of the law, the other moves the hands of authority; and now they seem to have sequestered in the course of a single week the only available funds and the only existing paper in the islands.

But there is one thing they forget. It is not the whites who menace the duration of their Government, and it is only the whites who read the newspaper. Mataafa sits hard by in his armed campa and sees. He sees the weakness, he counts the scandals of their Government. He sees his rival and "brother" sitting disconsidered at their doors, like Lazarus before the house of Dives, and, if he is not very fond of his "brother," he is very scrupulous of native dignities. He has seen his friends menaced with midnight destruction in the Government gaol, and deported without form of law. He is not himself a talker, and his thoughts are hid from us; but what is said by his more hasty partisans we know. On March 29, the day after the Chief Justice signed the secret judgment, three days before it was made public, and while the purchase of the newspaper was yet in treaty, a native orator stood up in an assembly. "Who asked the Great Powers to make laws for us; to bring strangers here to rule us?" he cried. "We want no white officials to bind us in the bondage of taxation." Here is the changed spirit which these gentlemen have produced by a misgovernment of fifteen months. Here is their peril, which no purchase of newspapers and no subsequent editorial suppressions can avert.

It may be asked if it be still time to do anything. It is, indeed, already late; and these gentlemen, arriving in a golden moment, have fatally squandered opportunity and perhaps fatally damaged white prestige. Even the whites themselves they have not only embittered, but corrupted. We were pained the other day when our municipal councillors refused, by a majority, to make the production of invoices obligatory at the Custom-house. Yet who shall blame them, when the Chief Justice, with a smallness of capacity at which all men wondered, refused to pay, and, I believe, still withholds, the duties on his imports? He was above the law, being the head of it; and this was how he preached by example. He refused to pay his customs; the white councillors, following in his wake, refused to take measures to enforce them against others; and the natives, following in his wake, refused to pay their taxes. These taxes it may, perhaps, be never possible to raise again directly. Taxes have never been popular in Samoa; yet in the golden moment when this Government began its course, a majority of Samoans paid them. Every province should have seen some part of that money expended in its bounds; every nerve should have been strained to interest and gratify the natives in the manner of its expenditure. It has been spent instead on Mulinuu, to pay four white officials, two of whom came in the suite of the Chief Justice, and to build a so-called Government House, in which the President resides, and the very name of taxes is become abhorrent. What can still be done, and what must be done immediately, is to give us a new Chief Justice—a lawyer, a man of honour, a man who will not commit himself to one side, whether in politics or in private causes, and who shall not have the appearance of trying to coin money at every joint of our affairs. So much the better if he be a man of talent, but we do not ask so much. With an ordinary appreciation of law, an ordinary discretion, and ordinary generosity, he may still, in the course of time, and with good fortune, restore confidence and repair the breaches in the prestige of the whites. As for the President, there is much discussion. Some think the office is superfluous, still more the salary to be excessive; some regard the present man, who is young and personally pleasing, as a tool and scapegoat for another, and these are tempted to suppose that, with a new and firm Chief Justice, he might yet redeem his character. He would require at least to clear himself of the affairs of the rouleaux, or all would be against him.—I am Sir, your obedient servant,

ROBERT LOUIS STEVENSON

Appendix C

A List of Over-inkings

1. Page 31	(Ms. 22-23)	11. Page 120	(Ms. 92)
2. Page 38	(Ms. 27)	12. Page 124	(Ms. 95)
3. Page 38	(Ms. 28)	13. Page 125	(Ms. 96)
4. Page 107	(Ms. 81)	14. Page 213	(Ms. 158)
5. Page 109	(Ms. 82)	15. Page 214	(Ms. 158)
6. Page 116	(Ms. 88)	16. Page 214	(Ms. 159)
7. Page 117	(Ms. 89)	17. Page 215	(Ms. 160)
8. Page 118	(Ms. 90)	18. Page 221	(Ms. 165)
9. Page 119	(Ms. 91)	19. Page 223	(Ms. 166)
10. Page 120	(Ms. 91)		

Appendix D

A Note on the Special Photography

The negative for Print A of page 90 of Fanny Stevenson's diary was made in actual size from the original manuscript on 8 x 10″ Contrast Process Ortho Film. A Cook 9.5″ lens was used at F.32 and an exposure of 10 seconds was given. No filter was used. Four photofloods were the light source. The film was developed in D-11 for about five minutes.

The negative for Print B was made in actual size from the original manuscript on 35mm infrared film at 10:1 reduction. An Ektra 63mm lens was used at F.8 and an exposure of ⅕ second was given. An 89-A filter was used. Four photofloods were the light source. The film was developed in D-11 for about four minutes.

The negative for Print C was made in actual size from the original manuscript on 35mm infrared film at 10:1 reduction. An Ektra 63mm lens was used at F.9 and an exposure of 20 seconds was given. A Corning Glass filter was used. An ultraviolet quartz lamp was the light source. The film was developed in D-11 for about three minutes.

Index

Consuls, 193, 196, 201, 207, 211, 250 ff.
  see also William Blacklock, Thomas Cusack-Smith, Mr. St. John, Harold M. Sewall, Dr. Stuebel
Cordelia, 103
Cruise of the Janet Nichol, The, 149 n.
Cupping glass, 25, 143
Curaçoa, 177
Cusack-Smith, Thomas, 68, 127-28, 148, 217, 219, 225, 227
Customs and ceremonies, Samoan, see Feasts, Fono, Kava, Maid of the village, Manners, Melaga, Presents, Song, War paint

Daplyn, A. J., 208, 223
David Balfour, 152, 179, 183, 190
Decker, Bella, 177, 194
Devils, see Superstition
Diary, of Fanny, xiii
  editor's work on, xvi-xx
  see also Suppression of manuscript of Robert Louis Stevenson, xiv
Dowdney, Mr., 109, 124, 134
Dress, native, 147
Dumet, Mr., 117, 164

Earthquakes, 69, 75, 131
Ebb Tide, The, 190
Ebon, 105
Eggert, Mr., 109
Einfürer, Paul, 1-2, 13, 15, 25, 29, 40, 51, 69 ff., 80 f., 84, 89, 91 f., 106 f., 110
  clumsiness, 30, 32, 35
  drinking, 22, 24, 70
  RLS's description, 1 n.
Elena, 151, 153, 161, 166 f., 170, 178
Elephantiasis, 82, 107, 174
Emma, 81 f., 85, 92, 94
Employees and servants, see Ah Fu, Arrick, Ben, Mary Carter, Paul Einfürer, Elena, Emma, Faauma, Fusi, Mr. Hay, Mr. Henderson, Innes, Iopo, Java, Mr. King, Lafaele, Lauilo, Leuelo, Mat, Misifolo, Mitaele, Monga, Paatalise, Polu, Robert Ratke, Abdul Razzuk, Savea, Simi, Henry Simile, Sina, Mr. Skelton, Sosimo, Talolo, Tomas, Pussy Wilson, Yoseppi

Equator, xii, 8

Faamoina, see Poor White Man
Faauma, 93, 95, 112, 115, 124, 126 f., 129-30, 140, 151 f., 166 f., 185
Fanua (Mrs. Gurr), 106, 114, 120 ff., 129, 203, 207, 226
Fatulia, 198, 203, 207, 209
Feasts, 44, 151, 153
  at Vailima, 173-74, 177
Field, Isobel, xxii, 27 n., 28, 91, 120, 147 f., 210
  divorce, 185
  sketches of the war, 199, 209
Fiji, 98-103, 104
Folau, 190
Folk-lore, see Superstition
Fono (ceremony), 94, 127, 168 ff.
Fono (a native), 201, 204
Food, 3, 9, 12-13, 15, 34, 73, 84, 117
Footnote to History, A, xxi, 16 n., 17, 155, 163 n.
Foss, Captain, 111
Funk, Dr., 29, 88, 235
Fusi, 133, 139

Games, 17
Gavet, Père, 3 f.
Government, of Fatuna, 82-83
  of Fiji, 102-103
Green, Madame, 183
Gurr, E. W., 97, 109 f., 120-23, 128-29, 140, 226, 228
Gurr, Ethel, 114, 116, 120 ff.
Gurr, Mrs. see Fanua

Haggard, Bazett M., 104, 117, 124 f., 134, 153, 164-65, 180 ff., 199-200, 202, 214, 224 f., 226-27
Hamilton, Captain, 88
Hamilton, Mary, 145, 147 f.
Harvey, Mr., 100-101
Hay, Mr., 48, 66 f., 76, 89
Head hunting, 114, 196, 200, 202, 211-212, 219
  protest against, 222, 225
  women, 203 f., 206, 209 f., 211-12
Henderson, Mr., 115-16, 173
Henley, W. E., xi, 118
Henry, see Simile, Henry
Henry, Captain, 55
Hird, Ben, 55, 106